likeable
social media

likeable
social media

How to Delight Your Customers,
Create an Irresistible Brand,
and Be Amazing on Facebook,
Twitter, LinkedIn, Instagram,
Pinterest, and More

Revised and Expanded
Second Edition

DAVE KERPEN

with Mallorie Rosenbluth
and Meg Riedinger

New Foreword by Carrie Kerpen

Mc
Graw
Hill
Education

New York   Chicago   San Francisco   Athens   London
Madrid   Mexico City   Milan   New Delhi
Singapore   Sydney   Toronto

3 4 5 6 7 8 9 0   QFR   21 20 19 18 17 16

ISBN   978-0-07-183632-6
MHID   0-07-183632-2

e-ISBN   978-0-07-183633-3
e-MHID   0-07-183633-0

Library of Congress Cataloging-in-Publication Data

Kerpen, Dave.
  Likeable social media : how to delight your customers, create an irresistible brand, and be amazing on facebook, twitter, linkedin, instagram, pinterest, and more / Dave Kerpen. — Revised and expanded second edition.
     pages cm
  ISBN 978-0-07-183632-6 (alk. paper) — ISBN 0-07-183632-2 (alk. paper)
  1. Internet marketing. 2. Online social networks. 3. Social media—Economic aspects.
  4. Customer relations. 5. Branding (Marketing) I. Title.
  HF5415.1265.K425 2015
  658.8'72—dc23
                                                                                          2015001178

Interior design by THINK Book Works

McGraw-Hill Education books are available at special quantity discounts to use as premiums and sales promotions or for use in corporate training programs. To contact a representative, please visit the Contact Us pages at www.mhprofessional.com.

Thank you
so much for purchasing
the second edition of

*Likeable
Social Media*!

As a special bonus just for you,
please visit
http://www.likeablebonus.com
to download 3 free ebook singles:

- How to Leverage Mobile to Win at Social Media
- Facebook Is Pay to Play: What's Your Strategy?
- The 10 Commandments of Content Creation

For my amazing girls, Charlotte and Kate.
May you grow up in a more likeable world.

And for my amazing wife, Carrie,
my partner in all things.

Contents

Change is inevitable. Growth is optional. —John Maxwell

Author John Maxwell made this statement about the concept of leadership, but I believe that it is applicable in a variety of circumstances—including but not limited to social media.

When Dave first wrote this book in 2011, social media was in its infancy. Relatively uncrowded, brands were able to shine as they built and joined online groups of interest. They could organically become a part of the communities that they served. Built upon 18 seemingly simple principles, the book was revolutionary, and it was filled with success stories from businesses large and small. It soon became a staple on every marketer's must-read list.

As I write this just three years later, the social media landscape has changed drastically. Social media is more fragmented, and new major networks like Vine, Pinterest, and Instagram are still emerging. Brands have become just part of a very noisy space. And the seismic shift of networks requiring a paid advertising strategy for brands in order to see success has been felt across the business world.

Who *wasn't* surprised when, after spending time and effort to build a business's Facebook page, you were expected to pay to reach those fans? The landscape is radically different than it once was.

And yet, despite all of those changes, Dave Kerpen's evergreen principles remain true.

In this book, Dave applies his principles to current-day situations—case studies that move beyond Facebook and Twitter, for businesses of any size. He addresses how, even though the applications of these principles may have shifted, your social media strategy can and should be rooted in the concepts of listening, responding, and being authentic (to name a few).

As Dave's wife and business partner, I've watched him walk the walk of Likeable Social Media. First, he used these strategies together with me at Likeable Media, focusing on crafting impactful strategies and execution for big brands. But for Dave, something was missing. He felt that small business owners needed help most of all—they hadn't the time nor the energy to make social media work for them. He knew that he could have greater impact on the world by educating Main Street, as well as Wall Street. Through his books, he's been able to break down the fear around social media marketing. He transforms high-level concepts into simple, actionable, results-oriented tips that benefit social media marketers at businesses large and small.

As you read this book, think about your own business and how well your social media work meets the core principles of likeability. With Dave Kerpen in your corner, you're sure to improve your efforts and see great results.

—Carrie Kerpen
Cofounder and CEO
Likeable Media

Acknowledgments

Those of you who know me (and know the giant social media universe) know that there are literally thousands of people I'd like to thank here. But since that wouldn't make for very good reading material, I'll summarize by key categories. If your name isn't listed but you're among my extended group of friends, family, colleagues, and supporters, please know how appreciative I am of you and your impact on my life.

MY LIKEABLE PUBLISHING FAMILY

Thanks to all of the editors and staff at McGraw-Hill Professional who worked on the book and showed me there is still room for traditional publishers today. Thanks especially to Julia Baxter, my marketing rep and the first person at McGraw-Hill to accept my Facebook friendship—it meant a lot. To Zach Gajewski, my developmental editor and BU brother, thank you for being my ambassador of book quan. Thanks to Mary Glenn, Jane Palmieri, and Cheryl Ringer, who helped to make this second edition a reality.

Thanks to my agent, Celeste Fine at Sterling Lord, a likeable agent who helped me navigate the crazy new waters of publishing, and to her associate John Mass, a welcome addition to the team.

There would be no book whatsoever had my acquisitions editor Niki Papadopoulos not e-mailed me, encouraged me, signed me, and challenged me. Thanks.

MY LIKEABLE WORK FAMILY

I am so incredibly fortunate to be surrounded by an amazing team at my company, Likeable Local. Thanks to Meg Riedinger, my amazing chief-of-staff, and my coauthor on

this edition. I appreciate you more than you know. Thanks to
Hugh Morgenbesser, my partner at Likeable Local and one of
the smartest, more likeable people I've ever known. Thanks to
all of you for your support, you're the best team! Gaby Piazza,
Nicole Kroese, Daryle Lamoureux, Sam Sudakoff, Alexa
Pfeffer, Ben Wasser, Beth Henderson, Dana Wade, David Jolly,
Donna Parisi, Ethan Gavurin, Haley Forman, Hannah Baker,
Julia Hogan, Julian Wyzykowski, Karla Cobos, Krista Demato,
Kurt Schwanda, Laura Williams, Leah Tran, Lisa Markuson,
Mackenzie Porter, Matt Christie, Michael Braha, Mike Imperiale,
Rachael Chiarella, Ricky Ryan, Ryan Malone, Sam Waisbren,
Sara Murali, Stefanie Peterson, Thomas Miller, Tim Zerone, and
Zac O'Neill.

And to my incredible Likeable Media family: Thanks to
Mallorie Rosenbluth, Likeable Media's VP of client services and
my coauthor on this edition. You are outstanding in every way,
Mal. Thanks also to key Likeable Media employees, past and
present: Candie Harris, Brian Murray, Megan McMahon, Jenna
Lebel, Michele Weisman, Amy Kattan, Mandy Cudahy, Cara
Friedman, Clay Darrohn, Carrie Tylawsky, Devin Sugameli,
Rachel Hadley, Tim Bosch, Theresa Braun, and all the rest of
the team.

You—and the whole Likeable team—rule!

Thanks to our investors and advisors as well – without you,
we wouldn't have had two companies and hundreds of clients
to write about. You're all awesome: Dave McClure and the
team at 500 Startups, Tom DiBenedetto, Maurice Reznik, Roy
Rodenstein, Verne Harnish, Mark Roberge, Milind Mehere,
Nihal Mehta, Peg Jackson, Craig Gibson, Robb High, Christian
McMahan, Jeff Hayzlett, Chris McCann, Michael Lasky, Julie
Fenster, and Ed Zuckerberg. Thanks to all of our Likeable customers as well. Your faith and trust in us is invaluable.

Thanks to my most Likeable EO Forum—Andy Cohen, Ben
Rosner, Vinny Cannariato, Kevin Gilbert, Dana Haddad, and
Jeff Bernstein—and the rest of my friends from Entrepreneurs'
Organization (EO), who have changed my life in so many ways.

MY LIKEABLE ONLINE FAMILY

There are dozens of social media thought leaders who have influenced me, taught me, shared with me, and inspired me. Some I'm close friends with, others I've never met, but all of you on this list (and beyond) have had a profound impact on my view of the world. (They should all be followed on Twitter, too!) So thanks to Mari Smith, John Bell, Jason Keath, Peter Shankman, Sarah Evans, Jeremiah Owyang, Chris Brogan, Scott Stratten, Jay Baer, Guy Kawasaki, Clara Shih, David Kirkpatrick, Scott Monty, David Armano, Erik Qualman, Brian Solis, Aaron Lee, Tony Hsieh, Josh Bernoff, Nick O'Neill, Justin Smith, Amber Naslund, Liz Strauss, Sarah Evans, Todd Defren, Charlene Li, David Berkowitz, Geno Church, Jeff Pulver, Jeffrey Hayzlett, Philip Hotchkiss, Stacey Monk, Leslie Bradshaw, Jesse Thomas, John Jantsch, David Meerman Scott, Brian Carter, Shiv Singh, Ashton Kutcher, Greg Verdino, Ann Handley, Bonin Bough, Andy Sernovitz, Pete Blackshaw, Robert Scoble, Michael Stelzner, B. J. Emerson, Seth Godin, Julien Smith, Mark Zuckerberg, Ev Williams, Biz Stone, Dennis Crowley, Chris Treadaway, Jim Tobin, David Spinks, and B. L. Ochman. Thank you, and keep up the amazing work.

MY LOVEABLE FAMILY

OK, I'm counting close friends here, too. Thanks to my World Tour friends, Steve Evangelista, Kevin Annanab, Tad Bruneau, and Andy Kaufmann, for allowing me to take a break and have some fun during the crazy writing process. Thanks to Aunt Lisa and Uncle Mark for being a steady, positive family influence, to my Da for her unconditional love and support, my brother Phil, the smartest person I've ever met, my brother Dan, my resident marketing devil's advocate, and my brother Danny, a source of unending strength. Thanks to my mom, who taught me how to write, and my dad, who taught me how to think. Last but not least, thanks to my women at home. To my girls, Charlotte and Kate, thanks for putting up with Daddy being so busy when this book was written. I am so proud of you both and love you so much. To Seth, I love you and can't wait to meet you!

To Carrie, my partner in marriage, business, parenthood, and life, for you I am most thankful. You believed in me when I didn't. You left me alone when I needed it and were right beside me when I needed it. You made sacrifices to allow this book to be written, and I will forever remember and appreciate that. ILYSMNAF.

Thanks to all of the amazing, likeable people who helped get *Likeable Social Media* into your hands.

likeable
social media

I was standing in line to check in at Las Vegas's then-trendiest hotel in town, the Aria, for nearly an hour. It was June 2010, and I had just arrived after a twice-delayed six-hour flight from New York. I was tired and annoyed, and the last thing I wanted to do was waste an hour of my life waiting in line. Frustrated, I pulled out my smartphone and tweeted, "No Vegas hotel could be worth this long wait. Over an hour to check in at the Aria. #Fail."

Interestingly enough, the Aria didn't tweet back to me, but a competitor did. I saw a tweet from the Rio Hotel just two minutes later. If you're anything like most people with whom I've shared this story, you're probably thinking, "What did the Rio tweet, 'Come on over, we have no line'?" Indeed, many a small business owner and corporate senior executive who have heard this story have thought that this was the Rio's ROI moment, and that was surely what the Rio tweeted back.

Had the Rio tweeted such a message, I would have likely felt annoyed by two things: "First, why are they stalking me like a creepy character looking to manipulate me and benefit from my bad experience? Second, why is it jam-packed and happening at the Aria while it's wide open at the Rio?" On the contrary, however, the Rio Las Vegas tweeted the following to me: "Sorry about the bad experience, Dave. Hope the rest of your stay in Vegas goes well."

Guess where I ended up staying the next time I went to Las Vegas? And the time after that, and the time after that?

The hotel used social media to listen and to be responsive, showing a little empathy to the right person at the right time. An ad or a push-marketing message simply wouldn't have worked. But its ability to listen, to respond, and to be empathic did.

The Rio essentially earned a $600 sale from one tweet, one message that got my attention and ended up being integral in my decision as to where to stay next time I was in the city. Not a single person reading this could argue that the tweet was a marketing or sales message from the Rio either—because it wasn't. That would be considered an excellent return on investment (ROI) by anyone's standards. But the story doesn't end there.

Before even arriving at the Rio, I *liked* it on Facebook by clicking the Like button at Facebook.com/RioVegas, thereby letting my 3,500 friends, and the world at large, know of my endorsement of its customer-friendly practices. A few months later, my friend Erin was looking for a hotel to stay at in Las Vegas over the New Year's holiday, and I received the following message from her on Facebook: "Hey, Dave, I noticed you liked the Rio's page. Thinking about staying there for New Year's. What do you think?"

A friend's recommendation is more powerful than any advertisement, and Erin ended up staying at the Rio as well, along with 10 family members. Dozens of other friends have surely noticed my tweets and Facebook *likes* about the Rio and have been influenced since. So, one tweet led to one *like* on Facebook and, in fact, many *thousands of dollars worth of business*.

It used to be said that happy customers tell three people about their good experiences and unhappy customers tell ten about their bad ones. But as my experiences with the Aria and Rio hotels demonstrate, today, thanks to social media, happy customers *and* unhappy customers can tell thousands of people their feelings about a company's service or products with just a few clicks, relying on the Like button as a virtual endorsement. The Rio leveraged this fact to its advantage, while the Aria did not.

FROM ADAM AND EVE TO MASS MEDIA TO THE DAWN OF A NEW ERA IN COMMUNICATIONS

In the beginning, there was Adam and Eve. Eve said to Adam, "You've got to try this apple," and the first marketing interaction in the history of the world had taken place. It was simple and effective, from one trusted person's lips to another's ears, and it resulted in a successful, if free, "transaction."

Word-of-mouth marketing had begun, and it would remain the best, purest, most efficient form of marketing for thousands of years (see the timeline in Figure I.1). Then, in the year 1450,

FIGURE I.1 History of Marketing Timeline

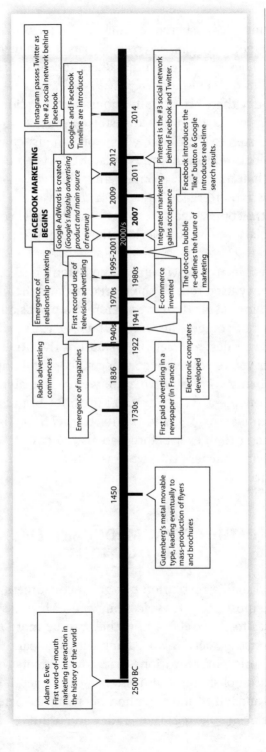

Adam & Eve: First word-of-mouth marketing interaction in the history of the world

2500 BC

1450 — Gutenberg's metal movable type, leading eventually to mass-production of flyers and brochures

1730s — First paid advertising in a newspaper (in France)

1836 — Emergence of magazines

1922 — Radio advertising commences

Electronic computers developed

1940s

1941 — First recorded use of television advertising

1970s — Emergence of relationship marketing

E-commerce invented

1980s — The dot-com bubble re-defines the future of marketing

1995-2001 — Google AdWords is created (Google's flagship advertising product and main source of revenue)

2000/s — Integrated marketing gains acceptance

FACEBOOK MARKETING BEGINS

2007

2009 — Google+ and Facebook Timeline are introduced.

2011 — Facebook introduces the "like" button & Google introduces real-time search results.

2012 — Instagram passes Twitter as the #2 social network behind Facebook

2014 — Pinterest is the #3 social network behind Facebook and Twitter.

the printing press ushered in a new era of mass marketing and media. Direct mail, followed by newspapers and magazines, and radio and television, allowed marketers and advertisers to target huge groups of people at once.

But today there are literally thousands of radio stations you can listen to—or free ways to listen to music—so why would you ever listen to a radio ad, when you can just change the station? There are literally thousands of television channels you can watch at any given moment and—better yet—technology that allows you to record your favorite shows and fast-forward through the commercials. So why on earth would you watch the commercials, unless you work in the industry and have professional interest?

No, people are not watching and listening to commercials the way they used to, and the marketing and media industries are changing faster than ever before. So what's a marketer to do? How can you get the word out about your product, drive trials, drive sales, and accomplish all of the other marketing objectives you've got? How do you get people talking about you without being so disruptive, and, well, unlikeable? The good news is, people are already talking about brands like yours more than ever before, and thanks to social media, word can spread faster than ever before—so all you have to do is listen, respond, and harness that word to allow consumers to drive the action.

THE SOCIAL MEDIA AND *LIKE* REVOLUTIONS

The social media revolution has given consumers around the world the most powerful voice they've ever had. It's also forced companies to think about how they can be more transparent and responsive. Social media, along with a global recession, has led companies, organizations, and governments to figure out how to accomplish more with less money—to get their messages out there and talked about, without spending as many dollars on declining media like television, radio, and print.

Word-of-mouth marketing has always been considered the purest and best form of marketing, and social media has continued to prove this fact in many ways. People like to share with and feel connected to each other, brands, organizations, and even governments they like and trust.

Facebook's Like button, introduced in April 2010, has already been added by more than 5 million distinct websites (see Figure I.2). The Like button allows Facebook's more than 1 billion users, with one click, to express approval of companies, organizations, articles, or ideas. Whether it's a friend's picture of her baby you *like*, an article shared from the *New York Times*, a video from a local organization, or a contest from a global brand, the Like button gets more than 2 billion clicks per day.

Yet as astounding as these numbers are, it's the new personalization of the Web that matters most in the social media revolution, both to companies and consumers. It's Facebook's ability to show you exactly what your friends and friends of friends *like* that makes the *like* function such a powerful tool. If you have a new baby, for example, you don't care what stroller is advertised on television, and in fact, you probably don't care if 50, 500, or 5,000 people *like* a new stroller on Facebook. But if a friend of yours *likes* that stroller, you are more apt to feel that you can trust the company that made the item and you will be more comfortable buying a stroller from that company.

Facebook isn't the only social network to adopt a *like* feature either. YouTube, LinkedIn, Pinterest, Instagram, and Foursquare have all added their own functionality that allows users to express approval of content, and Twitter has a Favorite button that allows users to approve of specific tweets. Content, companies, products, and ideas judged likeable by people you know and trust can be easily found throughout today's Internet. Companies

FIGURE I.2   **Facebook's Like Button**

and professionals who are worthy of people clicking their Like button will, in the short term, build trust and, in the long term, win the new Web in their respective categories.

As the cofounder and CEO of social media and word-of-mouth marketing firm Likeable Media, I've had the privilege of being an early adopter of social media technology and an eyewitness to the social media and *like* revolution. Likeable's mission is to help build more transparent and responsive companies, nonprofit organizations, and governments. We believe that social media, used well, is nothing short of transformational, not only in marketing but also in public relations, sales, customer service, and operations. We believe it has the potential to break down silos to better connect companies internally and externally.

We've worked to improve social media branding for more than 250 companies and organizations, such as 1-800-Flowers.com, Verizon, Neutrogena, the New York City Department of Health, and the National Multiple Sclerosis Society, and, through Likeable Local, over 1,000 small businesses, such as dentists, jewelers, and real estate firms. There are organizations of all sizes that have learned to really listen, deliver value, and respond to customers—brands that share and inspire social content that's worthy of being shared online and offline, and *liked*, literally and figuratively.

JOIN THE COCKTAIL PARTY

Social media is like the world's largest cocktail party, where people can listen to others talking and join the conversations with other people about any topic of their choice. There are two main distinctions, though, between a real cocktail party and an online one: First, there's no drinking online, of course. Second, but more important, whereas at an actual, in-person cocktail party, you can only have a few conversations with a handful of people in one night, online, and through social networks, you can have numerous conversations with potentially thousands or millions of people at once.

In both "parties," you will find a mix of likeable people and not-so-likeable people. At a cocktail party, you might encounter people who won't stop talking about themselves, but you'll also run into those who are great listeners and show you they're interested in what you're discussing. You'll find people who tell great stories and people who bore you to death. Who do you want to see again or maybe even do business with at a cocktail party: the sales guy who talks incessantly about how great his company and products are or the person who listens to the problems you face, has an open discussion with you, and maybe even makes you laugh?

We all intuitively know what makes some people at cocktail parties interesting and enjoyable to interact with. Yet most companies have not figured out how to be likeable in the cocktail party known as social media. Many companies still act like the sales guy who won't shut up about his products, or someone who tries too hard to dazzle people, or the person who bores everybody to death talking without listening and not asking other people what they want to have a conversation about.

The good news is, you, as a company, have an opportunity to do better, to be the organization that isn't "that guy" at the cocktail party. By applying the same set of rules you'd apply to be the person everyone wants to be involved with at the party, you can become the most likeable company or organization in your category—and end up the most profitable as well.

Listen carefully, be transparent, be responsive, be authentic, tell great stories—the qualities that would make you the hotshot at the party—and they'll make your organization a likeable one on social networks.

LIKE IS THE NEW LINK: HOW FACEBOOK IS REORGANIZING GOOGLE'S WEB

You wake up one morning, and your back really hurts. You've been putting off finding a new doctor ever since you moved to town, it's been forever since you've had a checkup, and now you're paying the price. The pain is too much to wait any longer, and you've got to find a chiropractor now. So you grab your computer, go to Google.com, and enter "back doctor" and your town's name. You see a list of 10 chiropractors who have paid Google to be listed there and dozens of others who come up in organic search results. But do you really want to trust your throbbing back to a complete stranger in an emergency?

Then you think of another idea, and you head to Facebook and again search "back doctor." At the top of the results is a doctor's listing with a sidebar telling you that three of your friends *like* this doctor. Beneath the top listing is a chiropractor, next to which you see two friends who *like* him. "Sweet," you think. "Someone I can trust because my friends *like* him." You make a quick call, and you're off to get your backache taken care of by a recommended doctor, a professional your friends *like*.

This scenario and scenarios like it are happening every day now, and the use of Facebook and the social graph (global mapping of people and how they're connected) for search and commerce isn't far off. Think about it: Why would you possibly make a decision about a doctor, an attorney, a mechanic, or any important product or service for that matter based on advertising or Google search placement when you can make this decision based on the preference and recommendations of trusted friends? Facebook and social media have made it infinitely easier to do the latter. *It's nothing short of a game changer for marketers and businesses of all sizes.*

The great news about the new world of communications we live in today is that everybody has a shot. Build a great product, get the word out to a few people, make it easy for people to share with their friends, and you can win without spending a boatload. Just five years ago, for instance, if you went to a new restaurant that you loved, you might have shared the experience with a few of your friends, family members, or neighbors. Perhaps if you really loved the restaurant, you might have raved about it for a week to as many as 10 or 15 friends. Today, you can share these thoughts with 350 Facebook friends, 300 Twitter followers, or 150 LinkedIn connections, all with one click on your computer or phone. Or you can post a picture of that appetizing, or unappetizing, meal and share it with hundreds of people on Pinterest, Instagram, or Google+.

No matter what the size of your business, organization, or your client's business, you too have the ability to follow the simple rules of social media outlined in this book to reap the rewards. Senior management, and anyone in a communications position for that matter, needs to know that marketing in a social media and Facebook world is not about broadcasting your message and getting the largest reach and frequency. It's about tapping into the conversation, listening, engaging, and empowering. The loudest, biggest spenders don't win anymore. The smartest, most flexible listeners do.

WHAT SOCIAL MEDIA CAN AND CAN'T DO

Before we move on, I'd like to share three key points about social media to dispel any myths you may have heard and make sure I manage your expectations from the start:

1. **Social media cannot make up for a bad product, company, or organization.** If you're marketing a bad service or widget, not only will social media not help you but it will actually *hurt* your cause because word will spread quickly. The good news is, if you're using social media well, you'll quickly know when you have bad products, employees, or processes. As a good businessperson or marketer, you can fix these problems before they cause any serious damage.
2. **Social media won't lead to overnight sales success.** Success will take time, and it will come in increased buzz, referrals, traffic, and eventually, sales. I wish I could tell you that after you read this book you'll have all of the tools to instantly turn on the social media revenue engine and watch the money pour in. I can't, of course. I'll demonstrate the return on investment of "likeable social media" in lots of case studies, but no matter what, social media is not an instant win. We're talking about *building relationships with people,* and that invariably takes time.
3. **Social media is not free.** It will take time and/or money to achieve sustained growth. Since it's free to join Facebook and any social network worth talking about, many marketers think social media is free, or at least cheap. Well, the good

news is, no matter how large your company is, it's nearly impossible to spend the kind of money on social media that large companies regularly have spent on network television in the last 20 years. But building and executing a likeable social media plan will take lots of time and work. Ultimately, such a plan can't be the sole effort of any one marketing or public relations department. Instead, it must be integrated across your entire company, its agencies, and vendors.

BOOKS CAN BE SOCIAL TOO

I write a lot in this book about the two-way interactive nature of social media and the importance of leveraging that potential. Of course, a book is typically as one-directional as a medium can be: author writes, and reader reads and digests. As a social media author, I simply won't allow that to be the case. So here's my promise to you: as you read this book, if you have any questions, you need clarification, you are uncertain about content, or you want to challenge me on the points or strategies within, *please do let me know*, using social media.

Ask me questions through Facebook.com/DKerpen or Twitter.com/DaveKerpen. For a speedier answer, if perhaps not one directly from me, post on our company page at Facebook.com/LikeableLocal or through Twitter.com/LikeableLocal or Twitter.com/LikeableBook. If you have a question, even if you think it applies only to you, there are probably many others out there with similar questions. So I truly hope you'll take me up on that offer, and ask away.

LET'S GET LIKEABLE

Facebook, Twitter, blogs, YouTube, LinkedIn, Foursquare, and other social media sites and tools are innovating and changing faster than any other communications technologies in history. It's important to understand the basics behind how each major network works and how marketers and businesses can best leverage each site. Before we delve into the following 18 strategies to help you create an irresistible brand through online social media networks, I urge you take a look at the recently updated Appendix first. This section provides a brief refresher course on Facebook, Twitter, Google+, Pinterest, Instagram, and other social networks, blogs, and tools that matter most. It contains insight on how to best think about them and use them in marketing and advertising. If you feel as if you don't need a refresher, read on, but strongly consider using the Appendix as a guide at any time and to provide further context.

While social media sites and tools will continue to change with every week that goes by, the 18 strategies discussed in this book will remain the same and help you utilize social media to become more transparent, responsive, engaging, and profitable.

Thanks for choosing to go on this journey with me. Let's get likeable.

CHAPTER 1

Listen First, and Never Stop Listening

You are angry.

You just got a letter in the mail from your car insurance company explaining that it will cover only half the cost of the recent work you did on your car following an accident. You're out $700, which stinks, but more important, you're wondering why you pay these high monthly premiums if not to cover situations just like this. So you call the company, and you're placed on hold for 30 minutes. Finally you get a representative who says, "I'm sorry, there's nothing I can do. This is the policy." As you sit there, frustrated and dejected, the telephone representative feeds you the next line in the script: "Is there anything else I can help you with today?"

"Of course not," you think. "How about paying for my car repairs? Maybe you should spend a little less money on your stupid TV ads I see all day and a little more time on your customer service." It's so frustrating not feeling listened to.

Then you post on Facebook or Twitter: "My car insurance company _____ sucks. Same old story." A few minutes later, you get a notification that someone responded to your post.

Surprisingly, you click to find a written response from your car insurance company: "We hear you. Please send us a quick e-mail about the particular issue, and we'll get to the bottom of it as quickly as we can." Somehow, you already feel a little bit better about the situation.

Did the company respond so positively only because you posted publicly? Maybe. The point is, a representative realized your frustration with the company's services and was forced to take notice of your post. Companies can no longer afford to ignore their customers' specific needs or complaints when the conversation can so easily be made public. Instead, they must listen, understand the issue, and respond appropriately.

EVERYBODY LOVES TO FEEL HEARD

Communication is 50 percent listening and 50 percent talking. Yet for many years, companies large and small have done a disproportionate amount of talking, shouting even. Customer service representatives, marketing researchers, and focus group organizers may listen, but budgets for these "listening" activities amount to little compared to the money spent on mass media "talking." Now, for the first time in our history, companies can listen, through social media, to conversations about them and their competitors.

You have a front row seat to spontaneous chatter of interest to your business. You have the ability to check in on prospective customers or prospects discussing problems your company solves. You can listen to existing customers talk about unrelated issues just to get to know them better. Checking in on your vendors, partners, or even your competitors' customers has never been easier. The amount of data you can gather and the number of conversations you can tap into through social media are nothing short of mind-boggling.

As tempting as it may be to "join the conversation," Facebook, Twitter, and other social networks aren't simply broadcast media. They're engagement media—that is, they are listening networks. Letting you listen to the conversation before you try to join in is an opportunity: How can you possibly know what to talk about in any conversation until you listen, at least a little bit?

Ask anyone who has ever dated or who has been in a successful relationship how important it is not only to listen to your partner but also to show him or her that you are truly listening. The guy on that first date who talks incessantly and does not listen—he strikes out every time. So does the woman at the cocktail party who talks only about herself. Increasingly, the same goes for the company that spends most of its marketing dollars talking and little time or money listening. Social media is the first communications channel that allows for such listening in large scale, and no matter what you sell or market, your customers are definitely talking.

Listen first before you talk back. You *can* join the conversation as a listener.

THE BENEFITS OF LISTENING: WHY DOES IT REALLY MATTER?

If and when customers or prospects acknowledge that you're listening, you immediately strengthen your relationships with them. We'll talk more about responding later, but clearly the ability to not only listen but also to acknowledge others makes them feel heard, which makes them happier, which is always a good thing. Even if you can't acknowledge customers (as is the case for highly regulated industries such as pharmaceutical and financial services companies in which only professionals can legally supply appropriate responses, if they can legally respond at all), there are other benefits to listening. A better understanding of how your customers use your products (or don't use them) can help you make critical changes in your offerings and in your communications with your customers. You can also uncover new opportunities you hadn't thought of, or you'll find out that some of the features you thought would be big hits have ended up not mattering to customers or failing altogether.

Knowing what's important to your customers can help you better plan your offers, promotions, and contests to further drive buzz and sales. Instead of expensive product launches, you can test new ideas carefully and receive feedback quickly, keeping your finger on the pulse of your customers. You'll be able to avoid pricey ad campaigns that champion things you *think* people will love about your product or service by listening to what people *actually want* before you spend a single dollar. Consider social listening the ultimate surveying and focus group tool—practically free, and running 24/7/365 for you.

LISTENING VERSUS MONITORING

Let's briefly compare the word *listening* to the word *monitoring*. A lot of companies and people use these words interchangeably to describe the process of seeing what people are saying about you, your products, and your competitors. Some may believe it is only a matter of semantics, but there is, in fact, an important distinction between the two.

Monitoring has an impersonal feel to it, imparting a certain amount of creepiness. When you hear "monitoring," you most likely think of the FBI or surveillance cameras. You think of negative situations: "Monitor that cough; it might get worse." *Listening*, on the other hand, is an important human process, and I've yet to meet someone who didn't like being listened to. Do you like being monitored? Do you like being listened to and heard?

How to Listen

There are lots of free ways to listen to what customers and prospects are saying online, and there are many paid enterprise systems available as well, with costs ranging from a few dollars to thousands of dollars per month. If you're new to listening, try these free ways first:

- Google Alerts
- Social Mention
- Twitter search
- Facebook search
- YouTube search
- TweetBeep

If you go to any social network and type a phrase or keyword into its search function, you will see what people are saying using that keyword in real time. National and global brands might search the entire Web, while local and regional organizations will want to use geographical filtering to find posts only in your coverage area. Remember, don't search just for your brand name but also for your competitors', and more important, for terms and words that your customers would use.

For instance, if you're a real estate broker, sure, you can search social networks for the name of your agency. But wouldn't it be more helpful to search for the phrase "want to buy a house" in conversations on social networks in your town so you can find real people in real time sharing their needs with others? If you're an attorney, you can search for your firm's name, but it might be more helpful to search for the phrase "need to hire a lawyer" to listen to potential future clients talk about what they are looking for in the way of legal services.

More advanced listeners, or brands with higher volumes of conversations to listen to, should consider a paid enterprise software solution. There are dozens of listening platforms available, but a couple of good ones to start with are Vocus and Sysomos. (See Table 1.1 for a number of others.)

TABLE 1.1 **Major Enterprise Listening Systems**

PLATFORMS	WEBSITE	PROS
Meltwater Buzz	Meltwater.com	Comprehensive tracking and analysis of user-generated content
Parature	Parature.com	Listen to and route customer comments to appropriate departments
Radian6	Radian6.com	Listen, measure, and engage with your customers across the entire social Web
Sysomos	Sysomos.com	Instant and unlimited access to all social media conversations
Vocus	Vocus.com	On-demand software for public relations management

Such products allow you to tap into large volumes of conversations across the social Web in a systematic, easy-to-follow way. You can generate real-time, daily, or weekly reports on mentions, competitive analysis, sentiment, and more. While solutions such as these are much more expensive than "free," they're a lot less expensive (and a lot more valuable) than traditional marketing research, such as surveying and working with focus groups.

I'm Listening; Now What?

It's important to keep an open mind about what data you'll find when you listen and, more important, what you can do with it. If your brand or product is being talked about in a negative way, it's urgent to fix the problems being discussed as efficiently as possible. If people are asking for something new, figure out a way to create that for them.

For instance, maybe your customers love a product but wish it came in a different flavor, color, or design. Or maybe they'd be willing to pay more for your service if you offered a new tool they need. If customers are revealing their favorite features about your product that you didn't realize were popular, consider accentuating these features in future marketing and communications materials. And of course, once you've begun to formally listen to what customers and prospects are saying, you'll want to formulate a plan to respond appropriately whenever possible (as will be discussed in detail in following chapters).

THE COST OF NOT LISTENING

At best, by not listening, you're not leveraging potential opportunities for growth, damage control, or both. At worst, you're causing your customers and prospects to turn to your competitors—those who *are* listening and will respond to customer needs. You're also allowing your brand reputation to be significantly hurt because by the time you get around to learning what people are saying, it may be too late to respond efficiently and make necessary changes to keep your company growing. Even if you're in a highly regulated industry and you're unable to fully join the conversation, it simply doesn't make sense not to leverage the resources available to find out what your customers and prospects are saying and to use that information to create better products, services, and processes.

I talked with Shel Horowitz, expert on ethical marketing, author, and longtime social media user, about the importance of listening, and he confessed that, at first, he didn't always take the concept to heart as he does today:

> The first discussion list I joined, I didn't listen first. I went in with keyboard blazing, did not take the time to understand the group, and ended up slinking off with my tail between my legs and leaving entirely. Since then, I've been in many groups, and I usually read all the posts for about two weeks before posting, and then I start with an introduction. I've developed a reputation as a friendly, caring, helpful, knowledgeable, and very transparent individual whose advice carries some weight.

Shel told me he can now safely attribute 15 to 20 percent of his book sales directly to his time spent listening and responding across social networks and online communities. So many marketers have taken to using new marketing channels to talk before listening, essentially filling each new channel that comes along with noise. Think about e-mail and most other forms of so-called interactive marketing. Is it really interactive, or is it mostly marketers talking? Social networks provide marketers with a massive opportunity to leverage the listening half of their communications.

NEVER STOP LISTENING

Remember, it's not about listening for a while and then talking to all of your new prospects and converting them into customers. Listening will always be 50 percent of the communication process, so you'll want to continue to refine your listening skills and processes throughout your work in social media. Always listen to the conversations in real time. In fact, sometimes the best daters, friends, businesspeople, and companies are the ones who do even more listening than talking, hearing what everyone has to say and speaking only when they have something really worthwhile to express.

In dating lore, there's always the guy who *thinks* he knows how important listening is, so he starts the date by saying, "Tell me about yourself." After his date talks for a minute or so about herself, she says, "How about you?" and he proceeds to talk her ear off for the rest of the date, telling her all about himself. The guy may claim he listened to what she said, but the truth is, he was just going through the motions, not really carrying it through in a meaningful way.

That's not listening. In order to be a likeable organization that effectively listens to its customers and prospects, you've got to fully integrate listening into your job or agency's functions.

When You Can Only Listen: Allergan Facial Aesthetics

Allergan, a Fortune 500 pharmaceutical organization, is like many pharma brands when it comes to social media. Because of the highly regulated nature of the industry and its products and offerings, the brand needs to be extremely careful about what they say and don't say online, especially when it comes to interactive social media sites. While some pharmaceutical organizations decided to ignore the conversations entirely, Allergan Medical Aesthetics (the division behind popular brands such as BOTOX Cosmetic, Latisse, Juvéderm, and others) recognized social conversations were happening about their brands, and they believed they could glean a significant understanding about their patients and the perception of their products if they paid attention to what was being said.

With the assistance of Likeable Media and the listening platform Sysomos, Allergan Medical Aesthetics identified a variety of keywords and categories that would allow the brand to capture key information. They now mine through tens of thousands of mentions of their brands every week. From this data, they are able to report and follow up on off-label uses of the brand (an important part of meeting FDA regulations for pharmaceutical brands) as well as track and measure the overall sentiment toward their brands. Key trends and themes can be identified and used to inform future marketing plans. Because a strong listening process is in place, the brand can be made quickly aware when any out-of-the-norm situations arise.

By keeping a finger on the pulse of and recognizing the importance of social media in understanding their patients, Allergan Medical Aesthetics can make more informed and better-educated decisions, which in turn positions their brands for success (Figure 1.1).

By listening and responding, greater sentiment comes from customers, whose loyalty grows. They, in turn, become better advocates for your products. It's as simple as this: the customer talks; the company listens and acknowledges; and the customer is happier, as is anyone else watching, since the conversation is public. Whom would *you* rather buy a product from: a company that obviously, publicly listens to its customers, or a company that seemingly ignores them by not utilizing social networks to directly interact with the public?

FIGURE 1.1   **A Snapshot of Allergan's Facebook Timeline**

THE ROI FOR SMALL BUSINESSES

Dr. Wendi Wardlaw of Stoneybrook Dental, a Likeable Local customer, had practiced dentistry for nearly 20 years before diving into social media. Today, as a dentist, missionary, and public speaker, Dr. Wardlaw understands the importance of listening on social media. Despite her hectic schedule, she manages and listens on Facebook every day (Figure 1.2).

"Everything happens really fast there. You have to listen," Dr. Wardlaw said.

In August 2014, Dr. Wardlaw was monitoring her Facebook newsfeed one night when she searched dental keywords and saw that one of her patients was posting about discomfort and pain. The patient in question had undergone a routine outpatient procedure earlier that week so her abnormal symptoms were concerning. Dr. Wardlaw private messaged the patient and asked her to send a picture of her mouth.

Upon seeing the photo, Dr. Wardlaw immediately sent the patient to the hospital where she received antibiotics to treat the start of a serious infection. After a few nights in the hospital, the patient was healthy enough to be released. Had Dr. Wardlaw not been listening on Facebook, the patient's health could have been much further compromised.

FIGURE 1.2   **Snapshot of Dr. Wardlaw's Facebook Page**

ACTION ITEMS

1. Write down a list of five phrases people might use that would identify themselves as potential customers of yours. Conduct Twitter and Facebook searches for each of these phrases.
2. Conduct Twitter, Facebook, and YouTube searches for your brand, competitors, products, and services. Take inventory of what people are saying.
3. Develop a plan and system to formally or informally listen on a regular basis throughout the social Web, and determine ways your organization can benefit from the insight and knowledge gained by listening.

LISTENING SHOULD ALWAYS BE 50 PERCENT OF THE CONVERSATION

Listening is the single most important skill in social media, and it's one that's easy to forget once you get started with all of the sexier, more exciting things you can do. So whatever you do, once you start, never stop listening. Even once you start talking, it doesn't mean you stop listening—it's quite the opposite actually. If you feel like you're running out of conversation to listen to, broaden your search terms and find new audiences—people who don't know you even exist yet but, based on what they're saying, probably should. Results will follow, and it won't be long until your company is the "coolest person" at the social media cocktail party (and more important, the most successful!).

CHAPTER 2

Way Beyond "Women 25 to 54"
Define Your Target Audience Better Than Ever

I was talking with friends at the South by Southwest Interactive conference in March 2009 about a concept I call *hypertargeting*, by which a company gears a marketing and advertising effort toward a specific group through individuals' social media profiles, activities, and networks. At the time, and even more so now, Facebook, Twitter, and LinkedIn held an unbelievable amount of data on hundreds of millions of people. From users' profiles and comments, you could advertise and market toward groups more efficiently than ever before. On Facebook alone, you could target people based on their age, gender, education, marital status, interests, job title, and employer.

For example, instead of a beer company randomly searching for men aged 21 to 23, the company could easily find 21- to 23-year-old males in key geographic markets who have listed "drinking," "partying," or "bars" as interests on their profiles. My friend Leslie Bradshaw overheard the conversation on hypertargeting and chimed in with her thoughts on what she called *nanotargeting*—a concept similar to hypertargeting but with search criteria so narrow that you can target just one individual among hundreds of millions.

"Cool," I thought. I raced back to my hotel room that night, jumped onto the Facebook ad platform, played around with targeting options, and took out an ad for 31-year-old, married, female employees of Likeable Media living in New York City. The ad copy read, "I love you and miss you Carrie. Be home from Texas soon."

That advertisement had a target audience of one (Figure 2.1). One person, out of hundreds of millions of people on Facebook, could see it. Of course, when my wife and business partner, Carrie, saw the ad, she immediately loved it, freaked out, and did what any social media marketing firm partner would do. She took out a Facebook ad targeting 31-year-old, married, *male* employees of Likeable Media living in New York: "Thanks, Dave. Love you too. This is pretty cool." We've been sending one another nanotargeted Facebook ads ever since.

Unless you just want to impress your spouse or friend, or you're a social media dork like this author, you probably don't have a target audience of one. Then again, maybe you do: would your brand benefit from engaging with the CEO of the largest company in town? Would your startup benefit from engaging

---

FIGURE 2.1   **Nanotargeted Ad**

I Love You Carrie

I love you and miss you Carrie. Be home from Texas soon.

with a partner in your city's more prestigious venture capital firm? Consider the possibilities of nanotargeting the marketing director of a key vendor or partner to further explore his or her current needs and overall expectations.

Whether your perfect target audience is 1, 10, 100, 1,000, or 1 million people, you can now engage them in a way that was virtually impossible only a few years ago. Once you find your target audience, listen to them (see Chapter 1), find out what they are looking for, and provide your product or service to meet their needs. You can build a relationship with your audience and even allow them to directly buy your goods or services, all using social media.

In the past, newspapers, magazines, television, and radio allowed marketers to tap into wide audiences of people, based on broad demographic criteria: 18- to 34-year-olds, 25- to 54-year-old females, or males 55 and older in New York, for example. But in hindsight, in almost every case, these categories were too sweeping. Specifics will help you hone in on your target audience, connecting you directly with the consumer. For instance, are you targeting parents or singles? Sports fans? Hockey fans only? Are you in every major market or only certain markets?

Traditional marketers may be naysayers here with regard to the advent of social media and its relation to reaching the right customers. They will argue that currently with cable TV networks, you can target people with specific interests, such as home decorating or cooking. They might believe that trade publications and conferences are the best way to find your niche audience in the business-to-business (B2B) space.

While clearly you can target your audience *better* using niche trade publications and cable television shows than you previously could with just network television or radio, magazines and specialized publications are quickly perishing. Also, everyone I know fast-forwards through TV commercials using DVR technology, no matter what specialized network they're watching. With the introduction of commercial-free, audience-targeted podcasts, music and news blogs, and online user-friendly music listening sites, such as Spotify and Pandora, fewer and fewer people are tuning into traditional radio broadcasts. Besides, just because targeting through traditional media is *better* than it used to be doesn't mean it is *the best*. And why settle for anything but the best in your search for the perfect audience for your product or service? Let's take a look at a few examples of how to find this ideal audience on Facebook, LinkedIn, and Twitter.

FACEBOOK: REACH AS MANY USERS AS YOU WANT (OR AS FEW!)

In the movie *The Social Network*, the Sean Parker character played by Justin Timberlake has a famous line: "You know what's cooler than a million dollars? A billion dollars." My line on Facebook marketing is the opposite: "You know what's cooler than reaching a billion people on Facebook? Reaching the perfect 1,000 prospects or 100 or 1." Facebook's ads aren't free to run, of course. Facebook earned more than $3 billion in ad revenue in the third quarter of 2014[1] but its self-serve ad platform *is* free to explore. (We'll talk a lot more about Facebook ads in Chapter 15.) This means that anyone who wants to can easily research exactly how many people on Facebook fit into whatever targeting criteria he or she desires, free of charge. In other words, without even running any ads, you can find your target population among hundreds of millions of people simply by feeding Facebook the exact attributes you're looking for in an audience.

I've included a screenshot (Figure 2.2) of various targeting criteria available to advertisers. The basics—gender, age, and location—allow you to quickly target millions of people at scale the way you would using traditional media. (And before you tell me Facebook is solely for young people, note that in the United States alone, there are more than 50 million users over age 60.)

So, even though it's very general, if you're looking for your audience based only on age, gender, or location, you can certainly find it easily. It's the other categories, however, that allow you to drill deep down to identify your perfect audience. Let's focus on the two key targeting categories in this process: interests and workplace (see Figure 2.3).

FIGURE 2.2   **Basic Targeting Criteria**

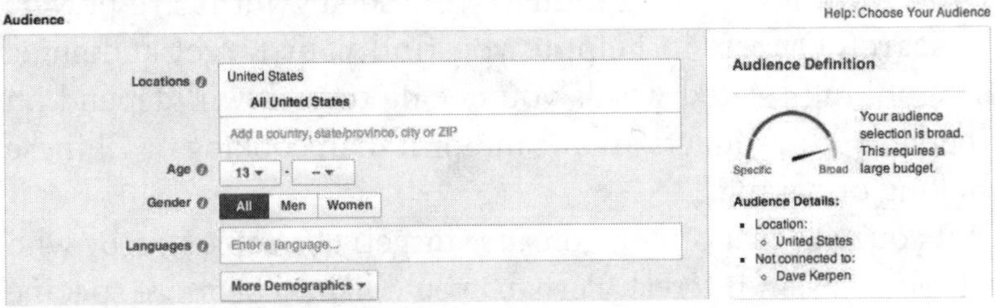

In the "Interests" category, you can input literally any interest that at least 100 people have listed on their profile. Note: there are *hundreds of thousands of options* here. Type in "cooking," for instance, then more specifically "Italian cooking," "Chinese cooking," or "French cooking." You could also go with "baking,"

FIGURE 2.3   **Targeting by Interests and Workplace**

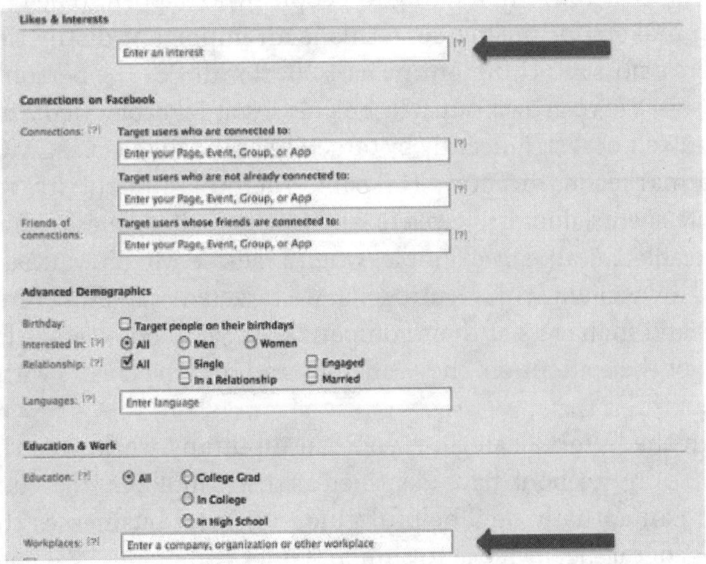

then "baking pies" or "baking cakes." There are of course many possibilities and dozens of other cooking-related keywords. If you work in the food industry, these keywords are powerful search criteria in helping you find your target audience. The cooking-related words you decide to pick will depend on whether your products are meant for Italian cooking or Chinese cooking or baking.

If you're a yoga center, consider targeting people nearby who list "yoga" as an interest. Perhaps you'd like to be more specific and target people who list "Bikram yoga" or "Reiki," depending on the services you offer or are researching offering in the future. If you represent a nonprofit, consider targeting the thousands of people who list "philanthropy" as an interest. Then take it a step further, and check for specific causes that are relevant or reach out to other nonprofit workers who share a similar mission, locally or even globally.

In the "More Demographics" section, you can also select a job title. Perhaps you want to target retail buyers, distributors, HR managers, journalists, doctors, dentists, or maybe CEOs. This search function is especially helpful in the B2B space.

Remember, even in the B2B space, you're not marketing to businesses. You're marketing to people, who happen to be decision makers for businesses—this is an important distinction. There's no such thing online as B2B. It's all P2P, or person to person. We've grown our B2B businesses at Likeable Media and Likeable Local significantly by targeting brand managers, CMOs, and marketing directors (Likeable Media) and dentists, real estate agents, doctors, jewelers, and other small business owners (Likeable Local). For example, when Likeable Media wanted to land an account with Neutrogena, we targeted marketing directors and managers at their company using Facebook ads. After we got their attention, they called us and became clients within a month.

In the "Work" category, you can input any workplace that people on Facebook have identified as their employer. This function can actually be a helpful guide for local businesses that are geographically close to similar, larger companies. We had a chiropractor client in San Francisco, for instance, who targets employees of nearby offices. You can also use this function for internal marketing and communications. Imagine telling the whole staff, "You're doing a great job, keep up the good work," just by sending out a Facebook message. Get creative with this function, and you'll figure out how to best utilize it for your organization.

When you combine the "Job Title" category with "Work," as well as other specifications like "Industry" or "Office Type," then you can pinpoint your key audience with precision. Imagine, for instance, searching for only CIOs at Fortune 500 companies in the medical industry, or targeting real estate agents at the top five firms in town.

Whether you're a small business, huge brand, nonprofit, or government agency, your perfect target audience will be found on Facebook. Frankly, I've yet to find an organization anywhere whose target audience *isn't* on Facebook. Be sure to listen, and then find and engage your share of the hundreds of millions of people across the world who communicate via Facebook—the share that makes sense for *your* organization.

LINKEDIN: FOR MAXIMUM IMPACT, TARGET PROFESSIONALS ONLY

While Facebook may boast 1.23 billion monthly users, LinkedIn boasts over 300 million professionals and business users. If you're in the business-to-business space, it's well worth looking at specific targeting options on LinkedIn. Such information provided includes the obvious, again—age, gender, and location—but LinkedIn also utilizes criteria that allow you to determine exactly who your audience should be, based on job title, school or degree, skills, group affiliations, industry, seniority, and company size.

Software marketers might target information technology professionals. Financial planners might target C-level senior management in markets where the financial planners have offices. We use LinkedIn to target senior marketing professionals in New York, Boston, and Chicago. Also, the reality is that there are still some professionals, especially senior ones, who aren't on Facebook, and if you're going to find these folks at all online, LinkedIn is a great place to start.

FORGET DEMOGRAPHICS: TARGETING ON TWITTER

We've been talking about the amazing demographic targeting capabilities of Facebook and LinkedIn's ad platforms. But what about targeting people *based on actual needs they have expressly shared*? In other words, who cares about people's age or their job title or interests if you know that they are looking for a service or product you provide? You can find such people using Google, but the current leading platform for finding conversation is Twitter. All tweets are, by default, public. There is an immensely high volume of tweets every day—more than 500 million![2] By utilizing Twitter, your target audience becomes based on what people are actually saying, not simply on what you glean from demographic research.

Say, for instance, you're an entertainment lawyer, or you're in the marketing department for an entertainment law firm. You can target movie producers or actors or others you *think* might need your services. Or you can do a Twitter search, such as the one featured in Figure 2.4. In this example, a search for the keywords "need entertainment lawyer" yields three people who in the last 18 hours actually asked for an entertainment lawyer!

How much potential revenue would three inbound leads mean to most law firms?

FIGURE 2.4   Entertainment Law Firm Twitter Search

If you haven't done one before, take a moment to try a Twitter search on your smartphone. Just go to Search.Twitter .com, and type in the search bar "need [your product, service, or category]" or "I want [something you have]." You may be happily surprised with how large a perfect target audience you find out there practically begging for you. This method of targeting is not going to scale for low-priced, high-frequency products, but for anyone selling or marketing a high-end product or service (jewelry, real estate, or financial or other professional services, to name a few), it's the ultimate in targeting. Imagine communicating only with the people who want to hear from you or who are sharing problems you can solve. The time spent targeting on Twitter will quickly pay off. Stop guessing what your audience wants and start searching—and listen to what they are saying.

HOW DO *YOU* LIKE TO BE TARGETED
AS A CONSUMER?

Take off your marketing hat and put on your consumer cap for a moment. Do *you* like being targeted broadly by marketers and advertisers? Do you enjoy watching incessant car commercials interrupting your favorite TV shows? Or would you rather see ads and marketing materials from car companies when you are actually looking to buy a new car and have expressed interest in doing so? Similarly, if you're single, it doesn't necessarily mean you want to see ads for dating sites, and the fact that you're a woman doesn't mean you want to hear about department store sales.

And for goodness sake, just because you're a man doesn't mean you want to be bombarded by men's sexual health companies. No, you likely want to hear from companies and organizations based on your specific stated needs and interests. Now that it's possible to more narrowly target people using social networks, put your marketing hat back on and leverage the opportunity.

HOW WELL DO YOU KNOW YOUR TARGET AUDIENCE?

The last few decades have brought numerous improvements in marketing intelligence and research. But until you had today's ability to target such specific groups of people, you may have had no need to identify your target audience so narrowly. For example, you might have known your audience loved playing sports, but perhaps they preferred one sport to another. Or maybe young women loved your product, but you didn't know that 21- to 22-year-olds were far more likely to buy it than 23- to 24-year-olds. Today you can run the appropriate Facebook or Twitter searches to target your audience precisely and find out who the consumers for your products and services actually are.

While some businesses have narrower and more well-defined target audiences than others, you can always refine the notion of who is part of your ideal audience. You will likely find that there is more than just one group of people who are looking for your goods or services. Huge global brands, for example, have certain categories of customers that are more common than others. Perhaps female lawyers spend more on your product than stay-at-home moms, for instance. If you don't know the specifics, you can always ask too: If you have 1,000 Facebook fans, ask what their favorite sport is. If you find out for some reason that 9 out of 10 of them prefer baseball, you might consider sponsoring a local Little League team. Social media will help you find your target audience and provide you with further insight about these groups.

Put an End to Wasteful Marketing Spending

There's a common axiom about advertising among key marketing executives: "Fifty percent of my advertising works. I just don't know which 50 percent."

Search marketing and social media have rendered it possible to target exactly the people you know are your customers and best prospects, not the people you *think* are in those groups based on your intuition and vague understanding of market research. You can continue to spend your marketing and advertising dollars on less targeted media in the name of greater reach and awareness, or you can focus on a narrower but much more potent audience. When you tap into that unique target audience, you'll never again want to waste precious marketing dollars on less accountable, out-of-focus media.

Targeting Is Just the Beginning of the Conversation

Remember, we're not talking about advertising repeatedly in the hopes of eventually finding the right person at the right time who may happen to need to buy your product or service. We're talking about defining and finding the narrowly targeted, correct audience and then beginning to engage them in a conversation, so that *when they are ready to buy*, you're the obvious, logical choice. If you've targeted them correctly and then engaged with them along the way, when it comes time to buy, they won't even need to search, and they certainly won't need to respond to a television or radio ad. They'll already know you, trust you, and like you, so they'll turn right to you. And of course, you don't need to be peddling a physical product. Take, for example, Likeable's work with the Fibromyalgia & Fatigue Centers (FFC) and the steps we took in helping people afflicted with fibromyalgia and chronic fatigue syndrome and the FFC connect.

Fibromyalgia and Fatigue Centers
Target Just the People in Need

Millions of Americans suffer from fibromyalgia and chronic fatigue syndrome. The Fibromyalgia & Fatigue Centers of America is one of the leading treatment facilities in the country. They provide help in the form of doctors, nurses, counselors, and group support with 12 physical locations throughout the country. The typical broad profile of someone who suffers from one of these illnesses is a female between the ages of 35 and 60, and in the past, FFC has used mass targeting initiatives in the form of television ads, radio commercials, and print ads in the hope of reaching these and other people who can benefit from their services.

That kind of advertising is expensive and wasteful, however, so we developed a narrower targeting initiative. We used Facebook to target people who actually listed "fibromyalgia" in their profiles as an interest because we assumed that, aside from a few doctors and researchers, most people who list it as an interest suffer from the illness or have a close family member who does. We also listened on Twitter for people actually talking about one of the illnesses, regularly searching for keywords such as "fibromyalgia," "tired all of the time," "chronic fatigue," and "why am I so tired?"

Equally important, we set up a community on Facebook called Fibro 360, where anyone who has been affected by fibromyalgia or chronic fatigue syndrome can share stories, support one another, and get news, tips, research, and information on the illnesses. We didn't link online ads and marketing messages to FFC's website or to its phone number. Instead, we linked all communications to the community on Facebook. Nine months later, the results were astounding: tens of thousands of people had joined the community on Facebook.

Now hundreds of people connect and talk with one another each and every day, and if and when people in the community want additional help, they turn to Fibromyalgia & Fatigue Centers and often hire our client. Hundreds have done this, resulting in a greater than 20 percent sales lift, attributed to Facebook.

LIKEABLE'S OWN TARGETING

The best B2B targeting we've done using social media is for our own companies, Likeable Media and Likeable Local. We may be smaller than lots of big agencies, but with more than 39,000 *likes* on Facebook, we've grown one of the largest fan bases of any marketing agency in the world. More important than the number of fans we have, though, is who they are. From the start, we've targeted people on Facebook with job titles such as "chief marketing officer," "vice president of marketing," "brand manager," and "marketing director." These key decision makers are our perfect customers, so we've focused our efforts on them and geared our ads toward them. They've become fans, they've interacted with us over time, and many of them have called or e-mailed asking to do business with us. For Likeable Local, we've targeted and acquired over 10,000 small business fans on our Facebook page.

No matter whom your organization is looking to reach, you can find them on Facebook, and, increasingly, on Twitter. There are several more examples in Table 2.1 of types of companies and the narrow audience targeted for them using both social media sites.

So, who are *your* perfect customers? How narrowly can you define your target audience?

TABLE 2.1 **Targeted Audience for Various Companies**

CLIENT	TARGETED AUDIENCE
Real estate coach	Real estate agents and brokers across the country
Beachside hotel in south Florida	Engaged women living in colder, northern states who might be looking for a destination wedding location
Telecommunications provider	Users complaining on Twitter about problems with the client's competitors
New shopping center	People within a 10-mile radius of the center who list "shopping" or "buying new things" as an interest in their profiles
Cat accessory company	Users who list "cat lover," "cat," and "I have a cat" in their profiles
Author	Fans of authors with similar writing styles and book types
Public relations firm	Publicity managers and public relations directors at the 100 biggest companies in the client's city

ACTION ITEMS

1. Write down a description of your perfect target audience. Define your customers and prospects as narrowly as you can. What is their age and gender? Are they married, engaged, or single? Where do they live? What are their interests? What are their job titles? Where do they work? What do they talk about? If the answer to some of these questions is, "That doesn't matter," then that's OK. But try to paint as detailed a picture of who your customers are, and who you want them to be, as you can.

2. Once you've defined this audience, look for and find them on social networks. Dive into the Facebook advertising platform, and see if you can determine how many people fit all of the criteria that you've written down. Search LinkedIn by job title or industry if you're in the B2B space. Search Twitter and Facebook for people talking about whatever it is that you think your customers talk about.

3. Write down a list of places in your marketing budget where you're spending too much money targeting too wide an audience. How can you cut back from other marketing and advertising expenses that are reaching a broader group in favor of more narrow targeting using social networks?

HASTE MAKES WASTE; SO DOES TRADITIONAL MARKETING AND ADVERTISING

I understand that after reading this chapter, you won't go out and immediately cut your entire advertising budget because you're targeting too wide an audience. You don't have to. But surely you can think of somewhere to cut back in order to start targeting the right people through social networks, those who will become your customers, advocates even, in the future. Find them, bring them into the conversation, and when they're ready, you'll be their first choice.

CHAPTER 3

Think—and Act—Like Your Consumer

Do you like being disrupted? Do you enjoy when you're reading something online and a pop-up banner ad gets in the way of the next paragraph? What about when you're working on a project at the office, the phone rings, and you answer to find a sales guy on the other end of the line trying to pitch his wares?

When I speak at conferences, clubs, and meetings, I often tell my audiences, many of whom are marketers, to place themselves in the role of the consumer. I then ask, "How many of you listen to and enjoy radio commercials?"

No hands.

"How many of you watch and enjoy television commercials?"

A couple of hands usually come up at this point, and normally, upon further review, these people are, in fact, ad guys.

"How many of you use and enjoy Facebook or another social network?"

Here, hands shoot up in the air, anywhere between 50 and 90 percent of the room.

Is this because Facebook, or social media as a whole, is the newest, shiniest product in town? I don't think so. I believe it's because people fundamentally want to use media to relax, enjoy themselves, and connect with others—*not* to be interrupted. Here are a few marketing and advertising tools and methods that are available today. Placing yourself in the role of the consumer, think about how you feel when you receive or experience the following:

- Direct mail
- Magazine ads
- TV ads
- Radio ads
- Packaging (that is, "Free Toy Inside" on the cereal box)
- Flyers handed to you on the street
- Billboards off the highway
- Automated messages when you're on hold, telling you to visit the company website
- Mobile and/or text-messaging ads
- Ten minutes of ads before the trailers even start at the movie theater
- E-mails constantly arriving in your inbox from marketing lists you don't remember signing up for
- Telemarketing and cold-calling to your home and office

Advertisements and marketing ploys are found just about everywhere we go. From the television in our living room to the stall in the public bathroom, from a drive down the interstate to a walk through the city's streets, from your phone line at work to your personal cell number: nowhere is safe from ads! And while some ads are funny, interesting, and even compelling—if you consider the consumer's viewpoint, you'll agree that most are simply disruptive and unwanted.

So what's a marketer to do? How can you possibly avoid joining the endless parade of marketing and advertising disruptions in the quest to find your consumers?

All you have to do is stop thinking like a marketer and start thinking like your consumer.

RULE OF THUMB: WHAT DO YOUR CUSTOMERS REALLY WANT?

Laura Fitton of HubSpot has a saying: "Your entire social media strategy can be summed up in two words: Be useful." With every Facebook message you send out, with every tweet you post, even with every e-mail or radio and television advertisement you write, ask yourself the following:

- Will the recipients of this message truly find it of value, or will they find it annoying and disruptive?
- Would I want to receive this message as a consumer?

If you respond that yes, as *a consumer*, this message is of value and you would indeed want to receive it, then it is a message worth communicating to your customers and the world. On the other hand, if you cannot see any *true* value to the consumer or you believe the message will be only an annoyance, then it's simply not worth sending. Why spend money, time, and effort only to contribute to mass advertising, marketing, and information noise that the consumer does not want or need in the first place?

Sure, even a poorly conceived message can generate some Web traffic, phone calls, awareness, or even sales, but it can also erode your brand. In the long run, the organizations that will win are the organizations that engage in positive, useful communications with their customers and prospects. Today, the most effective way to do so is to utilize the tools offered by social media.

The Brilliance of the Facebook News Feed

On Facebook, when you log in as a user, you are brought to a home page that displays your News Feed. The News Feed is a stream of information from your Facebook social connections, including your Facebook friends, Facebook groups you've joined, and Facebook pages that you've *liked*. Not every piece of information posted by every one of your friends is included, but since the Top News pops up as the default for users when they log on, that's one of the first things you see, and it is your main source of information.

The brilliance of Facebook's News Feed is that it serves you individualized content based on three factors:

1. How recently the content occurred or was created
2. The strength of your relationship with the person or organization who shared the content
3. How much engagement (*likes* and comments) it received

Most important for marketers to consider is the third factor because it directly affects whether or not a company's content will be seen in the users' News Feeds. The more people who are interested in the content, or the more people who have had a positive experience with a product or service relating to the content, the more *likes* it will receive, and the more prominent it will be in the feed.

Figure 3.1 shows a formula describing the original News Feed Optimization algorithm, also known as EdgeRank, from a presentation given by Facebook engineers Ruchi Sanghvi and Ari Steinberg at Facebook's 2010 f8 developer conference.

FIGURE 3.1   **News Feed Optimization**

$$\sum_{edges\ e} u_e w_e d_e$$

u_e affinity score between viewing user and edge creator

w_e weight for this edge type (create, comment, like, tag, etc.)

d_e time for decay factor based on how long ago the edge was created

---

In 2013, Facebook abandoned the original EdgeRank formula, but Facebook continues to optimize content based on relevancy, time, focus, quality, and variety.

Want your Facebook posts to be seen? Ask yourself these four key questions:

1. **When and how often should I post content?** In order to optimize, you'll need to determine when your fans, friends, and prospects are most likely to be logged on and using Facebook. If your customers are teenagers, for instance, you shouldn't share content during weekday mornings and early afternoons when they're at school. If you are targeting a nine-to-five office crowd, sharing content in the morning may be to your advantage because many Facebook users in this audience are likely to check their pages as they settle in at their desks. Or if your customers are mostly teachers, you'll want to share updates between 3 and 5 p.m. when they're likely working but not in front of their classes. In general, however, more users are logged in on weekend days and fewer companies are working then, so weekends are the best time to share content.

2. **Do these users interact with me often?** If a user *liked* your page through a Facebook ad but never actually visited that page and didn't have friends who interacted with your page, that user is not likely to see any of your content updates. If a user visits your page from time to time, has *liked* the occasional post, or has even viewed photos from your company, your chances of showing up in his or her News Feed increase dramatically. Keep this setup in mind because this is why getting *likes* initially on your content is so very important—once you get someone engaged, a dialogue between you and the consumer or prospect is created, one that can be built upon and continued.

3. **How interactive are the engagements with the post?** This edge is the simplest and most worth focusing on. Facebook's algorithm determines the level of interest or relevancy of an object based on the number of comments and *likes* it receives. The greater the response to the object, the more likely it is to

show up in users' News Feeds. Of course, this is a powerful momentum-gathering, cyclical concept: if a piece of Facebook content receives enough comments and *likes*, it will rise to the top of users' News Feeds, where it will be more likely to generate an even greater number of positive responses. If, on the other hand, the content doesn't quickly catch on, it won't rise to the top of users' News Feeds, and it will remain virtually invisible.

4. **Have I boosted the post?** One foolproof way to get your content seen is to *boost* the post (which we'll talk about in more depth in Chapter 15). At Likeable Local, we've found that an investment of even just a few dollars to boost a particular post can result in thousands of people seeing that client's content. Facebook's new algorithm makes it more difficult for people to see content organically. The first three factors are still very important, but post boosts are increasingly important.

How to Make the Algorithm Work for You

Facebook's News Feed algorithm is nothing short of revolutionary. Imagine if television commercials that people didn't want to watch disappeared or if direct mail that the first few recipients didn't open stopped being sent out, never making it to anyone else's door. Consider how much you would pay to have e-mails other people hadn't responded to positively remain out of your inbox. Facebook has effectively created a system that filters out all the junk the user couldn't care less about or, worse yet, will respond to negatively. This situation forces companies, and individuals, to think very carefully about the content they share: it's a great thing for users and a powerful tool for marketers and advertisers who understand what their consumers want and don't want. Let's look at an example.

Conglomerate A is a global sneaker brand that has spent millions of dollars in advertising to grow a Facebook fan base of 1 million fans. Your similar, though much smaller, organization has far fewer resources and currently has only 5,000 fans, half of whom happen to also be fans of Conglomerate A.

Conglomerate A shares a traditional marketing message with its fans: "Check out our new running shoes on our website and buy them now!" Only a handful of people click the Like button or comment on the content. Since the company has failed to engage its audience, only a few hundred people will end up seeing the update because it will not be moved up into users' Top News.

Your company, however, posts a link to your website with the following update at the same time as Conglomerate A's: "Click 'Like' if you're excited about going running this weekend! Anybody going running?" with a beautiful picture. Here, you attempt to engage the users with a more personalized, friendly, and less demanding message. You are not just telling them to "go buy shoes." Your update then generates comments and *likes*, enough to stay at the top of thousands of people's News Feeds for a day. This placement, in turn, generates greater clicks and higher sales. More important, the comments left lead to a conversation that will aid your success in the *next* update you share. You've outdone Conglomerate A. While it was busy marketing, you were thinking like your consumers. You were engaging them and building an invaluable audience.

WHAT DO YOUR CONSUMERS LIKE?

The important question is, What do your consumers truly like? Consider what they care about. What do they value? What content will get them to authentically click Like and increase your visibility among users? Keep in mind that you can't just keep sharing updates that ask people to *like* the content because that would quickly get as annoying and disruptive as many of the traditional marketing tactics you've grown to know and hate.

For the answers, look to what you already know about your consumers—and if you don't know something, ask!

For instance, say you have a male-focused customer base. You suspect these consumers are big sports fans, but you're not sure what sports or teams they are most interested in. You could simply ask on Facebook, "What's your favorite major sporting event of the year? Who did you root for this past season?" If your fans overwhelmingly say the Super Bowl and provide their favorite football teams, you'll want to share content about that sport in the future, even if your product has nothing to do with football.

If *you* were your consumer, what would make *you* click Like or leave a comment? An appetizing photo? A funny video? A fact nobody knew about you?

One thing users are sure *not* to respond to positively is a press release about your latest earnings statement, new hire, or new product. There may be an audience who cares enough about this information to warrant sharing it elsewhere, but that audience is not the group to target on Facebook. The Facebook audience doesn't care. Social media networks such as Facebook, Twitter, and LinkedIn are not broadcast media. I can't stress this enough. Engage. Don't broadcast!

IT'S ABOUT YOUR CUSTOMERS, NOT YOUR BRAND

In the past, traditional marketers didn't have the luxury of having a two-way conversation with customers, but they did have a captive audience. Consequently, traditional marketers pounded consumers over the head with marketing messages until the public bought from them. If you're over the age of 40, for example, you probably know the Jolly Green Giant jingle—not because it's a great song but because you were exposed to it so many times through television and radio ads that you couldn't help but learn it.

In a crowded marketing and advertising world, *mindshare* is how much your customers are thinking about your product or service. In order to win your customers' mindshare now, your marketing can't be *solely* about your brand, or products, or features and benefits anymore. More than anything, you have to get your customers talking, or you have to get involved in their already ongoing conversation. If they're talking and you're at the top of their News Feeds on Facebook, you've got some mindshare—and that's more valuable than paid advertising, which customers can readily choose to ignore. Messaging has to be about *your customers*. What are their hopes and dreams? What do they want to do, hear about, talk about, and share? What's actually relevant to them?

This lesson is a hard one for companies to learn because it involves unlearning much of what they know about marketing, promotion, and publicity. They'll ask, "What about our brand? How can we spend precious marketing dollars and time on messaging that has nothing to do with our brand or company?"

It's the results that matter, so remind yourself about the News Feed, for example. If the message is all about your brand and people don't find that message interesting or relevant, then they won't even see it. On the bright side, even if the message isn't about your brand at all, if it's being commented on and *liked*, your Facebook page name will still be seen by your fans, and it will garner attention from others. Your brand will not only be at the top of people's News Feeds but also at the top of their minds. Let's take a look at a couple of real-life examples of the power of thinking like your customers and appropriately using social media to engage them.

The Pampered Chef: Cooking Up Content Their Fans *Like*

The Pampered Chef (TPC) is one of the largest and best-known direct sales organizations in the country. Based in Chicago, it has a huge sales force of independent consultants who sell cooking and dining products through house parties and other events. The Pampered Chef joined Facebook as an organization after most of its direct-selling competition had already established their own pages and generated thousands of fans. TPC wanted to build an effective Facebook presence quickly for its overall brand and salespeople. It didn't have a budget for Facebook ads, which its competitors, and many other companies, were using to drive initial *likes* to their fan pages.

The Pampered Chef's team members thought carefully about the kinds of content TPC's customers would like, and what they wouldn't like, and they worked together to build a fan page, applications, and a daily content calendar that would be about neither the brand nor selling but instead all about the consumers. The result was that the team now shares useful content such as recipes and recipe contests, and they encourage visitors to their fan page to share their stories about their own great meals and pictures of their own culinary masterpieces. A virtual gift application allows fans to share a picture of a scrumptious cake on their friends' Facebook walls on their birthdays or to celebrate other occasions. All of this content is loosely related to the brand and its mission, of course, but it isn't *about* the brand. It's about the *consumers*, and it is designed to be as intriguing as possible. By generating hundreds of comments and *likes* through consumer interaction (see Figure 3.2), the Pampered Chef remains at the top of its fans' News Feeds for as long as possible, generating more eyeballs, mindshare, clicks, and sales.

More than a hundred thousand people *liked* the page in the first two months, *without any paid advertising*, and hundreds of people comment on every daily update. The rich content shared by the Pampered Chef each day generates not only *likes* but lots of sharing as well, which in turn drives more and more people

---

FIGURE 3.2   **A Facebook Post from the Pampered Chef**

 The Pampered Chef Hey pampered friends, we want to hear from ✕ you! In honor of our 30th anniversary, tell us what your favorite Pampered Chef recipe is! (Pssst...did you know you could win your own Pampered Chef business? Enter to win our Your Life. Your Way. Sweepstakes through the Join Us tab today!)
October 18 at 12:17pm · Like · Comment

👍 Amy Slife and 370 others like this.

💬 View all 303 comments

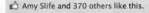

back to the page. While the company did not reveal revenue numbers generated by the initial Facebook engagement, rest assured that sales figures were very likeable too.

Century 21 Real Estate

It's safe to say most people are familiar with Century 21 Real Estate, the brand behind the ubiquitous black and gold property signs. On its website, Century 21 describes itself this way:

> Century 21 Real Estate LLC (century21.com) is the franchisor of the world's largest residential real estate franchise sales organization, providing brand marks, comprehensive training and marketing support for the CENTURY 21® System. The System is comprised of more than 102,000 affiliated sales professionals in approximately 6,900 offices in 75 countries and territories worldwide.

You'll notice that "homeowners" and "home buyers" are not mentioned in that description. That's because the brand's primary goal and focus is on franchise growth and agent acquisition. A brand whose business focus is on franchise acquisition would seemingly not place a marketing focus on all homeowners, right? Maybe for a brand that isn't Century 21.

Instead of creating social media properties that are solely focused on acquiring future franchise owners or real estate agents, Century 21 decided to appeal to the masses. With regular social media postings and blog entries tying real estate themes to DIY, pop culture, and current events, Century 21 has positioned itself as one of the most engaging real estate brands, generating more website traffic than its competitors and appealing to prospects as people first. While tips for how to zombie-proof your home (posted in honor of a season premiere of AMC's hit show *The Walking Dead*) might not scream "Be a franchise owner!" it does let Century 21's customers know that they're a real brand, with a sense of humor, and they are different from the competition (Figure 3.3).

FIGURE 3.3   A Facebook Post from Century 21 Real Estate

 **CENTURY 21** ✔
@CENTURY21   ⚙   +☺ Follow

5 Zombie-Proof Houses Your Family Won't
Be Caught Dead In. buff.ly/1boNcMD

↩ Reply   ⇄ Retweet   ★ Favorite   ••• More

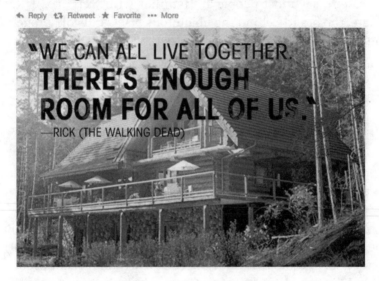

ACTION ITEMS

1. Write down what your typical customers like. Try to avoid writing things your customers like about your company, organization, or products, and instead focus on their interests. Then imagine what specific content would make you click the Like button if you saw it as a consumer. Write down 10 examples of such likeable content.

2. Take messaging that your organization has used in written marketing materials in the past, and rewrite it for social media, making the material more valuable or interesting to the audience. It should be short and sweet, and it should be something you'd want to receive as the consumer, not something you would have wanted to send as the marketer.

3. Develop a plan for how you might create valued content not just for social networks but for all marketing and communications content. What would you change in your e-mail marketing, direct mail, Web content, and ad copy if you thought like a consumer instead of a marketer? Can you create better content in all of your communication?

BE LIKEABLE, NOT DISRUPTIVE

We are all bombarded by more marketing messages every day than we can even count. You have an opportunity to rise to the top of the clutter, not by coming up with a more creative disruption but by producing content that people actually want to receive. Facebook's News Feed forces you to think like a consumer and challenges you to share content that will be truly valued or enjoyed by your consumers. If you don't want to be invisible, you'll have to be likeable, at least in social media. Remember, on Facebook, you're not competing with your competitors for the consumers' attention. You're competing with pictures of my best friend's baby!

CHAPTER 4

Invite Your Customers to Be Your First Fans

You've started a Facebook page and a Twitter account for your company. You've put up a YouTube channel, started a blog, sharpened your LinkedIn profile, and you've even added a button on your website promoting your Facebook page. You're doing everything you're supposed to do to "join the conversation" with social media.

Yet up until now, the results have been dismal. You have a ridiculously low number of fans, considering the size of your business, and the only person you're having a conversation with is yourself. (OK, maybe the guy in the cubicle next to you has joined in too.) But the promise of social media that you've heard so much about is far from being fulfilled. You don't know what you've done wrong or what you need to do to get on the right track to social network success. Where are all of your Facebook fans? Why isn't everyone giving you the *like* stamp of approval?

There's no reason to worry. No matter the size of your organization, gaining lots of fans on Facebook, followers on Twitter, and subscribers on your blog and YouTube is far from automatic. The bad news is that you're going to have to work for fans, friends, and followers, but the good news is that everyone else has to as well. There are international brands that spend millions of dollars in marketing each year with fewer than a thousand fans on Facebook and no official Twitter presence at all—so whatever situation you're in right now, you're in good company and still have time for improvement.

The Internet is nothing like it was 10 years ago, when people endlessly surfed the Web. Many people just don't access information on the Web in that way anymore. If anything, users surf the Web using their own personalized Facebook, Twitter, and LinkedIn filters to look for relevant and recommended content. Moreover, people are increasingly accessing the Web through their smartphones and favorite mobile apps. What that means for you, as a company, is that whether you're a huge brand or brand-new, people who don't know your product or service already are unlikely to be your first Facebook fans or Twitter followers.

So who will become your first social media brand advocates? Your strongest assets are customers, staff, partners, and vendors. However, to leverage this goodwill, you have to ask them to support the company through social networking *and* tell them why they should. Explain the benefits of social networking to your current supporters. Tell them why it is imperative that your company move forward with social media initiatives. Describe the ways their actions will help your company in your marketing and advertising efforts, and make sure they understand how valuable their participation is in this process.

THE *LIKE* IS MORE IMPORTANT THAN THE LINK

Ten years ago, if you built a website for your company, you didn't expect thousands of strangers to just visit it, did you? Instead, you used other marketing initiatives and assets to direct people to your website and to publicize the website address or link wherever you could. Sometimes people checked it out, and if they were interested in your content and trusted you enough, maybe they even stayed a while or purchased your products and services. Or if other related companies found your content useful, it was possible that they would link your website to theirs, in exchange for you linking their website to yours. This linking took place in the hope of creating more "link value," greater search engine optimization, and more website traffic. Today, however, the *like* is more important than the "link." Getting people to your website may help them learn about your company and maybe even buy something, but getting them to *like* you on Facebook does two additional things that will contribute to your company's long-term success.

First, when people use the *like* function, they subscribe to your updates, allowing you to have a conversation with them on Facebook forever, unless you erode their trust and they unsubscribe. Second, it introduces and endorses you *to every one of the users' friends.* The average person on Facebook has 350 friends, so with every *like*, you're exposing your brand to another 350 potential customers, or more. Can you imagine if every time one individual visited your website, she shared that fact with 350 of her friends? ("Hey ladies, I just visited this site. Check it out. It's so great!") The same phenomenon is true for followers on Twitter, subscribers on YouTube or your blog, and other social networking outlets, but the numbers aren't as big as those on Facebook.

Simply put, the more *likes* the content receives, the more often it will be viewed, and the number of people seeing and accessing the content will grow over time. There are long-lasting effects of the *like* in Facebook search optimization: once you acquire a *like* on your page, any of that person's friends will see this during future searches. So if you're an attorney and one of your clients has *liked* you on Facebook, any time one of his friends searches for an attorney in the future and finds your page, your client's testimonial ("Your friend John *likes* Bob the attorney") will be right there waiting for him. If you represent a children's car seat company, once one happy mommy customer *likes* your product on Facebook, her friends will quickly see her endorsement, and that will be more powerful than any impersonal advertisement.

HOW TO GET THE LIKE:
DEVELOP YOUR VALUE PROPOSITION

Before you started reading this book, maybe you already understood the capabilities and importance of Facebook's *like* function. The question you might have now, however, is how do you get people to actually *like* you on Facebook? No matter how well known your brand is currently, you'll need to provide a value proposition to your customers, staff, vendors, and partners, some sort of benefit they will receive from becoming your fans. In other words, don't just tell them to *like* you. Tell them what's in it for them, and tell them in a way that's about them, not you.

Consider the following two different calls to action:

**Like us on Facebook now at
FB.com/LikeableLocal.**

versus

**Ask us your social media questions anytime at
FB.com/LikeableLocal.**

The first one is totally brand-centric. Why would you read that and decide to *like* our company unless you already knew us, loved us, and trusted us? The second call is consumer-centric, and it is likely to generate a lot more action, not only from people who already love us and trust us but also from casual, first-time customers and maybe even prospects. Remember, it's not about you. It's about your customers. Whatever you can do to encourage activity on your Facebook page will in fact encourage *likes*, without actually asking for them. For instance, Oreo asks customers on the company's packaging: "To dunk or not to dunk? Let us know at Facebook.com/Oreo." The company is encouraging people to share their opinions. It is not just telling them to *like* Oreo's online content—yet, more than 37 million people have *liked* the company on Facebook.

The value proposition might be different for each constituency. For example, you may want to invite your own staff to *like* your page with the incentive that they can post questions to the

CEO, some of which will receive responses. For customers, however, you may invite them to access a discount.

By giving people a value proposition for joining you and then surrounding your customers with that value proposition, or others, at every opportunity, you'll convert customers into fans, and that's where things begin to get interesting.

Why should people *like* you on Facebook or follow you on Twitter or LinkedIn? What's in it for them that's of value? How can you summarize that value in a short, easy-to-understand call to action? The answer is, it depends on your business or organization. Here are several real calls to action from clients to help you think about why people should *like* you:

- Share your feedback with us at FB.com/VerizonFiOS.
- Win prizes and join the conversation at FB.com/1800Flowers.
- Your medical questions answered at FB.com/KenRedcrossMD.
- Free support for quitting smoking at FB.com/NYCquits.
- Connect with other moms like you at FB.com/striderite.
- Get some at FB.com/NYCcondom.

It's not about you. It's about your customers (see Table 4.1). In the same way that the Web quickly became too big for you to tell people to visit your website without telling them why,

TABLE 4.1 Top 10 Reasons Consumers *Like* Fan Pages on Facebook*

1. To receive discounts and promos
2. To show support for brand to friends
3. To get a "freebie" (e.g., free samples, coupons)
4. To stay informed about company activities
5. For updates on future projects
6. For updates on upcoming sales
7. Just for fun
8. To get access to exclusive content
9. To learn more about the company
10. For education about company topics

*Source: Based on a report from CoTweet and ExactTarget, cited in Paloma Vazquez, "Why Do People 'Like' a Company or Brand?" *PSFK*, November 1, 2010, PSFK.com/2010/11/why-do-people-like-a-company-or-brand.html.

Facebook is too big to tell people—even your customers—to *like* you without telling them why. It's essential to develop that value proposition and then integrate it into your communications with customers and prospects.

Getting the *like* approval is essential for everyone, but it is even more important for smaller businesses and new organizations, which can utilize such free social media and word-of-mouth marketing to grow their fledgling companies. Don't be afraid to ask anyone in your organization's circle of influence to *like* you. Just don't do it without creating value for whoever that audience is. You're not going to get *likes* from anyone without giving him or her a valid reason. On the other hand, you're also not going to get *likes* from anyone without reminding him or her to *like* you. Give them value and opportunity, and your vendors, partners, staff, and friends will join you.

Where Should You Tell Customers to *Like* You?

You should provide potential followers and fans with value propositions to *like* you in as many places as possible. Here are a number of places to consider integrating the call to action to your customers:

1. On your website
2. On every e-mail you send out as a company
3. On every staff person's e-mail signature
4. On every business card you hand out
5. On every brochure you print
6. On every receipt you hand out
7. On every piece of snail mail you send out
8. On every inbound phone call to your company
9. On every outbound phone call from your company
10. On all of your packaging (as in the Oreo example)
11. On all of your in-location signage

Some of these more antiquated techniques—snail mail and brochures, for example—are given new vitality and purpose both for you and your consumers if you can connect them directly to your online social network.

Text to Like

Most people don't carry their computers around with them wherever they go, but just about everyone has their smartphone with them almost all the time. Facebook has a little-known "Text to Like" feature that's powerful in converting anyone to *like* your page without being in front of a computer. Simply type "like [page name]" from anywhere in the United States, and send it to FBOOK (32665) from any mobile phone connected to your Facebook account, and you'll *like* that page. Don't believe me? Test it out right now—I don't mind. Grab your phone and text "like LikeableLocal" to 32665. Then you'll be able to ask our company any questions you have about social media or this book, and you'll receive a quick response. (Thanks for the *like!*)

The "Text to Like" feature has vast implications for any business with real-life physical locations, any product sold in stores, and any retail or restaurant locations or government services. Imagine if you're waiting in line at a deli or a department store, and you see a note posted near the register that reads, "Text 'Like OurStore' to connect to us on Facebook, and get 20 percent off your next purchase." As a customer, you are getting an incentive that makes this offer compelling, and it is likely you will probably check it out. As a marketer, consider how to integrate such marketing and advertising into your customers' experience.

If you take a long view on such activity, the rewards are bountiful. By focusing on getting the *like* instead of making an immediate sale of a particular product, it's true that you might not sell as much product to that customer as fast as you had wanted to. But with the power of Facebook's social graph, you will create an average of 200 potential new customers for every user who *likes* you. If that customer comes back to you weeks later and brings a friend or two, isn't that more valuable than a single, initial sale? More long-term opportunities are therefore created for marketers less focused on immediate sales and more focused on obtaining *likes*.

A NEW INTERNET SALES CYCLE IS BORN

A prolonged recession and an increased focus on, and ability to measure, every click on the Internet has led to the marketer's obsession with driving subscriptions and sales through Web and e-mail marketing. But if you step back and consider the value of the *like* compared to the immediate sale, you'll see that a long view will yield a better return.

E-commerce: Sales Now or *Likes* Now?

The typical e-commerce site features dozens, hundreds, or thousands of products for sale, many of which are often purchased as gifts. Every piece of text and graphics on such a site has been carefully optimized to drive as many clicks to the shopping cart as possible, attempting to maximize immediate sales. This strategy made sense before the arrival of the social Web, but what if that same e-commerce site were optimized for people to share what they *liked* by clicking the Like button on as many products or categories as possible? This function would create a permanent record of each visitor's interests. Then, friends of the visitor could go to the site, see the exact products their friend indicated he *liked*, and they could then buy it for him for a birthday, holiday, or some other reason. As a company, you'd get fewer immediate sales, but you'd set yourself up to significantly increase your *conversion rate* (the percentage of website visitors who buy your products or take further actions) in the future.

Wouldn't you be more likely to buy something online for your husband or your wife if you saw that he or she had already shown interest in it by *liking* it online?

Professional Services: Like as the New Referral

Websites for doctors, dentists, lawyers, accountants, and other service professionals are set up now to convince you to call them—to take action now. But what if these websites were set up to generate *likes*? If professionals took the time to say to all of their current clients, "If you are satisfied with our services and would like to let others know about your exceptional experience with our company, please *like* us on Facebook," or "Ask us questions on our LinkedIn page," these professionals would instantly begin creating a valuable network, not only growing their exposure but also building a clientele who highly trusts them.

Five years ago, if you wanted to find a lawyer or accountant, you might have done a Google search and found those practices that had spent money on search engine marketing so that their site would be the first to pop up on the screen. Now, to find a lawyer or accountant, you can do a Facebook or LinkedIn search of your trusted friends or colleagues and find a practice to which they have given their approval. Are you more likely to pick a lawyer or doctor at random online or rely on the recommendation of a friend?

Dr. Ed Zuckerberg and Aesthetic Family Dentistry (Even Dentists Can Be Likeable)

Edward Zuckerberg, DDS, is a practicing dentist, for many years based in Dobbs Ferry, New York, and now in Palo Alto, California. He also happens to be the father of Mark Zuckerberg, founder and chief executive officer of Facebook. Known as "Painless Dr. Z" by his patients, Dr. Zuckerberg is proof that anyone's business can benefit from utilizing social media. Dentists have always relied on word-of-mouth recommendations and referrals to increase their business—today, social media allows this to happen much more passively and efficiently.

Let's face it, most people don't like going to the dentist (sorry, Dr. Z). If you're anything like me, you consider a dentist appointment more like a tolerable, necessary evil than something you find the least bit enjoyable. Consequently, smart dentists everywhere have gone out of their way to make their practices as tolerable as possible, including friendly front office staff, bright colors on the walls, interesting magazines and other reading material, and toys for children's visits. In addition to these things, which make the physical experience better, Dr. Zuckerberg has taken the steps necessary to make his practice more likeable on Facebook.

When you first walk into the office, you'll see a sign saying, "Like us? Then Like us on Facebook at Facebook.com /PainlessDrZ or text 'like PainlessDrZ' to 32665 to join the conversation." This action alone is more effective than the actions taken by 99 percent of all dental practices in the world in driving *likes*. People sitting in the waiting room are a captive audience, and it's the perfect opportunity to convert customers into online fans. However, the conversion opportunities don't stop there.

Dr. Zuckerberg's e-mail appointment reminders include a call to action to ask questions about your upcoming visit on Facebook, and new patients are invited by phone to "get to know us better before you come in by checking out our bios on our Facebook page." These techniques lead to patients feeling more comfortable on their first visit, but they also lead to more likes.

So far, more than 60,000 people have *liked* Dr. Z on Facebook—which has led to more than two dozen new patients. I had a Facebook friend whom I don't know that well send me the following message: "Saw you like Dr. Zuckerberg. Is he a good dentist?" To which I replied, "Yes!"

She became a patient the next week of the world's most likeable dentist.

Another likeable dental practice is Aesthetic Family Dentistry in Port Jervis, New York. Dr. Seth Horn and his team encourage patients to *like* their Facebook page by sharing pictures of their patients on their Facebook wall. Almost every patient who comes in for an appointment gets his or her picture taken with various props. At the end of the appointment, the patient gets an FB business card that says, "Tag your photo on FB.com /AestheticFamilyDentistry."

Aesthetic Family Dentistry went from having just a few *likes* to having over 350 *likes* in a matter of just two months. Although they haven't quite caught up with Mark Zuckerberg's dad, for a small practice, that is great organic progress. Parents especially love tagging their kids in the dentist's chair with a giant foam thumb (Figure 4.1), and now the practice has nearly all their clientele as Facebook connections. Think about how much easier

FIGURE 4.1   Happy Patient in Her Likeable Dentist's Chair

it is for this practice to stay top of mind with their patients on a daily basis.

WHAT IF YOU DON'T CONVERT YOUR CURRENT CUSTOMERS?

There is a risk in focusing on converting your current customers to fans. Seasoned Internet marketers will argue that there's no guaranteed ROI on generating *likes* from your consumers or prospects. They will also claim that by focusing on generating more *likes* on Facebook, you're inherently decreasing your immediate sales.

Every time someone clicks Like, they'll say, that's one less click on *buy now*. This may be true, and you may see a dip initially in online conversions when you first shift some of your marketing strategy to gaining *likes* as compared to *buy nows*, but you don't really have a choice. If you want to grow a social presence, you have to take the time and energy to attract the low-hanging fruit: your current customers and other people who know you. From there, you'll gain other fans and followers who are likely to eventually buy from you. But you have to start with your current customers.

Uno E-mail from Uno Pizzeria & Grill Leads to 100,000 Fans

Uno Pizzeria & Grill is a large chain of family-friendly restaurants throughout the country but concentrated in the Northeast and the Midwest. Known best for its deep-dish pizza, Uno serves up a wide variety of lunch and dinner foods to many thousands of people each week. Uno had been on Facebook for longer than a year, but up until September 2010, it had just 30,000 people who had *liked* it on Facebook. That's a decent number to be sure, but considering how many customers they serve and how many fans competitors like Chili's and Applebee's had, it was a number Uno Pizzeria & Grill wanted to increase dramatically.

The company had placed a call to action to *like* Uno both on its website and at the bottom of every weekly e-mail it sent out to a large subscriber list. But Uno believed that a dedicated e-mail with a strong value proposition to its customers would drive action much more significantly than simply requesting to be *liked* by current fans. The company decided to offer a free appetizer to *all fans* if it reached 100,000 fans—more than tripling a number that had grown organically over the course of an entire year.

Instead of offering a coupon or call to action to visit a location or book a group or make a reservation, the company's weekly e-mail told recipients only to do the following: "Like us on Facebook to earn a free appetizer. Share this with your friends, and when we hit 100,000 fans, everyone will win a free appetizer on us."

Within 24 hours of the e-mail message going out, Uno Pizzeria & Grill had gained more than 10,000 new fans, and within three months, it had reached its goal of 100,000. It didn't get as many sales from that one e-mail as it usually did, but that didn't matter for long. Many thousands of people enjoyed their free appetizer at Uno—and most of them stayed for dinner and dessert, far outpacing the sales lift that the e-mail message usually created. Uno e-mail, uno big return.

ACTION ITEMS

1. Work with your team to create your value proposition, not for a sale but for a *like*. Why should your customers *like* you on Facebook? What's in it for them? How can you craft this value proposition into a short, catchy call to action? What value proposition will you offer employees, vendors, and partners?

2. Brainstorm all of the ways you can integrate this call to action into your current marketing and communications practices. Write down anything and everything. Then, determine which are actionable immediately and which may be actionable over time. Operationalize the *like*.

3. Create a 15-second elevator pitch to tell your customers and anyone you come into contact with why they should *like* you on Facebook and follow you on Twitter. Make sure it's a reason that would resonate with *you as a consumer.*

THE ROAD TO LIKEABLE SOCIAL MEDIA SUCCESS IS PAVED BY YOUR CURRENT CUSTOMERS

Once your current customers have *liked* you, you can begin to earn momentum using content, ads, promotions, and the organic virality of the social graph. But until that happens, you'll be listening and talking in a vacuum. Don't just tell your customers to *like* you. Tell them *why* they should *like* you. Make it about them, not about you, and you'll get the *likes* and follows you're craving to grow your social media network and sales overall.

CHAPTER 5

Engage
Create True Dialogue with,
and Between, Your Customers

Do you remember in college when you attended classes held in large lecture halls where professors talked at you for two hours at a time? You also likely had some classes that were a lot smaller and involved a workshop or discussion component. Which type of class did you find more valuable? Which one did you talk about at length, share with friends, and learn from more?

No matter how brilliant the professor of the large lecture was, undoubtedly there were people literally sleeping during the class. And no matter how uninspiring the teacher of the small discussion group was (often, it was a graduate student or teaching assistant in charge), you couldn't help but learn because you were actively engaged in thinking about, talking about, and discussing the subject matter at hand. In fact, you probably learned as much from fellow students and dialogue with others in your class as you did from those professors or instructors who supposedly "held the knowledge."

Just as more engaging classes at a university provide more value to students, the companies and organizations that stand out are those that use social media to meaningfully engage customers and foster dialogue, instead of those who rely on simply, and repeatedly, talking *at* consumers. Companies that can foster communication, not only between organization and consumer but also between consumer and consumer, will reap the greatest benefits of the most connected world we've ever had.

TALKING WITH YOUR CHILDREN INSTEAD OF TALKING TO YOUR BABIES

The twenty-first-century model of truly engaging customers publicly is quite different from marketing and communications models of the past.

Let's say you're a parent. Think about the way you would talk to your children when they are babies versus when they become older. When you speak to a baby, she can't talk back, though she can give you nonverbal cues about how she feels. She won't necessarily understand what you're saying, so as the great parent you are, you'll put on a show to elicit a reaction from her. You make funny faces, talk in loud or silly voices, and sing to her until you get a laugh or a smile or some other desired result. This situation is like the television commercial of the past (or even present, perhaps). The goal of the commercial is to grab the viewer's attention and produce some sort of response, often using humor, outrageousness, surprise, or song.

When a child gets old enough to talk, as any parent knows, dynamics between the parent and child change. The good news, and bad news, is that the child can talk back to you. Now you get instant verbal feedback on everything you verbally express— you know exactly how well your children understand what you're saying and typically whether they're going to listen to you or not. Of course, sometimes parents don't like what their children say, or how they say it, but as the parent, you have to respond. With the ability to understand what your children are trying to express to you comes greater responsibility and accountability for how you will continue to communicate in the future. Now you're not just talking to your children. You're engaging with them. You're in the conversation for the rest or your life—that's part of your job as a parent.

Consider how this analogy relates to the forms of marketing and advertising that are quickly becoming outdated with the advent of social media. The loudest, costliest advertising formats, such as TV commercials, don't dominate the conversation anymore because, in fact, they no longer own the conversation. The conversation exists on social networks. By engaging the audience directly, you will find that the smartest, most flexible listeners win over the audience. They help create and develop the conversation; they do not attempt to dictate it. Those companies that talk at their customers are less likely to create followers, while those that engage consumers find they will be part of the conversation for life—and that's part of the job of a marketer.

GROWING YOUR CUSTOMER RELATIONSHIPS

So what does "being engaged" really mean?

To be engaged means to be genuinely interested in what your customers have to say. You have to want, even crave, feedback of all kinds because you know it gives you important data to build a better organization. Each individual at your company has to provide his or her full attention, mind, and energy with the customer or task at hand while maintaining the mission and core values of the organization. Anyone can send out an e-mail or a Facebook or Twitter message, but it takes commitment and focus to actually connect with people.

You simply can't "be engaged" on the social Web because it's "the thing to do" now, or you read about it in a book, or you think it will lead to increased sales. You have to authentically believe that being active in growing your social network will lead to deeper, stronger relationships with your customers. You have to be interested in your consumers and prospects, and the creation of a solid bond with them must be your goal.

When two people make a promise to one another that they are to be married, they are said to be "engaged." Similarly, when a company chooses to be engaged with its customers, it commits to being truly concerned about what they say, think, and feel. For many organizations, this connection may be a fundamental shift in how they see and value customers. Instead of creating or outsourcing a customer service department, you want to know firsthand what customers think, how they feel, and what they are looking for from you.

Getting Back to Your Core Values

Most companies, at least when they are first formed, have the best of intentions. Many times, entrepreneurs' original motivation is to create a solution in an attempt to solve a problem. Companies don't necessarily start off by seeing people as dollar signs or statistics. But as organizations grow, they get harder to manage. It becomes easy to lose the initial mindset of authentically wanting to be there, fully present, for your customers and even easier to drift away from your fundamentals and core values.

What is your organization like now? Are you the kind of company that truly cares about its customers and values feedback? Does the marketing arm of your organization act more like an old professor at a large university lecture or like a young, interested teaching assistant leading a group into discovery and learning *together*? It may be hard to honestly and accurately assess yourself and your company, but it's imperative if you plan to survive in the social media age, in which a direct relationship with your customers is becoming the only way to succeed.

If your organization looks like the tired old professor, the good news is that you're certainly not alone. The bad news is that it's going to take a lot of work and a commitment from senior management for the company to get seriously engaged with its constituents and return to the core values of simply being a business catering to the consumers' wants, needs, and desires. You can certainly follow the rules to *look* more engaged, but until you *are* more engaged, you run the risk of being known as only feigning interest in your consumer base. Authenticity is necessary in creating long-lasting connections through the social Web.

Building Communities Around Trust and Loyalty

When you make the commitment to listen to and engage with your customers and prospects, it fosters a genuine sense of trust and loyalty between you and them, and *among them*. Think about the university analogy: In a large lecture, how comfortable would you feel disagreeing with the professor in front of the whole class? How would you feel being the *second* person to speak up, after someone with a dissenting opinion talks? You probably wouldn't feel very comfortable speaking up at all, and neither would others, which is why day after day in that lecture, the professor talks and the students listen and take notes. This setup doesn't really facilitate a valuable relationship or learning experience.

However, if in a smaller discussion class the instructor makes it clear on the first day that the atmosphere is one in which all opinions and comments are respected, where dialogue and dissent is welcomed and even encouraged, and where the teacher hopes to demonstrate that she is as interested in what everyone has to say as they are interested in her, then the class will become community based around respect and trust. This teacher, whether she's a TA, grad student, or full-time professor, is seeking to create a discussion, not just lecture at the audience. Students will feel safe and empowered to speak up. They may also continue the dialogue without the instructor and beyond class time.

That smaller discussion class is building a community with value far beyond what the professor may have provided solely by way of imparting knowledge. If you can similarly build and engage an authentic community in this way, your community will bring your brand value beyond what you may see right now. Engaging your customers or prospects and getting them involved in your brand community will create a sense of trust and loyalty between you and your customers. An authentic, engaged brand community can live anywhere online—on a blog, through Twitter, or on YouTube, for instance. However, most brand communities are on Facebook pages, the predominant social media site. Brand communities are usually started by companies, but when they are run well, they can take off, almost on their own, as more and more customers join the conversation. How well you talk to your fans and stimulate conversation without pushing product will determine how large your community grows and how much they trust and value you.

Customers Solving Customer Service Issues

One example of the benefits of building an engaged community is that customers will help one another out. If you create a place on Facebook or Twitter for people to ask questions, share feedback, and interact with not only you but one another, you will engender trust and loyalty and help the community grow. Customers or prospects will take notice and appreciate when you answer questions on a timely basis and in an authentic way.

If you provide a place for consumers to connect and to gripe, to share information and to learn and to grow, people will realize you are committed to them and the community you are fostering, and they will return that commitment to you. So now when someone unfamiliar with your company comes to the community, a potentially huge new prospect, and posts a question, another member of the community might answer the prospect's question before you have time to. Or when an unsatisfied customer comes to the Facebook page to complain, the community is likely to rally behind you without your even having to ask. How valuable might each of those things be to the bottom line? An engaged community grows your stakeholders in the company way beyond the staff and shareholders. These stakeholders will show support for you throughout their online social network and beyond. Your company's reputation and visibility will grow, and in return, your online, and offline, community will flourish.

ENGAGING: EASIER SAID THAN DONE

Despite the vision of an engaged company, it is far easier to discuss than to actually implement. You will find that unless you are the leader of a small business or organization, the commitment to be engaged cannot happen immediately. Senior managers need to invest themselves fully in the change toward greater customer interaction and community building.

Is it devastating to your organization to not be fully engaged with its customers? The answer to that question is probably not, for a while at least. However, in an increasingly transparent and social world, by not being authentically involved and concerned about your consumers, you risk having one horrible customer experience totally erode your reputation, and eventually your bottom line, regardless of the size of your company. If your senior managers aren't sold on building an engaged community, tell them about "United Breaks Guitars."

In July 2009, country singer Dave Carroll was on a United Airlines flight when his guitar was broken. Dave put a claim into United, and it not only refused to replace the guitar but also refused to apologize. So, he took to YouTube, quickly making the "United Breaks Guitars" video, criticizing the company for its lack of accountability. It was an instant hit. After one day, the video had more than 100,000 views. A United spokesperson called Carroll up and offered to pay for the guitar, but Dave refused the offer, suggesting the company instead give to a charity in his name. United did not respond publicly on YouTube, Facebook, or Twitter. Within four days of the video being posted online, it had more than 1 million views, and it had received national news coverage. By that time, United Airlines' stock price had fallen 10 percent, costing stockholders about $180 million in value. Four years later, however, the video had more than 20 million views on YouTube, and United never did address the issue through social media. Its brand's reputation remains damaged.

Do you think if United Airlines had engendered an engaged community through social media that the devastating fallout would have happened? If lots of United consumers felt loyal to

United, they would have stood by the company when an online crisis developed.

There are countless other examples. Search online for "Motrin Moms" or "Comcast Technician Sleeping" for two great ones. There will certainly be more. You can avoid being *forced* to become engaged by proactively making the commitment to your consumers.

ENGAGEMENT FOR NONPROFITS AND GOVERNMENTS

As valuable as customer engagement is for companies, it is crucial for nonprofits and governments. Social media is tailor-made for such organizations, and the success of a nonprofit in fulfilling its mission, or a government organization in launching an initiative, is entirely dependent on an engaged constituent base. Nonprofits and governments in the past had to create movements offline, without the luxury of a built-in online community of people ready to support one another and fulfill the mission. Now, a strong nonprofit or local government can build an engaged community using Facebook or Twitter, and it can raise money or effect positive change in faster, more efficient ways than ever before. How can your company replicate this effect? How can your company grow a *movement* online?

New York State Takes Control

The New York State Department of Health (NYSDOH) is a government agency serving the people of New York State, one of the most populated states in the world. The NYSDOH runs many public health initiatives funded by the government, including the Take Control! program, designed to provide New York State teens and young adults with information and local resources to promote positive sexual health. This program is unique because it's about teens connecting with other people like them in a nonjudgmental way. They can get information and have their questions answered without feeling like they're being lectured by adults. So it would make sense that when it came time to build out a marketing strategy for this initiative, the tried-and-true television advertisements, radio spots, subway posters, and online banner ads simply couldn't be at the core of the marketing strategy. That's not where or how teens talk to other teens, so the NYSDOH took to social media where these digital natives spend a lot of their time.

The original objective of the NYSDOH's 2012 launch of the Take Control! Facebook page was to increase awareness of the program, drive traffic to the informational website, and provide teens with content they could relate to and learn from. The DOH agency built the page for the program at Facebook.com /TakeControl, and its staff members worked to create and share daily content, listen to and respond to all questions and posts from New York teens, and build a highly engaged community. Suddenly, humorous content that looked like the images their friends regularly shared—but with a safe sex–healthy relationship spin to it—was getting tens of thousands of comments, *likes*, and shares. Most parents can't get an answer to "How was your day?" from their teens, and these teens were talking about their sexual choices.

But far more important than the conversations and engagement with the program, the Facebook page evolved into a community in which teens could talk to other teens. If a piece of content was posted that didn't resonate with the community, the members let the DOH know. When a question was posed, the community members weren't answering a state government organization. They were answering each other and having conversations with each other. Once a teen spoke up about something, more soon followed. The page became an online forum, a place where friends hung out after school, and the "cool" spot to access funny images about being a teen (and about sex!). Teens began to ask important questions, learn where to get condoms and where to get tested for STDs; and they felt comfortable letting 30,000 of their peers know they were virgins. They received support and guidance not just from the DOH but from each other. What started as a marketing hunch (teens are spending a lot of time on Facebook, so let's build there!) accomplished a seemingly impossible feat—teens voluntarily joined a group and started talking about safe sex. In a time when bullying is running rampant, there is support, humor, education, and acceptance taking place.

Stride Rite Creates an Engaged Mommy Movement

Starting a movement is easier for a cause, a mission-related nonprofit group, or a government organization than it is for a business, but you should never underestimate the potential of any passionate community united around beliefs, commonalities, or shared interests. One such group online is moms, who, in general, love to share with one another.

Stride Rite is a leading shoe brand that makes and distributes footwear for babies and children across the United States. The company sells its shoes through retail locations as well as online, but in 2009 it decided it wanted to build a more engaged community on Facebook.

Stride Rite knew it already had a strong brand that many people were familiar with and loved. The bond between the brand and its customers was good, but in order to build an engaged community, Stride Rite had to leverage stronger bonds: those between mother and baby and between fellow moms. This required an initial shift in strategic thinking from the company, as it would have to make the community a lot less about its shoes and more about the kids wearing the shoes, and their moms, than they had ever originally planned.

The online conversation started strong in late 2009, and frankly, it hasn't slowed down at the time of this writing. More than 210,000 fans have joined the community at Facebook.com /striderite, the vast majority of whom are young moms. If you visit the page on any given day, you'll see customers talking with each other and with the brand—usually not even about shoes but about their kids and babies. Thousands of moms have posted pictures and videos of their babies' first steps, and Stride Rite always responds to comments, questions, and shared items.

Moms also help each other out with lots of baby- and child-rearing questions that have nothing to do with walking or feet, and the company *welcomes* that dialogue too. Moms feel empowered, engaged, and proud to be part of the Stride Rite community. In turn, the company provides opportunities to buy Stride Rite's shoes. Online sales have increased steadily, week after week, since the program launched.

By putting an engaged community ahead of sales, Stride Rite was able to generate better long-term sales, along with 210,000 brand advocates.

ACTION ITEMS

1. Determine what resources you have to put toward a social media program through which your organization can become authentically engaged with its consumers. Based on the size of the company, it may take a long time to foster an online social community— time that will have to come from existing employees, new hires, or outside agencies. Determine who at your company can, and will, make the commitment to authentic engagement, and get those people in a room together to start the conversation.
2. Hire an online community manager if you don't yet have one. This person's main role should be to build and grow an engaged community. If you are a small business owner, figure out a way to devote 10 minutes a day to increasing engagement.
3. Write a list of five ways that your communications could be more engaging than they are right now. How can you be less like the old college lecturer and more like the enthusiastic workshop leader?

THE PROCESS OF GETTING ENGAGED HAS TO START WITH ONE ACTION

Whether your organization is already deeply engaged with its customers or is far from it, the process of becoming further involved starts with one person, and one action. Just because you're not able to turn your company upside down doesn't mean you can't take positive steps toward using social media to foster better dialogue between your brand and your customers and between your customers themselves. Now stop stalling, go buy that ring, and get engaged.

CHAPTER 6

Respond Quickly to All Bad Comments

You've worked hard for months with your team and a consulting firm on creating social media best practices, and you've planned how to integrate social media into your business. You've built a Facebook page, a Twitter account, a LinkedIn company page, and a blog, and you're excited to join the online conversation and foster a burgeoning community. Several coworkers have rallied behind you and your commitment to engaging customers throughout every step of their relationship with your company. Then, the night before the big launch day, you receive a phone call from your frantic chief executive officer:

"Remind me, what the hell are we going to do if people write bad things about us on our Facebook page? We can delete those, right? Because if we can't delete those negative comments, I don't think we're ready for Facebook."

The answer is simple: if you're not ready to respond to negative comments, then no, you're not ready for Facebook yet. If your company is not prepared to embrace the good, the bad, and the ugly, then social media in general isn't right for you now. If you are prepared to handle criticism and respond appropriately, however, then having your own social network community where people post positive and negative comments will be a huge asset.

EMBRACE WHAT YOU CAN'T CONTROL: SOCIAL MEDIA COMMENTS ARE THE NEW COMMENT CARDS

Remember those comment cards every business used to have with a box you could drop them in? Many small businesses and restaurants still have them today. Whether your company officially has comment cards or not, they exist in the form of Facebook, Twitter, LinkedIn, blogs, and other online social outlets. The good news for the customer is that today's consumer base is the most empowered in history. If you have a negative experience with any company or professional, you can fill out "a comment card" from your smartphone that instant and then immediately share your comment not only with hundreds of friends but also with complete strangers throughout the world.

Of course, if you consider this situation from the standpoint of a company, this is a scary proposition. Just as the aforementioned CEO is freaking out, so are marketers, public relations executives, and small business owners everywhere. For years, it's been the role of communications professionals to control public perception of their companies, and now any kid with a Twitter account or Facebook profile can ruin it all. That said, as a marketer, once you accept and embrace the fact that you cannot control the online posting of negative comments about your company, you can begin to formulate a plan for what you're going to do to respond to criticism.

You could try to ignore it, of course. There are still plenty of companies that refuse to accept the fact that people are talking negatively about them. You could also try to delete things online—sure, on your own Facebook page, you can delete whatever you want—and perhaps your company's lawyers could write letters to every Web publisher who ever allows negative comments to be published about you, demanding that those comments come down.

But the truth is, there's no way to entirely stop people from making negative posts about your company, whether you have an official Facebook page or not. So, why not prepare yourself and, instead of avoiding it, embrace negative feedback, comments, and criticism? Especially if *you* are the frantic CEO in our example, the following idea might sound like a radical and potentially damaging one—so take a deep breath, and brace yourself.

The Do-Not-Delete Rule

The do-not-delete (DND) rule states that *unless a comment is obscene, profane, or bigoted, or it contains someone's personal and private information, it should never be deleted from a social network site.* It might be best to illustrate the wisdom of the DND rule by first playing out a scenario in which you *don't* follow it.

Johnny Customer posts on Control Freak Inc.'s Facebook page, "I just got a bill for $100 more than I was supposed to. You guys suck!" The frantic CEO insists that the comment be deleted right away so nobody else sees it, and the comment is promptly removed from the page. Johnny Customer logs on later that day to find his comment deleted. He is infuriated that the company has censored his complaint, and he reacts by starting a new Facebook group called "I Hate Control Freak Inc.! Boycott Them!" He also makes a YouTube video singing about his hatred for the company and detailing his bad experience, and he starts a Twitter trend with hashtag #controlfreakincsucks.

As it turns out, Johnny Customer happens to be the captain of the football team at his school and the lead singer for a popular rock band in town. Within 24 hours, thousands of people are posting negative comments on Control Freak Inc.'s wall, and worse yet, customers are canceling orders, and sales are down.

Sure, this is a dramatic rendition of the situation, and it may not be the most likely occurrence, but is it really worth taking the risk (remember "United Breaks Guitars" from the last chapter)? The point is, when you delete someone's comment, it is the ultimate "Screw you." It's like collecting a customer's comment card, reading it in front of the customer, and then ripping it up in his or her face. You wouldn't do that, would you? Plus, the Internet is infinite. Anyone who feels wronged or not heard can turn elsewhere to gripe, finding more energy (and maybe more sympathizers) to vent than he or she had before.

Not Responding Is a Response

The second gut reaction of some executives after wanting to delete the negative comment is to ignore it. "Maybe by ignoring the problem, it will go away," they might think. Or, "We don't want to give this issue credence because it might lead to more negativity from customers."

If deleting a comment is the equivalent of ripping up a comment card in someone's face, ignoring a negative comment is the equivalent of putting a caller on hold and never getting back on the line (with thousands of people watching the phone call!). No, it's not as bad as hanging up on him, but he'll still get the impression that you don't care about him. Worse yet, everyone else who sees the comment and lack of response from the company will conclude that your organization just doesn't care. By not responding, you're actually sending out a strong message: the customer's opinion doesn't matter to you. This is a dangerous message to convey to your current consumers, prospects, and the general public, many of whom would interpret a lack of response in just this way. You don't want to make matters worse, so what's a company to do?

THE SOLUTION: RESPOND QUICKLY AND PUBLICLY, AND THEN TAKE THE ISSUE PRIVATE

In the situation just mentioned, Johnny Customer wants a reply to the apparent $100 discrepancy on his bill. What do you think of the following response?

First, one of your company's representatives publicly posts, "I'm sorry you had an issue, Johnny. Please see the private message we

sent you to resolve the matter." Next, this post is followed immediately by a private message sent directly to Johnny, "Sorry you
had a bad experience, Johnny. If you e-mail us with your account
information to wecare@controlfreakinc.com, we'll try to resolve
the issue as quickly as possible."

By responding quickly and publicly, you not only respond to
someone's complaint or concern but you also send the message
out to the world at large that you're the kind of company that
listens to its customers and fixes problems promptly. By taking the individual matter private, you avoid a public back-and-
forth between company and customer, which wouldn't help
anyone involved but only prolong the negative situation. And
when you're apologizing, refer to people by name: it goes a long
way toward helping them feel heard and understood. We're all
human, and we all make mistakes. Even the angriest of customers will recognize this truth and will be quick to forgive you, but
only if you apologize and fix the problem as soon as possible.

Depending on the size of your organization, you'll need to
make sure you have enough internal or external resources to
handle complaints in a timely manner. You probably already
have a sense of just how many complaints you typically
receive, maybe from those traditional comment cards if you
have them. Of course, comment cards used to get forwarded
to a department where someone would read them, write
replies, and mail them out a week later. In the online world,
things happen a lot faster.

Put on your consumer cap. If you had a complaint or question
about something, how quickly would you want to be, or expect
to be, answered? Of course you'd like to receive a response
almost immediately, so you should answer your customers
right away as well. As a rule of thumb, make sure you have the
resources in place to answer people's negative comments within
24 hours or sooner if possible. Even if your initial response is,
"I'm sorry, and we'll look into that and get back to you with a private message within 72 hours," at least you're immediately telling
the customer that you care and you're going to fix the problem as
quickly as you can. After all, an angry customer is just like all of
us: she wants to feel heard, and understood.

"I'm Sorry" Is Not an Admission of Guilt

Many legal departments are reticent in allowing marketers to say "I'm sorry" on Facebook and Twitter. It's as though lawyers are convinced that apologizing is an admission of guilt and makes a company liable for damages. Some industries are more highly regulated than others, and sometimes, it's just not feasible to apologize. (For instance, as mentioned in Chapter 1, often pharmaceutical companies can't legally apologize in response to online complaints made about their products.) But, in general, the words "I'm sorry" or "We're sorry" can go a long way in helping a customer feel heard and diffusing a potentially hazardous situation. There are lots of ways to put an apology in writing without admitting any wrongdoing:

- "I'm sorry you had this experience."
- "We're sorry you feel this way."
- "I'm so sorry you've had a problem."
- "That sounds so frustrating. Sorry you felt like that."

Responding with a short but genuine apology is a great start, but equally important, *you've got to be able to fix the problem.* For many companies, this means that the marketing and public relations departments have to work closely with the customer service team to resolve people's complaints in a timely manner. Remember, customers don't care about what department you're in—they care only about whether you can solve their problem or not. There's really no difference to customers between a public relations associate and a customer service rep.

Prioritize Your Response Based on the Commenter's Online Influence

It's easy to say, "Respond to every customer who complains," and though this should be the goal, it is not always possible. Some organizations are so vast they don't yet have the resources to answer every single person's complaint. Take online social networks, for instance, such as Facebook and Twitter—that is, the companies themselves. Each has hundreds of millions of users but fewer than 2,500 employees. There's simply no way they have the ability to answer every complaint made. In these situations, and perhaps for your company, you may consider prioritizing how quickly you respond based on the customer's online influence.

Klout (Klout.com) and other services rank people online based on how many friends and followers they have. Just as you'd probably respond a little faster to celebrities who filled out comment cards years ago, you might consider prioritizing your response time based on how influential the customer is. The harsh reality is that if Johnny Customer has 40,000 followers on Twitter, he can do far more damage to your reputation online than if he has 4. Again, in an ideal world, you could respond to every Johnny Customer's complaint, but you may not have the ideal resources to do so currently.

TURN COMPLAINERS INTO SUPPORTERS

Depending on how efficiently and effectively you can solve a customer's problem, you just might turn a hater into an admirer or even a major brand supporter. Consider if Johnny Customer, from our example, heard back from you immediately, and you were able to address his specific complaint with ease. His mind is likely to be changed about your company, and he might be so impressed and pleased that he recommends you to his peers. Consider the following real-life example of an unsatisfied Verizon customer.

A Foe of FiOS Becomes a Fan

Verizon FiOS is the television, Internet, and phone bundle offered by Fortune 500 company Verizon in select areas across the country. The Fans of FiOS Facebook page has been a marketing, promotions, and customer service asset for Verizon since 2008. When first launched, the page was designed to provide regional support for Verizon FiOS's marketing and promotions initiatives. Customers, however, are typically more concerned about their own service problems than about the marketing and promotional material posted—and they're not afraid to publicly share their issues. The FiOS team always attempts to quickly resolve such customer issues in conjunction with Verizon policies and procedures. My favorite interaction was with Ray Umstot-Einolf, who posted the following on the FiOS fan page on March 22, 2009:

> Hey Verizon why won't you give me my money back!!! I signed up for your Verizon Bundle Pack and I'm paying $300.00 a month and my service is supposed to cost about $120.00. We call you every month and the problem is never fixed. Funny thing is I know of about 10 other people you are doing this to. Telling them one price and billing them another and not refunding when you admit you are wrong. You guys Suck!!! And a lawsuit may be in your near future. Have a great day, you bunch of crooks!!!!

Members of the Verizon team breathed and quickly considered their options. There were admittedly a couple of individuals who suggested the dreaded "delete" tactic, in fear of giving credence to such a complaint. But cooler heads prevailed, and the do-not-delete rule won out. They responded this way:

> So sorry you've had a problem, Ray. We've sent you a private message and someone from Verizon will be in touch with you shortly. —Devin, from the Fans of FiOS

Ray was put directly in touch with the customer support team. A few days passed, and Verizon worried the next post from Ray might be even worse than the first. Then, on March 26, 2009, Ray posted the following on the page:

> I wanna thank Fans of FiOS for fixing my billing Problem. Devin was awesome and I would like to thank her for her help. Had a Regional Manager call us today and went over the bill and corrected our bill. Thank you!!!

And for the Record. I love the FiOS service and the Extreme Internet package makes me jump up and down every time I download anything or play a game. Thank you Verizon FiOS. No more Crookcast for Us.

It was difficult to believe, looking at both posts, that Ray was the same person. And yet there they were, in front of Verizon and thousands of fans on the page. In a few days, Ray went from being a raving hater to being a full-on supporter with an audience of thousands. In this situation, customer service and marketing were blurred together, resulting in a great promotion of the company and an incredibly satisfied consumer.

CONSIDER RESPONDING WITH SURPRISE AND DELIGHT

Responding with an apology and a quick solution to the problem is essential. But remember, unlike the comment card, which is a private matter, social media is of a public nature, so there's more at stake here when replying. Is there a way you can go above and beyond to fix the problem—exceeding the unsatisfied customer's original expectations? Maybe you send a bonus gift in the mail, or you refund the customer's invoice without telling her, or you give her a deep discount on the next month's service. Consider the options, get creative, and the customer's next comment to all of her friends may be raving about the amazing company you are.

1-800-Flowers.com Responds by Surprising

1-800-Flowers.com is the world's leading online and phone service providing and delivering floral and other gifts to customers across the country. It provides services all year long, but its two busiest weeks of the year, as you might expect, are around Valentine's Day and Mother's Day.

While the conversation in its online communities is usually quite positive, occasionally customers post complaints that we at Likeable respond to in conjunction with the customer care team. During the two key holidays, the stakes are raised, as many competitors are advertising in the market. The last thing we want is for complaints to go unanswered at this time. Any complaint could quickly snowball and have a major negative effect on sales.

1-800-Flowers.com decided to staff up its Facebook community 24/7 for key holidays beginning in 2010, and it committed to responding publicly within an hour of any complaint. Further, it resolved to not only fix customers' problems but to also over-deliver, with larger bouquets and orders than the complaining customers had paid for. It was a risk because customers could potentially take advantage of the situation, and profit margins could easily slip. However, the results were great. There were just as many complaints as in the past, but they were responded to quickly, and when the orders did arrive, recipients (and senders!) were surprised and delighted. Many of them ended up posting online again, much more positively this second time. The added spending paid off in keeping the public brand reputation at a high during a critical time.

ACTION ITEMS

1. Determine how you will allocate resources to respond to negative comments posted on social networks. Is it the responsibility of the marketing department, the customer service department, an agency, or all three?
2. Develop a plan to respond swiftly and publicly. Work with your lawyers to develop language that is OK by them and is as customer friendly as possible.
3. Make sure you have enough resources to manage negative comments in a timely manner. Have the resources to not only respond to comments but also to actually fix the problems efficiently.
4. Write a list of five ways you can respond to negative situations positively, turn around customer complaints, and use "surprise and delight" to leverage otherwise negative situations.

ACCEPT THAT COMPLAINTS ARE UNAVOIDABLE, AND REACT QUICKLY: TURN YOUR CUSTOMER CARE INTO A MARKETING ASSET

No human being is perfect, and therefore no organization is either. Your company will surely make errors, and now, thanks to social networks, the whole world can easily find out about these mistakes. But you also have the ability to show the world how responsive a company you are. If you can respond quickly and authentically, with an apology and a solution, you can avoid any damage to your reputation. Further, if you provide an additional reward to your customers when tackling the issue, you can actually turn your response and customer care into a marketing asset. Wouldn't you rather have people like Ray on your side?

CHAPTER 7

Respond to the Good Comments Too

"Excuse me, sir," a well-dressed woman says to you in the aisle of your department store. "I just wanted to take a moment to thank you for everything you and your company have done for me throughout the years. I am a longtime, happy customer—and you've truly brought joy to my life. Thanks, and keep up the great work." You stare at her with a blank expression on your face, then turn and quickly walk away in fear there may be a complaining customer that you need to attend to elsewhere in the store.

This situation is absurd, of course, and it would never happen. You'd never reject a happy customer. Instead, you would welcome her with open arms and invite her to share more. Heck, you'd probably give her a hug or a free T-shirt, or both!

You likely embrace your happiest customers—they remind you of what you're doing well and what your organization is all about. They're also the best unplanned part of your marketing agenda. Word-of-mouth endorsements and conversations with satisfied customers remain the most potentially powerful marketing tools you have.

Yet each day, millions of positive comments to and about brands on social networks go unnoticed or are given no response. Visit the Facebook pages of most big organizations and you'll find people sharing stories, asking questions, and praising products or services—almost always without a response. Do companies not have enough resources to address these posts? Are they so focused on maintaining a defensive posture with regard to all of the negative comments that they decide not to reply to any comments at all? Do companies not see value in responding to positive posts?

Whatever the reasons, they are making a mistake, possibly to your company's advantage. If *your* organization begins to follow not only negative posts and comments but also positive ones, and if it takes action in responding, you are ahead of the game. In fact, if other companies aren't doing a good job interacting with their customers or prospects through online social networking, your company looks even better to consumers when you take the initiative.

ACKNOWLEDGMENT ALONE GOES A LONG WAY—GET CREATIVE!

Just as the two simple words "I'm sorry" go a long way when a customer complains, so do the words "Thank you" when a customer has something nice to say. "Thank you" says "You matter." "Thank you" says "We're listening." "Thank you" says "We appreciate you." It's best to further personalize your response as well, sharing your brand personality a little bit.

Develop Your Social Personality

Brand personality is formed by giving your brand human traits when presenting your company to the public. Your brand's social personality sets you apart from other brands, giving your company unique features in an attempt to connect more directly, and more humanly, with your consumer. For example, the voice (or wording) you use to respond to posts helps shape your personality. Here are several different ways to say thanks to a positive comment, expressing the personality behind the brand:

- "Thanks a lot, Johnny. You rule!"
- "Thank you for taking the time to share."
- "Thanks for liking us. We like you too."
- "Thanks for your feedback, Johnny. We're listening."
- "Thanks for your comment, and keep spreading the good word!"

Acknowledging your customers' positive feedback is easier today than it has ever been before. With the advent of the social Web, connecting directly to your consumer while showing that, as a brand, you truly care about your public persona ingratiates your company to current and potential customers.

Responding in Your Brand's Voice

Language is a major part of your brand identity. Would a bank talk to its customers face-to-face using the same language that a pizzeria would? Would a pediatrician discuss a medical condition with her patients using the same language an oncologist would with his? Would a major brand target its teenage customers using the same language it uses in its ads for adults? Just as you use different language to talk to different customers face-to-face, or in advertising and marketing, and you choose that language based on who your customers are and what your organization is all about, so too must you consider the language you use on social networks in your responses.

In fact, without the advantage you have in face-to-face conversation to inflect different emotions in your voice or use nonverbal communications, the tone of your written words on Facebook or Twitter is incredibly important. Think about how differently you read these two messages:

Thank you very much for your feedback, sir.
We appreciate your support.

versus

Thanks, man. You rule!

FIGURE 7.1 Chill Zone Response

Ben ▨▨▨ sometimes, I just lay under the faucet and chug chill zone until i pass out
November 1 at 3:43pm · Like · Comment

👍 3 people like this.

Cumberland Farms Chill Zone Hahaha what a baller.
November 1 at 3:50pm · Like · 👍 1 person · Flag

What kind of brand does your organization have? Are you serious or fun? Friendly? Humorous? Outrageous? Warm? More important, what are your customers and prospects like? Are they young, adventurous adults, or are they cautious, serious seniors? Are they teens having fun, or nervous moms, or time-starved business professionals, or another category of people? Depending on the nature of your audience, your words and the way in which you respond, even to positive comments, are integral to the way in which they will be received.

For example, Cumberland Farms Chill Zone is a really popular product for teenagers, and virtually nobody else outside that demographic. So when they reply to fans in social media, they aim to represent the irreverent teen spirit of their customers. See Figure 7.1 for a great example of their responsiveness in action.

Seamless Has Fun with Its Fans

One company whose social media pages take its brand's voice to heart is Seamless (Facebook.com/Seamless and @Seamless on Twitter and Instagram). Seamless is an online food delivery service (think: all the ease of delivery without the annoying phone calls). The company was started in New York City, and it maintains its strongest ties and most dense penetration in the city that never sleeps. As such, the brand's voice and tone is a bit snarky and very witty. Seamless is your cool friend who has everyone laughing in the middle of the party—even though he just met everyone five minutes before. Seamless understands what it's like to live in a big city. It's a relatable brand that's way more than just online food delivery. From subway signs to television spots, the brand maintains its persona in all the messaging it creates.

But the company didn't use this technique only when it was in its startup phase. It also used the same approach to real-time engagement and content on all its social media properties. So when a customer posts a comment on a Facebook post and says "I love you Seamless," the staff do some digging and find out the person is a fan of the TV show *Absolutely Fabulous*, and they respond with a GIF expressing their mutual adoration (Figure 7.2). And then that customer and her friends come back and *like* it. You know how they'll be getting their lunch delivered to the office tomorrow.

FIGURE 7.2   **Seamless's Communications with Its Facebook Audience**

KEEP SPREADING THE GOOD WORD

Facebook is the single most viral platform in marketing history. Most marketers are so concerned with squashing or limiting the spread of negative comments that they lose sight of the power of spreading the positive ones. The truth is, people are more likely to buy your products or services if they feel they know you, trust you, and like you (both in general and in an online context). They are therefore much more apt to want to see something positive than negative about your company. If you can authentically amplify and accelerate positive word of mouth about your organization, online social media provides the best tools for accomplishing this on a huge scale.

In the offline world, if a customer shares positive feedback with you, it's the perfect time to ask for a referral: "Do you have any friends who would be appropriate for me to talk to?" or more passively, "Thanks. Please let your friends know."

On Facebook, when you receive a compliment, it's the perfect time to say, "Thanks. Please suggest this page to your friends!" The average person on Facebook has about 350 friends, but some people have as many as 5,000! It is likely that your happy customer has more than a few friends who might also be interested in your page and will show their endorsements as well, creating a cycle of approval.

The situation is similar with Twitter. On Twitter, if you receive positive feedback, reply and ask the user to retweet, or share you with the user's followers. The average person on Twitter has 120 followers, and some have as many as *100,000* or more. Again, one recommendation on Twitter can go a long way toward building a base of new followers.

None of this can happen however, if you don't recognize and thank your customers who actively follow and interact with you—each and every one of them.

IT'S A CONVERSATION—KEEP TALKING

In the days of comment cards, organizations responded to complaints, and most good organizations replied to every comment. But then, the communication likely ended there. With social networks, the conversation continues forever. Once you respond to the first comment, the customer can continue engaging with you. Who knows where things might lead? Think of this process as an ongoing discussion rather than a set of comments to respond to. You want public conversations begun by happy customers to go on for as long as possible while maintaining high visibility. How can you keep the conversation going? How can you surprise and delight the *positive* posters?

From a Tweet to a Job

Aimee Ertley of Sage North America provided an example of how to keep the conversation going with satisfied customers. Sage is a leading business management software and services group with offices throughout the United States. The Sage Peachtree Accounting product marketing team has an active presence on Facebook and Twitter, as well as an active online product community. Ertley told me the following:

> Last fall, a student named Andrew tweeted about us in a class one day. Our social media team saw his tweet, responded, and sent him a goodie bag as a thank you, to help him with finals. He blogged about it and talked about how Sage is "hip to the funk," as a result.
>
> Earlier this year, we actually flew him to our offices for an internal meeting about the importance and power of social media for our employees. He mentioned while he was here that he was interested in getting an internship, and it went on from there. This summer, he interned with us and did a phenomenal job. So, from one tweet, Andrew got a fun package, an internship, and valuable experience. Sage got a fantastic summer intern and created a die-hard fan.

Of course, all of that didn't really happen "from one tweet." It happened from a company having a positive attitude about responding to all comments, then responding to a tweet, going the extra mile, and continuing the conversation. Who knows—your next key hire might be the customer who just posted on your Facebook page.

ACTIVATE YOUR BRAND AMBASSADORS

Every small business knows that handful of customers who are its die-hard fans—the people who swear by your service, who are there all the time, or who consistently refer others to your business. Big brands hopefully have even more of these people—folks I call "brand ambassadors." Brand ambassadors are those customers who love your organization no matter what. They are happy to tell others about your company without any special incentive, and without you even asking them to. Still, they would be more likely to spread the word if you asked, so why wouldn't you?

Picture Rod Tidwell telling Jerry Maguire (in the movie of the same name): "Jerry Maguire, my agent. You're my ambassador of quan." Tidwell describes "quan" as "the entire package" made up of "love, respect, community, and the dollars too." Come the end of the day, this quality, quan, is what all companies are searching for: a community built of mutual respect resulting in financial growth for the business and satisfied, loyal customers. Brand ambassadors, or so-called ambassadors of quan, want to share the "special sauce" that you've got—all you have to do is tell them to. It helps that now, thanks to social networks and privacy settings, you can quickly tell how many online friends people have. Online influence varies greatly from one person to the next, and since all organizations have limited resources, you'll want to find brand ambassadors who not only adore you *but also* have lots of friends, fans, or followers.

Once you've identified your brand ambassadors, you can do much more than just thank them for being customers. You can reward them with incentives, special perks, and exclusive content. For example, provide them with online tools or samples of your product so they can share them with friends or hand the products out at parties they might host with your help. You can give them multimedia content such as pictures and videos and encourage them to create "mashups," adding their own voice and interpretation to your material before passing it along to friends and followers. The goal is to activate your customers who love you enough to regularly share their passion for you publicly.

Full Disclosure

You'll want to amplify your brand ambassadors' voices as much as possible—just make sure you have them disclose their relationship with you. If you end up giving them anything of material value, the Federal Trade Commission requires that reviewers disclose they received something in exchange for posting a review or other comments. For instance, you can't give someone a trip to your resort in exchange for them blogging or writing on Facebook about their experience, unless they clearly disclose that they received a free trip in exchange for the review. (More on transparency in Chapter 9.)

Word-of-mouth marketing has always been good business practice, but today, the ability to effectively and efficiently utilize it through social networks is unparalleled. In the past, if a celebrity visited your store, you certainly treated him exceptionally well and asked him to spread the word about his experience. Today, it is important to think of every customer as an online celebrity with followers, friends, and, above all, influence. Sure, not everyone who posts on your Facebook wall or tweets about you has as much sway or trendsetting ability as some celebrities, but they certainly can spread the word on your behalf—easily and quickly—especially if you thank and encourage them. (Some users probably have more online influence than some so-called celebrities too!)

A Toast to Responsiveness

One small business in North Carolina takes pride in answering all customer comments and inquiries on Facebook. Toast Café of Cary (FB.com/toastcafecary) is a small American breakfast and brunch café that serves food made with the freshest ingredients. During the summer of 2014, Toast Café of Cary was rebuilding its location. The construction was supposed to be quick and painless, but it took much longer than anticipated. The restaurant's employees were anxious to be in business, and the residents were anxious to be served.

In the midst of construction, the owners of Toast Café created their brand values. Authenticity, responsiveness, family, community, and speed were a few of them. Originally, responsiveness pertained to their servers. Dean from the restaurant explained that the whole staff is there to help every customer. "Every server is your server," he said. Dean and his team then took this core value online, incorporating it into their social media strategy.

Today every customer comment or question is responded to in a timely manner. All queries are answered, and the complaints are responded to, but most important, every customer's comment receives a reply (Figure 7.3). Toast Café has gained a

FIGURE 7.3   Toast Café's Communications with Its Facebook Fans

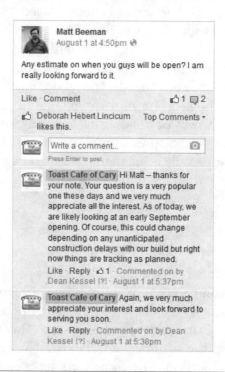

reputation online as a local business that cares about its customers and everything they have to say. In fact, customers who have shared positive experiences and who are subsequently embraced and thanked by Toast Café are often the first to post on the page when other customers post negative comments.

Who is better able to defend you against negative posters: you or your thousands of happy customers? What kind of company would you rather do business with as a consumer: a company that publicly answers every single customer, or one that seemingly ignores its customers?

ACTION ITEMS

1. Create a social brand bible for response. Determine what your brand's voice should be like in its responses to customers on social networks. Fun? Serious? Personal? Professional? Write down several different specific ways, based on this brand voice, that you would say "Thank you" to a happy customer.

2. Determine what resources are necessary to enable you to respond to every customer who posts on a social network with a comment or question. Base your estimates on your understanding of the organization's current number of customers, fans, and followers. How will your staff do this? Will you do it internally or use an outside vendor? What about nights and weekends?

3. Determine formal or informal ways you can reward your most loyal and influential customers in order to accelerate the positive word-of-mouth recommendations they will make. What assets can you offer? What expectations will you have? How can you be assured that they are following the laws of the land and disclosing to their friends what they have received from you?

TRULY VALUING ALL YOUR CUSTOMERS

Every company says it cares about its customers, but so many don't actually back up this claim on social networks, let alone elsewhere. You wouldn't hang up the phone on customers, or walk away from people you were face-to-face with, so don't ignore them on Facebook, Twitter, or any other online social networking medium either. By valuing each customer at least enough to say, "Thanks," you show the world that you are truly an organization that cares about its customers. By throwing in some surprise and delight and getting your biggest fans to further spread the word, your quan can travel a long way.

CHAPTER 8

Be Authentic

"Thank you for calling us. This is your customer care advocate, how can I be of service to you today?" you hear on the opposite end of the line.

"Great," you think. "This sounds like someone who can help me."

"I'd like to dispute part of my bill that I don't understand," you reply.

"Account number, please," the customer care advocate responds. Though you entered that number into your phone keypad just moments ago when you first called, you proceed to give the representative the information anyhow.

"I'm sorry," the customer care advocate replies. "There's nothing I can do about that problem. You'll have to speak with the billing department, and they're only open Monday through Friday. Can I help you with anything else today?"

The employee is just doing his job, of course, but all his job entails is following a script. Not only does this interaction leave you frustrated at the company's inability to help you with your problem but it also may leave you scratching your head about the inauthenticity of considering a phone agent a "customer care advocate." In no way does this employee's job seem to involve caring or advocating for you, the customer.

How about "financial counselors"? Have you ever received assistance from a "financial counselor" who in fact is an insurance salesperson concerned little, if at all, with helping you sort out your financial issues?

Not everybody with the job title of customer care advocate or financial counselor is inauthentic. There are likely lots of great folks doing those jobs. But the *job titles* themselves are misleading, intentionally or not. Of course, this inauthenticity does not apply only to job titles: brand promises from slogans, advertisements, and websites are often guilty of the same inaccuracies or false representations.

Many large companies have a hard time being authentic in their interactions with customers. As organizations get larger, it becomes difficult to manage higher volumes of staff and clients. To deal with this growth, managers develop models and processes, and customer service centers create scripts. These attempts at efficiency might cause some aspects of the organization to run smoothly, but in dealing with customers, they make it easy to miss the mark. Models, processes, and scripts will not help you connect with your consumer. Instead, such impersonal devices create a division between your service or product and your customer because there is a loss of valuable human interaction.

Social media provides an opportunity to reverse this trend for larger organizations and to showcase authenticity for smaller ones. If your company can actually "be human" in dealing with its customers through current social networks, you'll find that your customers will respond positively and appreciate your more personal attitude. Be warned, however, that if you try to deal with huge numbers of customers on social networks in an inauthentic, highly processed way, your actions can and will backfire.

Before going any further, I should point out specifically what I mean when I say that you have to be "authentic" on social networks. Overall, you have to be human and demonstrate a personality. No one wants to feel as if she is talking to a machine or dealing with someone who cannot empathize with her situation. The online social Web is all about human interaction—connecting with one another on some level. As a company, you need to want to connect with your consumers or prospects in a personal or individual manner. You also have to be flexible and responsive, with the ability to cater to customers' various or changing needs, wants, opinions, and ideas. Become part of the online conversation and truly seek to understand your consumers and the role your product or service plays, or could play, in their actual lives. While in the context of representing your brand, you, and anyone else connected with your organization, have to be the person you really are—you can't fake it anymore when it comes to dealing with the consumer.

Aaron Sorkin, who wrote the screenplay for the hit movie *The Social Network*, about the founding of Facebook and its early days, told Stephen Colbert in a television interview (aired September 30, 2010) that social networking is more of a performance than a reality.[1] He so glaringly missed the point. On the contrary, social networking, done well, is authentic and real, unlike Sorkin's scripts.

Others have speculated that social network users are narcissists, sharing their every move with the world (think when users post what kind of cereal they had for breakfast this morning). Yes, there are some people, and companies, who use social networks for such self-centered purposes and fail to see the true possibilities of harnessing the online social Web. Such users are short-sighted and in many ways tragic, as the promise of social network communication holds much greater potential. Facebook, for example, can in fact be a place for people to authentically connect with one another and for companies to build true and long-lasting relationships with customers and prospects.

BE AN IMPROV SHOW, NOT A MUSICAL

Musicals, plays, and operas are all wonderful, traditional forms of entertainment. Theatergoers attend, sit back, and relax, and the performers "put on a show." Performances can be subtle and nuanced but are often loud, larger-than-life productions, especially musicals. Most musicals include lots of color and sound and expensive scenery, props, and costumes in an attempt to dazzle the audience and leave a lasting impression. The same script is performed night after night, and with stellar writing, acting, singing, and directing, the show comes together and wins over the crowd.

Improvisation comedy shows, on the other hand, usually have little to no set and almost nothing scripted. Improv features several performers, who interact with the audience throughout each show by soliciting ideas for skits, then basing their performances on audience suggestions each night. Unlike a musical, every show is different, but as long as the audience brings creative or interesting ideas and high energy and the performers are talented, it makes for an incredible experience.

Your brand, company, or organization can create such an experience for your customers and prospects on social networks. Even better news is that this can be done without the huge budget of a Broadway show or a television commercial. It will, however, require a fundamental shift in the way you see media and marketing, now that social media has enabled a two-way conversation between the company and the consumer. You'll have to think less about "putting on a show" and more about building an excellent team that is flexible, able to go with the flow, responsive, and engaged. And unlike in improv, in which performers are playing different parts every night, your team needs to rely on its own authenticity as unique, individual people.

DEVELOP AN AUTHENTIC VOICE

Advertising has traditionally been more like a Broadway musical than an improv show. The goal has been to create a brilliant distraction to get people's attention, be noticeable, or generate buzz, even if the products or services offered often lack a sense of authenticity.

Consumers, however, have gotten used to talking to each other through social networks with a level of humanity they have come to expect from all users. Now, as an advertiser or company, you need to join in this conversation, and when you do so, your organization must keep your consumers' expectations in mind. You have to be an authentic human being in your interactions. Anything less and your consumers might consider your attempt at conversation nothing more than a marketing ploy, no better than if you repeated a bland corporate mantra. Consider what your brand or organization is really like. How can you convert your mission statement or the About Us page on your website into actual conversations you'll facilitate and be involved in each day on Facebook and Twitter? You need to let the world know about your company's, or brand's, personality while showing that you truly care about your consumers and are willing to put the time in to make a connection with them.

Regulating Discussions

Hopefully, your organization already has protocols for how customer service reps interact with customers, how salespeople pitch prospects, or how public relations executives talk to traditional media reps. With the advent of social networking, all of that "talk" online is a matter of public record *forever*. There is a tendency, especially in large organizations, to carefully regulate that speech, making sure it meets corporate and legal guidelines and that nobody says the "wrong thing." For example, corporate communications and legal departments may be concerned about their employees or representatives going "off message," making negative comments, or admitting liability through an apology.

That attitude is a mistake on social networks, and it renders authentic communication nearly impossible. The more you try to regulate brand conversations, the more impersonal you'll make them, and the less customers will respond. Worse still, the less flexible and authentic you are, the more it will show, and the less you'll be trusted. Remember, online, your trust and reputation with customers are everything.

So what can you do to keep the lawyers happy at your company but maintain that all-important authenticity? The best solution is to develop a set of guidelines for what tone of voice you will use and what you really can't say. Then, make sure that trustworthy people are representing the organization on social networks, whether it's your own staff or an agency's. You need to know that these representatives will make the right choices about what, or what not, to say during social network conversations. You can even put this new set of guidelines in a document and create a "social media policy" (the lawyers will really love that).

Making Mistakes

Will representatives make mistakes when speaking with customers? Of course they will. People mess up at your organization every day in their dealings with customers and prospects, but these mistakes are not a matter of public record the way they are on social networks. The pace of social media is too fast for people to not make mistakes occasionally, and some mistakes are obviously bigger than others. Before social media, many screwups by employees were forgivable, and others cost people and agencies their jobs. The same is true in social media. Remember, though, that it's a conversation. People are forgiving when you admit you were wrong and you fix your mishap quickly.

For example, if you make a typo in an update on Facebook or accidentally share a broken link on Twitter, just delete it, fix it, and then share it again along with a simple apology. These types of imperfection show vulnerability. This can bring your organization closer to customers and prospects because it helps show them that, hey, you're human too. Instead of attempting to perfectly manicure each status update and tweet you make, concentrate on authenticity in your voice, relationships, and overall presentation of your brand throughout the social Web. People are drawn to what is real, not what is fake or scripted. Be real.

Behind the Curtain: Letting People Know You

A great way to showcase your organization is to take pictures and video of your team and the space where you work and then share them online. Of course, your customers don't care enough about you to want to see such material every day, but surely they'd appreciate an occasional window into the people and culture at your company. You don't have to hire a professional film crew or write a script. Instead, once a month, you can take your iPhone to a new department, staff person, vendor, or executive, and ask them a few questions about themselves and their roles at the company on camera. (The sweet spot for videos on social networks is 30 to 60 seconds. Try not to go too much longer because few people will care enough to watch the whole thing.)

You can also share pictures or video from an organization's summer outing, the opening of a new location, or even an "insider's view" of the chief executive officer or the company's back offices. This slice-of-life video will be effective in humanizing your brand and letting customers get to know the people behind the company, hopefully building their trust in your organization. Just don't go overboard. Remember, on social networks, it's all about your customers—what they want to discuss, see, hear, learn, or understand. It's not about you.

AUTHENTICITY BREEDS TRUST; INAUTHENTICITY BREEDS FEAR

In relationships, with rare exception, we're drawn to people who are able to share their feelings and their true selves, admit their flaws, and be honest and open, or authentic. We feel a connection with such people because we know we can trust in and rely on them.

It's a huge turnoff when people are "fake"—putting on a show or holding something back. People don't want to continue getting to know someone if they think he's being artificial. If you do not feel like there is some type of openness between you and the other person, it is unlikely the relationship will grow. Feelings of inauthenticity breed mistrust and potentially fear, fear that this person is not right for you or that there's someone else out there with whom you would click on an immediate personal level.

The same dynamic takes place in social networks. When an organization shares and connects with customers in an authentic way, it breeds trust and allows customers to feel comfortable deepening their relationships with the organization.

Organizations that share highly produced content or that speak in a scripted manner appear inauthentic and breed mistrust. Such situations won't lead to the coveted *likes*, shares, and recommendations your company is trying to attain.

Just as in a relationship between two people, openness and trust helps a connection grow. The goal for your company is to nurture these relationships so customers will have better experiences and even put their personal reputations on the line by sharing and recommending your product or service to friends.

B1Example on Social Media

B1Example is a government agency project supported by the Boston Public Health Commission's Division of Violence Prevention and Office of Communications. Its mission is to show positive actions and behaviors that prevent violence while actively influencing and empowering youth to redefine "street cred," earn respect the right way, and feel proud of their communities.

The Boston Public Health Commission (BPHC) felt strongly that the government agency itself not be the voice on social networks for the project. They also thought that Likeable Media, even as the social media agency providing support, shouldn't be that voice either. We agreed. To preserve authenticity and speak directly to the target audience, we instead recruited and carefully trained a team of 10 Boston teenagers to run the Facebook page and YouTube channels for the project. These teens already had proven themselves as role models and were personally motivated to create an impact in the community. The nature of the objectives necessitated a total surrender of control about messaging—something many companies, and most government agencies, have an incredibly hard time doing. But what urban teenager would trust a local government official telling her to "stay in school" or "stay off the street"? For that matter, what urban teen would trust any adult, as compared to a peer, talking about such issues?

The BPHC paid little attention to the teens' grammar and punctuation. It concentrated on helping them develop the group's voice and their individual voices and to build a process for creating, sharing, and inspiring content. On Facebook you'd see text updates that would frighten English teachers and public relations executives everywhere, who for years have taught that there's a right and wrong way to write things and express yourself. But you'd also see dozens of videos created by kids looking to make a difference and thousands of Boston teenagers interacting with one another in order to prevent youth violence. You'd find kids talking to one another in a way marketers could never duplicate. You'd see the power of authenticity on social networks in action.

Omaha Steaks Reps on Twitter

Omaha Steaks is the largest online purveyor of steaks and other prepared foods in the United States. With its understanding of the benefits of harnessing social media tools, it decided to create an online presence through Twitter. Omaha Steaks wanted to make sure that each and every time someone shared content or answered a question on Twitter, authenticity was up front and center. Remember, every tweet, even from brands, comes from a person. Omaha Steaks decided to highlight the *people behind the brand* responding to and speaking with customers and prospects in an attempt to humanize every interaction.

After members of the Omaha Steaks customer service team, public relations team, and marketing team were trained, they began tweeting. At the beginning of each person's shift using the @OmahaSteaks Twitter account, the employee identified himself or herself with a tweet, such as: "Hi, everyone. Happy Sunday. My name is Paul, and I'm here to help."

Obviously, it's a lot easier to interact with "Paul" than with a nameless, faceless organization, and customers have actually responded better to the introductory tweets than to some tweets about the company in general or great deals on steaks. Many other brands have begun to adopt this personalized philosophy on Twitter, including Dunkin' Donuts, JetBlue, and Comcast.

BE AN AUTHENTIC CELEBRITY

Social media provides a platform for celebrities, who typically have had to hire marketers or publicists to promote them, to speak directly with consumers and fans. Actors, musicians, athletes, politicians, authors, and other public figures all have excellent opportunities to grow their fan bases, shape public perception, and accomplish their objectives by harnessing online social networking. Authenticity must be a key part of their plan though. Ideally, all public personas are Facebooking and tweeting for themselves, an authenticity that is impossible to top. Keep in mind that mobile phones allow anyone to share information on the run, opening a world of instant communication no matter where you are or what you are doing.

Of course there will be times when fan interaction may not be feasible, and it certainly is not possible for public figures to respond to each and every comment from admirers on their own. Agencies or staffers are commonly hired to help in this process, but they still attempt to make the response as personal as possible, sometimes indicating when they, and not the celebrity, are responding by sharing the initials of their name. Being up front as to who is actually responding on behalf of the public figure maintains authenticity.

A Likeable Singer: Lady Gaga

Of all the singers on the planet, can you guess who is the most authentic on social media? Here's a hint: you may be one of her "Little Monsters." Lady Gaga has changed the social media game for singers and actors alike. With more than 115 million fans and followers across the major social networks, Lady Gaga has taught her fans the value of authentic content.

While many singers have publicists, managers, and agents trying to shape their image, Lady Gaga is real with people. She shares pictures of herself in her pajamas with no makeup on, asking her Little Monsters questions and engaging herself with followers. If ever there were proof of the power of authenticity to drive connections, it's Lady Gaga and her many millions of fans.

Authenticity on Twitter: Ashton Kutcher

By actor Ashton Kutcher's own admission, he's not a good speller, and he often doesn't use proper grammar in his own tweets. Yet, with more than 16 million followers at Twitter.com/AplusK, he has had one of the leading Twitter accounts for years, with more followers than @NYTimes or @CNN. The reason for this? Ashton's authenticity, consistency, passion, and value.

Ashton tweets about causes he feels strongly about, such as ending human slavery, but he also tweets interesting and funny video content he discovers online. He's open to tweeting behind-the-scenes footage of his life in Hollywood. Most important, he consistently shares and tweets his actual, authentic self.

A Likeable Athlete: Nick Swisher

Professional athletes, similar to actors, have traditionally lacked an easy channel with which to communicate with fans. Athletes are typically represented by agents or occasionally public relations firms. Social media changes this setup. For the first time, athletes now have the ability to directly talk to fans at scale.

Major League Baseball player Nick Swisher is a prime example of this new ability to connect with people. He might not be the best player, but with more than 1.7 million Twitter followers at Twitter.com/NickSwisher, he's one of the top baseball players on Twitter. Why? Once again: authenticity. He not only shares photos and videos but also insights and thoughts directly from the dugout. His popularity comes from his ability to give fans behind-the-scenes access to somewhere they've not been before.

Nick's Twitter use is not just an exercise in ego either. Building huge legions of fans and followers through social media allows athletes to earn better endorsement deals, sell their own merchandise, and eliminate the hiring of middlemen. In 2009, Swisher was in a neck-and-neck race with Kevin Youkilis for the last spot on the American League All-Star team—a spot selected by majority fan vote—and a few tweets to Swisher's 1.5 million followers helped drive him to the top spot, making him an all-star!

ACTION ITEMS

1. If you're a one-person operation or a very small business, write down five things you could say that would seem inauthentic or that would sound like marketing-speak to a customer. Then write five examples of how you could convey the same messages in a more authentic way on Facebook.

2. If you are part of a large organization, create a plan for how to represent yourself authentically. Recognize that authenticity won't be easy but that it's essential. Meet with key stakeholders and management at your organization to determine how you can make communication more authentic across all channels, especially on social networks.

3. If you already have a social media policy, examine it carefully to ensure that it encourages authentic communication, and tweak it if it doesn't. If you don't yet have a social media policy, draft one now.

4. If many people are responding on Twitter on behalf of your organization, have each one sign tweets with his or her own name or initials.

JUST BE REAL

Just as people can usually tell the difference between someone who is being sincere and someone who is being insincere at a cocktail party, they can tell the difference between authentic communication and marketing- and PR-speak or legalese from your organization. If you are robotic or scripted in your social media interactions, despite the best of intentions, you will turn off customers and prospects. If you are real, authentic, and human in your interactions, customers and prospects will trust you, buy from you, and most important, share you with their friends.

CHAPTER 9

Be Honest and Transparent

Four years ago, I was friended by a New York State senator on Facebook. I accepted, despite not knowing the politician personally, because I admired a public servant using social media to broaden his knowledge and reach. Also, I had nearly run for New York public office myself at one point, and I figured that since I already knew a number of other state senators from that experience, I might eventually run into him, in New York City anyway. Who knows, maybe we'd become "real" friends then? So I was surprised, but not necessarily shocked, when one day while logged in on Facebook, a chat bubble popped up from the senator:

"Hey, Dave. What's going on?"

"Not much. How are you, Senator?" I responded via Facebook live chat.

"I'm good. Hey, can you contribute to my campaign please? Every donation counts, and the next filing deadline is tomorrow, so I could really use your help."

"Maybe," I replied somewhat suspiciously. "Wow, it's great that you're using social media for your own campaign."

"Thanks a lot. We have an event next week too. It would be great if you could come out to support me."

"Maybe," I said once again. Then I thought to ask, "Hey, this is the senator, right? I mean, you're not a staff person or volunteer impersonating the senator on Facebook in order to raise money, are you?"

Silence.

I continued, "As the CEO of a social media firm *and* a constituent, I'd really like you to level with me. If you don't respond at all, I'm going to assume that you're not really the senator."

More silence.

Then, I received the first honest message of the conversation: "I'm the senator's assistant, Dan. Sorry about that. The senator, he's not actually on Facebook, so we use this account on his behalf."

In such a situation, immediate and full disclosure is necessary—I shouldn't have had to ask whether or not I was actually speaking with the senator. I'm not sure just how much money that state senator raised through actions such as the one I experienced. Each time the campaign engaged with people under such false pretenses though, they took the chance of losing that election and tarnishing the reputation of the politician forever. Was it worth that risk just to solicit a few dollars from people on Facebook?

More recently, a Likeable Media employee had a bad experience with a major airline. After a flight full of complications, she finally arrived at her destination. Being a huge social media advocate, she posted an accurate but nonetheless damning account on the airline's Facebook page of what had transpired. Shortly thereafter, she got not one, but two private messages sent to her by users saying how much they love the airline. One user went so far as to say, "How dare you post that horrible comment on the page? What is wrong with you?"

She clicked on the profile of this sender, only to find that the user is an employee of the airline! In fact, the other private message was from another of the airline's employees as well. While the actions were obviously not officially sanctioned by the airline, they reflected poorly on the company, and the lack of disclosure in the messages sent to my employee was foolish and unethical at best and illegal and dangerous to the company's reputation at worst.

BUILDING TRUST: TRANSPARENCY IS NO LONGER NEGOTIABLE

Traditional marketers have worked for years at shaping people's opinions about brands and organizations using advertising and other linear marketing tactics. While marketers may be tempted to stretch the truth on social networks in order to achieve similar objectives, I can't stress this point any stronger: *You must be as honest and transparent as possible when using social media. Honesty and transparency build a direct relationship between you and the customer, and any deviation from these values can erode brand trust forever.*

In an age when it's virtually impossible to hide the truth, don't bother trying. If you're not ready to face the facts about your products or organization and share them with consumers, don't join the conversation yet. Once you're committed to creating a presence in social media outlets, there's no going back, and you really have no choice but to embrace transparency. If it seems intuitive to you to be honest, that's terrific. But too many marketers have employed dishonest tactics in trying to reach consumers, losing sight of the simple importance of telling the truth. With the advent of social media, consumers expect transparency from companies and organizations more than ever before.

Disclosure and the WOMMA Ethics Code

The Word of Mouth Marketing Association (WOMMA) is the leading trade organization for word-of-mouth marketing and social media. WOMMA has established an ethics code around what language and behavior are appropriate and inappropriate from organizations on social networks. The code is centered around honesty. From WOMMA's website:

> It's all about the Honesty ROI. Ethical word of mouth marketers always strive for transparency and honesty in all communications with consumers, with advocates, and with those people who advocates speak to on behalf of a product:

- **Honesty of Relationship**—you say who you're speaking for
- **Honesty of Opinion**—you say what you truly believe; you never shill
- **Honesty of Identity**—you say who you are; you never falsify your identity

It may seem intuitive, but think about how many marketers have broken this code through the years. They may have planted false reviews, pretended to be someone they weren't, paid for positive reviews, or asked employees to write reviews without disclosing their relationship.

All of these things not only violate the WOMMA code but are also generally unethical (and some of them may be illegal in the United States, according to the Federal Trade Commission's 2009 Guidelines, available at Bit.ly//FTC2009). Even if you're not caught by the FTC right away, which can impose tens of thousands of dollars of fines, the potential damage to your brand reputation is enough reason to never consider violating this code of ethics.

The Golden Rule

This concept is simple and intuitive (as are many areas of social media marketing): put on your consumer hat and do unto others, as a marketer, as you would want done unto you as a consumer. Would you want to be lied to, manipulated, or influenced by untruths? Of course not. So don't even consider these tactics as a marketer. If there's a gray area and you have to wonder whether something is ethical or not, it's probably not—take the high road, and don't do it.

Consider these four guidelines to maintain transparency and avoid potential ethical issues:

1. If you are being paid in product or other material value by a company or client, make note of it in your Facebook messages or tweets when writing about or supporting the company.
2. It's OK to ask customers to spread the word about your company, but if you're offering them free products in

exchange for their support, you must insist they disclose what they received in any reviews or other material they post about you.

3. If your company or organization is doing something you don't want people to know about, don't think you can cover it up on social networks. Instead, fix the problem.

4. When in doubt, disclose.

Remember, the world is so transparent now that you have to be honest and open from the very start of building your social media platform.

WHEN YOU DON'T KNOW THE ANSWER TO A QUESTION

Sometime between childhood and now, you were trained to try to answer people's questions honestly. But if you didn't know the answer, or sometimes out of sheer social grace, you may have learned to reply to people's questions with the response you thought they wanted to hear. When utilizing social media, don't tell people simply what they expect in an effort to please them. Instead, if you don't know an answer, just say, "I don't know—but I'll get back to you." People find honesty so refreshing (don't you?) that they may be happier to hear "I don't know" than anything else, especially a faulty response.

Transparent Banking: Educational Employees Credit Union

The Educational Employees Credit Union (EECU) is a medium-sized credit union with several dozen branches, and it is based in Fresno, California. In the highly regulated (and traditionally nontransparent!) financial industry, many institutions are struggling with how to best engage with customers using social media. For big banks using social media, the focus is not on banking itself but on the company's charitable giving or other service initiatives.

FIGURE 9.1 **EECU Deftly Handles a Difficult Situation on Its Facebook Wall**

 Melissa ▮▮▮▮ Will eecu be helping the state workers that are getting their wages cut to $7.25/hr in some way??
July 8 at 8:15pm · Like · Comment

 Educational Employees Credit Union | EECU Hi Melissa– Yes we will. We are in the process of finalizing the details of our action plan to help members with this hardship. As in the past, we will be able to assist our members with a 0% "emergency" loan to cover pay shortages while the state budget is being finalized. Our plan is to be able to start taking applications by July 15th.
July 9 at 1:32am · Like · 👍 1 person · Flag

 Melissa ▮▮▮▮ thank u so much for the info!! very much appreciated!!
July 9 at 10:40am · Like · Flag

The EECU wanted to stand out as a financial institution that really "got" social media and was willing to have an open conversation with its customers. After all, a credit union is by definition owned by its members. They, too, thought the focus of the conversation was better off being based around more interesting topics than banking—therefore much of the conversation on their Facebook and Twitter pages (Facebook.com/myEECU and Twitter.com/myEECU) focused on the Fresno area and exploring the culture and businesses nearby.

However, EECU never shied away from open and honest conversation about rates, customer service experiences, and activities with credit union staff. Take a look at the Facebook discussion in Figure 9.1.

The only topics EECU won't discuss publicly concern the personal financial information of individual customers—information that obviously requires security over transparency. At a time when most financial institutions of all sizes have been unable to create transparent communities for their customers, EECU has established itself as a market leader. Its members are more loyal to a bank they can trust online, and their policies have paid off in increased word of mouth and membership.

JUST LIKE DATING: THE MORE OPEN YOU ARE, THE BETTER . . . TO A POINT

Anyone who has ever dated knows that openness and honesty are key factors in establishing a relationship. When one person has trouble opening up to the other, the potential relationship is threatened—wouldn't you think someone had something to hide if he or she were not completely candid with you? The same situation applies to your company: if you have nothing to hide, only positive outcomes will result from increased transparency.

If a date completely opened up to you the first time you went out and shared her innermost secrets in the spirit of transparency, however, it would probably be uncomfortable and strange. Similarly, as a company, just because you're supposed to be transparent doesn't mean you have to share trade secrets, profit margins, or insider information with all of your customers. In fact, a lot of that information would be off-putting, even to the most curious customer.

In general, though, when you share insights into your company's values and culture and encourage an honest discussion of the decisions you've made, your customers will trust you more, feel closer to you, and want to strengthen their relationships with you—just like a dating relationship. Being transparent doesn't mean you have to share everything about your organization, but the more honest insight you provide, the better.

PUBLIC FIGURES, GOVERNMENT, AND DISCLOSURE

In no sector is transparency more important than in government. You, the taxpayers and voters, fund politicians, programs, and agencies. Therefore, they have an obligation to provide public access to honest information. Just as many big companies have been slow to adapt to the social media revolution, governments large and small have taken their time in building a platform or creating any social networking initiatives. But unlike many companies, whose first allegiance must be to shareholders, the government's first allegiance must be to constituents.

The example I began this chapter with is disturbing because the senator's staff person basically impersonated the senator in order to accomplish an objective. The correct way for public figures, such as politicians, actors, authors, and artists, to work with social media is for them to personally use the tools. However, if they think they're too busy to use Facebook and tweet and instead hire people to represent them, it's best to disclose who is (or isn't) responding to questions, starting conversations, and making posts on their behalf. Entertainer Britney Spears (Twitter.com/BritneySpears) does a great job of transparently letting the world know whether she or someone from her staff is tweeting by signing each tweet with the actual tweeter's initials. On the political front, from Washington DC, First Lady Michelle Obama's staff discloses who is tweeting on her behalf by doing the same thing at Twitter.com/FLOTUS.

While it's not necessary for brands and organizations to sign or initial every social media update, it does help build trust for followers to feel like they're communicating with an actual person behind the brand and not just a faceless organization. Ideally, your CEO feels comfortable using social media herself to connect with customers and prospects as well. The CEO is, after all, both a public figure and the top marketer at your organization.

A Transparent Politician: Cory Booker

President Barack Obama set the gold standard for using social media to help win the 2008 election—but it wasn't actually him tweeting and Facebooking his way to the top. While most people understood when it was revealed that Obama wasn't using social media himself, there was a discomfort level among some people due to the lack of complete transparency in the initial stages of his campaign. Cory Booker, a senator from New Jersey and the former mayor of Newark, New Jersey, on the other hand, has set the platinum standard for politicians' honest use of social media.

Despite the many duties of running the largest city in New Jersey, and one plagued by crime, unemployment, and a failing education system when he began as mayor, Booker has done a remarkable job using social media to connect to constituents, the media, and donors. His Twitter account, Twitter.com /CoryBooker, has amassed an amazing 1.48 million followers. In addition, he has set up city agencies with social media tools so that they too can connect to Newark residents openly. Though he began the friendship at a conference offline with Facebook CEO Mark Zuckerberg, it was the continued connection online, through Facebook, that culminated in Zuckerberg giving the Newark schools a gift of more than $100 million in September 2010, one of the largest private financial gifts ever made to a city.

However, no story better illustrates the power of elected officials to connect directly to constituents than what happened on December 31, 2009. Newark resident Ravie Rave tweeted during a New Year's Eve snowstorm that she was worried about her 65-year-old dad getting snowed in. Mayor Booker saw the tweet and tweeted back: "Please @BigSixxRaven don't worry bout ur dad. Just talked 2 him & I'll get his Driveway by noon. I've got salt, shovels & great volunteers."

He showed up at her dad's house an hour later and shoveled the snow. Note that Booker didn't care about proper grammar in his tweet. He was too busy listening, engaging, and responding to his constituents.

Booker continues to be an avid Twitter user and proponent of the open Web. We've come a long way from the days when letter-writing campaigns and petitions were the only ways to get the attention of elected officials, and many believe Booker is ushering in a new level of much-needed transparency for future politicians.

ACTION ITEMS

1. Create a social media policy that insists on honesty and transparency as the default expectations. Review with other key stakeholders in your organization what company information, if any, is off-limits and how you can better embrace openness and transparency while still keeping this in mind.

2. If you work at a large organization, determine whether your chief executive officer can effectively use social media tools such as Twitter and Facebook herself to be the ultimate transparent representative of your brand.

3. Closely examine your social media policy to make sure it is aligned with the values of honesty and transparency at its core. If it is not, consider what you could add to help instill these values. Include references to the Word of Mouth Marketing Association's Code of Ethics.

4. Write down three ways you could respond to questions and comments on social networks in a more transparent way in order to further build trust with your customers.

APPLY THE GOLDEN RULE, AND LET YOUR CUSTOMERS FALL IN LOVE WITH YOU

In an age of corporate secrets, a little honesty and transparency go a long way toward building trust with your prospects and long-term commitment from your customers. When in doubt, always disclose your objectives and who you are. Insist that anyone you have paid to talk about your company or products online be open and honest and fully disclose the situation.

Just as we fall in love with people who can listen to us and we can trust, we fall in love with companies that can do the same. Wouldn't it be nice if your customers fell in love with your transparent brand?

CHAPTER 10

Should You Ask a Lot of Questions?

Entenmann's is a baked goods company that started in Brooklyn, New York, around the turn of the twentieth century. The company has since grown to become a national brand, and it has created and discontinued tons of products over the years. It has a passionate fan base, whose loyalties sometimes lie with a specific tasty treat rather than with the brand itself.

Recently, an Entenmann's fan asked, "Why won't you bring back the Banana Crumb Cake?" on the Entenmann's Facebook wall. He posted this same question three times in one day. He was so distressed about the Banana Crumb Cake being discontinued, he actually began to rally fans to boycott his previously beloved Entenmann's brand. He wrote letters, created a petition, and posted all over the Facebook wall—where oh where had the Banana Crumb Cake gone?

Entenmann's is a forward-thinking company when it comes to social media, and it realizes that its customers are its most valued assets. Yet, the Banana Crumb Cake had not been selling in great enough volume to continue production, and Entenmann's had to give it the axe. So what's a brand to do? Senior executives at Entenmann's determined that the company would, in fact, resume production if *sales warranted the return* of the Banana Crumb Cake.

They placed a call to the disgruntled fan and let him know that they would be posting a poll on Entenmann's Facebook page so that fans could vote on whether or not to restart production of the cake. If 1,000 or more people voted to "bring back Banana Crumb," well then, he would have his way. This proposal empowered the customer and consumers everywhere, providing them with a stake in Entenmann's product line.

The next day, Entenmann's posted the question on its Facebook page: "Should we bring back the Banana Crumb Cake?" The fan (and anyone else who wanted to) had ample time to rally friends around answering the question. Not only did this provide the Entenmann's brand team with free insight into its current customers but it also ended up exposing many new people to the brand and its Facebook page.

Wondering what the results of the poll were? It turned out that the Banana Crumb Cake fan was not alone in his love for the product. Many fans voted to bring back the Banana Crumb Cake, and today, it is one of Entenmann's bestselling products. Moreover, Entenmann's has initiated a "Bring It Back" campaign through which Facebook fans vote on new products to bring back to market. Plus, the man continued to be a vocal fan of Entenmann's and enjoy their other products. One public question turned a disgruntled fan into one of the company's most positive and vocal fans today.

WHY ASK A LOT OF QUESTIONS?

People responsible for social media at organizations often lament, "Nobody's responding to our posts on Facebook and Twitter." Especially if you don't have a large organization with many thousands of fans, getting responses to, or comments on, your content can be challenging. To combat this issue, start with the basics. Consider whether *you* would be more likely to respond to a question or a statement in a conversation. Think about your reaction to the following two sentences:

- This book has provided valuable insight to you so far.
- Has this book provided valuable insight to you so far?

The first statement is likely to elicit a nod, a shake of your head, or the thought to yourself, "Eh? It's alright so far. Let me keep reading." No matter what, it's a light response, if any. The sentence also probably leads you to believe the author is a bit cocky and presumptuous for telling you what he wants you to think.

The second sentence, the question, is likely to yield a more definite response, such as, "Yes, I love it!" or "No, there's nothing here I didn't know already." Furthermore, the question conveys the impression that the author is genuinely interested in learning the answer and doesn't presume to know it.

In a traditional advertising and marketing setting, marketers have limited time and space to get their message out there. They have to tell customers what they want them to think. They can't afford to use that time and space to ask questions. In a social media setting, however, the opposite is true. You can't afford to tell people what you want them to think because they will not respond positively. Now, since you have unlimited time and space to help shape their perception, you can cater directly to them, learn about what they are looking for in a product or service, and understand what they like, dislike, want, and expect from your company. The way to meet this goal is to ask lots of questions—genuine ones, of course—and actually listen to the answers.

FIVE QUESTIONS YOU CAN ASK
YOUR COMMUNITY ANYTIME

1. What would you like to see more of in this community?
2. Who are you inspired by most?
3. Where is the most interesting place you've used our product?
4. When did you first use our service?
5. Why do you like this page?

What Is the Marketing Value of Questions?

Put on your consumer caps, and think about what companies say to you across marketing channels and how it makes you feel. Advertisers have always sought to make an emotional connection with their customers. Consider what better builds an emotional connection: when advertisers tell you about their companies, or when they ask you your opinions about them. Asking questions creates marketing value in these four ways:

1. Helping you guide the social media conversation without appearing forceful
2. Allowing you to become consumer-centric marketers rather than brand-centric marketers
3. Demonstrating that you value openness, honesty, and feedback (three values customers and prospects universally hold in high regard)
4. Showing that you care about what your customers have to say

Questions build an emotional connection between you and the consumer, and they generate conversations about your customers' pain points, problems, and needs. As customers have discussions with each other, and with you, you'll gain mindshare, increasing the likelihood that they'll turn to you for your products and services when needed.

What Is the Insight Value of Questions?

Questions on social networks lead to conversations that clearly have marketing value. But even if they didn't have such value, the insight you can glean alone from them is immense. Companies' research and development (R&D) departments routinely spend many thousands or even millions of dollars on programs, such as focus groups, surveys, and customer marketing research, to gain insight into their customers or prospects. Yet, once you've built up a following on Facebook, Twitter, or both, you can tap into these communities on a regular basis without spending a dime! These online networks are living, breathing focus groups. You can ask your customers questions about your products and services, about their perceptions and attitudes, their opinions, their knowledge of competitors, and an infinite number of other topics. Try asking simple questions such as the following to start:

- What can we do better?
- What were your best and worst experiences with us?
- What do you think of our recent advertisement?

Eventually you can also cut or limit the traditional focus group and research activity you do offline, saving money and providing you with a direct, real-time audience whose responses to your questions are almost instant.

In an age of growing transparency, asking questions publicly to gather insight is best. But what if you want to gather insights privately? Even in that case, you can create a private survey online and then solicit people to participate through your social communities. And when you solicit people, in order to generate a better response rate, ask a question! "Who'd like to participate in a survey about us?" will yield a better response than "Click here to participate in a survey about us" every time. Remember, questions have a natural tendency to elicit answers; statements do not.

WHAT DID LIKEABLE MEDIA'S RESEARCH FIND ABOUT QUESTIONS AND FACEBOOK ENGAGEMENT?

Our team at Likeable Media did a study on what makes a Facebook page update worthy of being *liked* by someone and the kinds of posts that generate the highest engagement rates. To find these answers, we looked at a month's worth of Facebook status updates for 10 of our clients ranging from independently owned Internet startups to national restaurant chains.

In *9 out of 10* cases, the interaction rate for status updates that posed a question directly to fans was *above the average rate for informational* posts. In *10 out of 10* cases, engagement rates for posts that talked exclusively about the company without posing a question were *below the overall average*. In terms of actual numbers, posts that posed a question or otherwise requested immediate feedback were up to *six times* more engaging than straight informational posts. Those posts asking fans to *like* the update were up to *5.5 times* more engaging. On one page, we actually found a "*like* this" update that was *26.6 times* more engaging than the page's informational posts.

Of course, if you simply post random questions, having nothing to do with your customers or products, those posts won't have much conversational staying power or engagement over the long term. The challenge is to find questions that encourage thought from your fan base. Though daunting, try asking customers what they think of a new product. Even more direct, pose questions inquiring about things consumers *don't* like about your latest products or services—you might get some real feedback you can use, or you still might get people sharing the coveted "I love everything about you" comment.

Ask people to *like* statuses if they agree with a point your brand is stressing. Finally, phrase updates in a way that's relevant to the values of your organization, and don't forget to help facilitate the conversation in a way that is not too sales heavy!

WHAT IS THE POWER OF CROWDSOURCING?

Crowdsourcing is the act of outsourcing tasks that are traditionally performed by employees at an organization to a large group of people or community (a crowd) through an *open call*.

The beauty of crowdsourcing is threefold:

- First, you find great solutions to problems from the people who know you best: your customers.
- Second, you tap into the wisdom of the crowd—as the saying goes, many heads are often better than one.
- Finally, most important, you get vested interest in the outcomes from a potentially huge group of people who are all waiting to potentially become your newest customers.

Crowdsourcing is the ultimate question. It's saying to your community, "We have a challenge. Can you help?"

Lay's Do Us a Flavor Contest

In 2012, Lay's, the international potato chip company, celebrated its seventy-fifth anniversary by crowdsourcing a new flavor. It began with a simple ask to its customers and fans: "Do Us a Flavor." Lay's fans were asked to submit their ideas for the next flavor for a chance to win $1 million and 1 percent of the new chip's sales. In just a few weeks, Lay's received millions of submissions, and the company then narrowed down the submissions to a few finalists. From there, the public voted on the next potato chip flavor, and Karen Weber-Mendham's Cheesy Garlic Bread won.

The money Lay's spent was far less than R&D would have cost, and since so many customers were involved throughout the process, when the new flavor launched, it had a built-in audience of more than 3.8 million people who had participated in the process to create it. Who wouldn't want to launch a new product that 3.8 million people already felt they had connected to before it even hit the shelves?

Tria Beauty

Involving your community in product development doesn't have to come in the form of a formal contest or large-scale campaign. Sometimes, with an engaged customer base, asking a simple question can garner intel—and an opportunity to surprise and delight your fans.

Tria Beauty, the revolutionary light-based skin care brand behind products that offer physician-quality skin care in convenient and affordable ways, was gearing up to introduce a new line of its flagship product: the Hair Removal Laser (HRL) 4X. Before the summer 2013 launch, the company asked its fans to vote on which colors the new version of the device should be offered in. Like the Entenmann's example above, Tria posed a simple question the fans could easily answer: "Which of these colors would you like to see in our new HRL 4X Colors line?" And Tria watched the responses roll in.

What Tria did next was what made this a special case. After announcing to the community that the brand had selected the two most-voted-on colors to be turned into products (the unnamed Color 6 and Color 7), they asked another question: "What would you name these colors?" What was simply an engaging question to generate conversation and excitement for the upcoming summer launch ended with Billi Smith commenting on February 4, 2013: "I wanna call her peony <3." When the Colors lines launched in July of that same year, the pink device carried the official name of Peony. Tria Beauty gave a special shout out to Billi Smith that day.

HOW SHOULD YOU ASK DISCUSSION-GENERATING QUESTIONS?

Crowdsourcing might work well when you have the right project and enough of an existing community to make it work, but asking questions through social media outlets on a regular basis can also keep fans interested, engaged, and having fun. It's important to stay creative, innovative even, to keep your customers interested and returning to your Facebook page or following your tweets regularly. You need to utilize your customers' growing mindshare and get them involved by posing intriguing questions that can create a full-on discussion.

What Talk Happens at Omaha Steaks' Table?

Omaha Steaks wanted to keep people talking by asking questions of its online community at Facebook.com/OmahaSteaks. However, after just a few weeks, asking questions about steaks, and even food, got repetitive fairly quickly. Omaha Steaks wanted a way to stimulate interesting conversation without making it irrelevant.

We determined that with any great meal, there's good conversation around the table, whether at a restaurant, at home with an Omaha Steaks product, or around the "virtual table" that is social media. We responded by designing "Table Talk." Table Talk is a weekly feature through which Omaha Steaks asks its fans a question that is likely to stimulate discussion, whether at the dinner table or online. The topics are occasionally about food, sometimes steaks, but they are most often about other topics likely to elicit interesting, lively conversation. The questions are often relevant to the time of year or holiday season, and they aim to always be interesting to the Omaha Steaks core audience.

Here are a few examples of questions asked at Table Talk, pulled right from its Facebook page:

- "Table Talk time! Some of us are seasoned Halloween veterans while others are still lacking ideas. So, what's the best Halloween costume that you or someone you know has ever worn?"
- "Time for Table Talk! It's officially premiere time for the Fall TV line-ups! What new or returning shows are you looking forward to the most?"
- "Time for some Table Talk! Did you know that New York City was once temporarily the United States capital? Have you ever visited the Big Apple? Did you catch any shows or just see the sights? Share here!"

None of the Table Talk questions are about the brand or what they do, but all of them stimulate conversation, creating hundreds of comments in discussions at times. Why bother, if you're Omaha Steaks? Remember, more *likes* or comments on any Facebook content drive that content to the top of people's News Feeds, leading to more impressions, and more top-of-mind awareness for Omaha Steaks for thousands of fans.

What are the concrete results of the Table Talk feature? Even without explicitly selling steaks to new customers, Table Talk has led to a higher frequency of annual purchases from the average customer.

ACTION ITEMS

1. Write down a list of the topics of conversation your customers typically talk about. Remember, when you brainstorm, nothing's wrong. Try to write about topics that have something to do with your brand or organization, and also some that have *nothing* to do with your brand. What do your customers like to talk about? What can they have a spirited discussion about?
2. Based on the topics your customers discuss, write a list of questions you could ask them publicly on Facebook or Twitter to stimulate interesting discussion.
3. What questions could you ask your fans to help you glean insight into what they want from you and how you could do a better job serving your customers? If your organization has done marketing research, surveying, or focus group testing in the past, consider how you might insert some of your findings into your social media communications.
4. Do you have any projects that might be well served by crowd-sourcing? Determine whether you have any upcoming design updates, new products or packaging, or other opportunities you could ask your customers and fans to help you with publicly.

WHY SHOULD YOU ASK A LOT OF QUESTIONS, AGAIN?

If social media is a conversation, you can't possibly be an active participant without asking questions. Asking your customers, prospects, and fans questions will get people talking and keep them talking, creating actual dialogue. And, ideally, they'll be talking about you in a positive light.

Asking questions on Facebook and other social networks can help you gain valuable insights about your organization, cut R&D costs, and gain access to ideas you may not have had from the people who know you best—your customers and prospects. Crowdsourcing allows you to ask the ultimate question of your community—"Can you help us?"—and builds a massive number of stakeholders in your success while providing your community with a valuable and often fun activity. Questions demonstrate your organization's fundamental openness to hearing answers, whether you like the answers or not. Can you think of any better way to engage your customers in dialogue online than asking questions?

CHAPTER 11

Provide Value (Yes, for Free!)

"Excuse, me, Dave, we've never met, but I wanted to introduce myself," Michael said confidently, as he stopped me at a large social media conference in New York. "I just wanted to thank you for all of the great value you and your company provide," he continued. "I mean, all of the links, resources, and tips your social media agency has shared, all of the articles you've written over the past year—they've just been so helpful that I've recently started my own social media agency with everything I've learned from you. Thanks again, Dave. Keep up the good work. I'll be watching!"

I felt devastated at first. I had always intuitively believed that providing value for free on social networks online was the way to demonstrate expertise and credibility, build a reputation, and become a "thought leader." But here, someone had the nerve (or transparency, at least) to tell me the value Likeable and I had provided for him, for free, was enough for him to start his own business doing what we did. It just seemed so unfair. I questioned my basic assumption that giving away a lot of what we sold built credibility and trust and provided the marketplace with the opportunity to organically spread the word about us. Maybe I had been wrong all along and was just a bad businessperson.

Luckily, only three days after the conference, I received a phone call that helped reaffirm our core beliefs about giving away valuable content online. The call came in from a key decision maker at one of the leading party and tent companies in the country. She was straightforward and to the point:

> Hello, Dave. You don't know me, but I've been following you guys on Facebook, Twitter, and your blog for several months now. I just read another excellent blog article from your staff, and it reminded me that I've been meaning to call you. We need a social media strategy and plan, and we could do an RFP (request for proposal), but honestly, I know we want to work with you because I've seen how you guys think in all these articles you've written and shared over the last few months. I have $250,000 in our budget. When can we get started?

The free value we had provided for months may have allowed competitors to learn from us—heck, it even spawned new competitors. But that same shared content had helped build our reputation and credibility over time so that we were able to attract *inbound* leads and grow exponentially without any outbound sales force. Had we not given away information for free, the $250,000 caller wouldn't even have known about us and certainly wouldn't have contacted us.

PROVIDING FREE VALUE BUILDS TRUST, REPUTATION, AND EVEN SALES

The more valuable content you can share with your fans and followers, the greater the trust and reputation you'll build with them. Share your expertise without expectation or marketing-speak, and you'll create an even better name for yourself.

For example, if you represent an accounting firm, write a blog article such as "Top 10 Tax-Saving Strategies for the Year Ahead" and share it on Facebook and Twitter. While it might be tempting to end the article by saying, "For more tax-saving help, call us," it's better to showcase your expertise without asking for anything in return. If a prospect wants more help, she can quickly figure out how to contact you from your website, I promise. If you're worried about not having enough to write about, you can always write shorter, more pointed articles instead. A "top 10" post could just as easily be a 10-part series in which you dive a little deeper into each of the top 10 strategies, examples, or reasons as well.

You don't need to write articles to showcase your expertise either. In fact, writing articles can be time-consuming and unnecessary. Simply finding helpful articles online and sharing them with your community will provide value that current and prospective customers will appreciate. The material doesn't have to be from you—just credit the source when you share it.

Provide Enough Value to Help People, *Without* Giving Away the Farm

Even if we did give away enough content to inspire others to start their own social media agencies, it's rare that you could ever give away so much information that people could afford to do everything on their own. Accountants can share general tax advice, law firms can present information about the impact of new laws, consultants can describe best practices, and doctors can provide health news and tips. Eventually, however, no matter how valuable people might find your research, tips, and articles, they are not experts, and they'll never know your content areas as well as you do. So when they need help, chances are they'll need *your* products or services—and that's when you can profit from all of the free value you've provided.

By consistently providing great content over time, you won't need to advertise how wonderful you are—your community will already know based on what you've shared. And when they're ready to buy your product or service, they won't need to respond to ads telling them whom to turn to. They won't even need to search Google to find what they're looking for. They'll already feel like they know you—they trust you and like you—so they'll turn to you to solve their problem.

Every Brand Is a Publisher Now

Articles are no longer solely written and shared by professional services firms. Now, every company and brand can post any articles they have written in-house or found elsewhere to their blogs and LinkedIn pages. They can tweet and retweet valuable information throughout their entire community simultaneously. You are essentially able to publish any amount of valuable information with the click of a button, and it has the potential to be seen by millions of users.

Venture capitalist Fred Wilson and many others have said that links are the economy of the social Web. Once you are connected through such links, your audience grows exponentially. Writing and sharing great articles can provide your community with valuable information, no matter what you're responsible for marketing. If it's a food product or restaurant, you can share great recipes. If you're marketing a clothing brand, you can share articles about the latest fashions. If it's a hotel or airline, you can share articles about travel tips. The most important thing is to think about your target audience and provide articles they will find valuable. What would *you* find useful if you were on the receiving end of a status update? What would *you* like to see from your company?

Keep in mind, no matter what your organization sells, you're not selling *that* here. Instead, you're selling your expertise. You're selling your reputation. You're selling your credibility. And, of course, you're not actually trading this content directly for something in return. You're giving it away. But is it worth it to become a thought leader in whatever space you're in? Is it worth it if in the future you never have to *sell* anything because people consider you the top expert in your niche and they come to you to *buy* your product or service before searching elsewhere?

Beyond Articles: Consider Other Ways to Provide Value

Though articles are an effective way to disseminate a plethora of information, other tactics are equally, if not more, helpful. For B2B organizations, for example, perhaps you want to write a white paper or share a research study. For consumer brands, you might want to create a fun game to play, a comic that makes people laugh, or a free mobile or Facebook application, all of which can provide entertainment and practical value. Be warned, however, that the cost of developing your own online game or application can be huge, and therefore it is riskier than writing a quick article.

Another way to provide valuable content is through videos. You may find it easier to create 60- to 120-second-long videos talking about how to do things yourself, top five tips, or any other content you might have traditionally written in an online post or article. For many, filming videos is easier than writing, and videos also have the added benefit of better showcasing your organization's personality than the written word might be able to. Here are a few quick guidelines for creating video content:

1. **Use an inexpensive camera.** There's usually no reason to waste money on high-end expensive equipment.
2. **Keep it short and sweet.** People's attention spans online are short—no longer than two minutes.
3. **Share the videos everywhere.** Share on YouTube and Facebook, and consider using Vine or Instagram videos to further spread your word.
4. **Have fun with it.** This shows in your final product. (It also shows if the person on camera is uncomfortable or anxious.)

No matter what medium you decide to use, content and value can be as simple or complex as you want. The main criterion, however, is that you deliver something useful to your customers or communities and truly ask for nothing in return.

THE IMPORTANCE OF CONSISTENCY

Creating and sharing valuable content will provide you with a great reputation and return—but only over time and through consistent effort and commitment. Think about it: The first time you come into contact with a new organization or author, do you trust him or her immediately? No, it takes time and repeated contact for him or her to gain your trust.

The same is true on the social Web. Unfortunately, many organizations try to create valuable content, but when there isn't an immediate return on their investment, they give up. Organizations that make a long-term commitment to regularly delivering value to their communities will succeed; those that put in minimal time and effort will fail.

FIVE PERCENT OFF IS INSULTING: COUPONS, AND THE DIFFERENCE BETWEEN VALUE AND MARKETING

Perhaps because marketers have for years used phrases such as "valuable coupons" and "valuable offers inside," we've grown to associate the words *coupons* and *discounts* with value. Indeed, e-mail marketing as a channel relies heavily on sending discounts on products and services to customers in hopes that the offers arrive in people's inboxes at the moment they want or need whatever the companies are selling. The question is whether or not such e-mails offer value or whether they are simply marketing ploys. Make no mistake: there is a difference between a *valuable* offer and a *marketing* offer.

Ten percent off is not really a value. It's a marketing offer. Five percent off is insulting. Fifteen percent off may or may not be perceived as valuable—it depends on your audience and product. It's of course OK to offer 5 or 10 percent off—just be aware that you're not really providing much value in the eyes of most consumers.

Can coupons provide real value? Free is always best, of course. No one can argue with the value of a free white paper download, game, sample, or gift with purchase. If you don't ever want to be perceived as a "value" or "discount" brand, a free gift with a purchase is the best compromise. Otherwise, 50 percent off, or greater, tells consumers that you are providing something of actual worth. While many companies won't want to offer any of their products or services at 50 percent off, an increasing number of them are using this model to attract new customers, reward loyal ones, and create buzz on social networks.

Every organization should be providing its fans and followers with valuable content on the social Web, and many are already.

The following examples are a few ways companies are providing value on a consistent basis.

GetResponse: Easy E-mail Marketing

GetResponse, the global e-mail marketing company helping over 300,000 organizations and marketers manage their e-mail and newsletter marketing needs, has built a highly engaged social media following around a topic that doesn't scream, "Like, comment, share, engage!" When GetResponse launched its social media presence, the company wanted to utilize these unique platforms to give its brand personality, provide customer service, and build a community for small business owners. The company now posts content regularly telling its marketers how to launch an Instagram channel to improve their marketing efforts, how to better design a landing page to entice sign-ups, and how to stay on top of the ever-changing world of search engine optimization (SEO).

You would think that providing this insight and knowledge would be a great consulting service for which GetResponse could charge its customers a premium, right? Wrong. GetResponse produces this content to ensure that its customers are successful, and it believes in the brand's ability to generate results for its customers because GetResponse is the expert in the industry. Instead of launching a new product, the company has built trust, and its customers stick around.

Anchor Associates: The Latest News and Laws

Anchor Associates is a dynamic real estate firm based in New York City. Far from being a mass-market company, Anchor Associates specializes in Manhattan apartment sales, rentals, and corporate relocations. Whether you're looking to buy or just rent for a semester of college, Anchor Associates works to fit your home to your needs.

Anchor Associates creates value by sharing the latest news articles about the real estate industry, as well as decorating tips and interesting events around the city. Could people in its target audience take the information and use it without hiring or even contacting Anchor Associates? Could competitors take the articles and repurpose them for their own use? Of course they could, and some probably do. However, even just a handful of prospects appreciating the information enough to contact the firm have provided Anchor Associates with a huge return on its investments—in the form of millions of dollars' worth of business.

Blendtec: Truly Entertaining Videos

If you haven't seen a Blendtec video yet and you're by your computer, it's worth putting the book down for a moment and visiting YouTube.com/Blendtec. Blendtec is the maker and distributor of the world's most powerful blenders, which it sells to restaurants, offices, and homes.

Blendtec isn't just great at blenders, though. It's great at entertainment too. Each short video the company produces asks the question, "Will it blend?" and it features an attempt at blending something you'd never think of—iPods, iPhones, and golf clubs are only a few (Figure 11.1). The videos don't try to sell blenders, and they don't try to provide any value to viewers beyond harmless humor and entertainment.

FIGURE 11.1 **Blendtec Asks, "Will It Blend?"**

But that harmless entertainment has led to this small company having one of the most popular corporate YouTube channels of all time. Millions of people have viewed Blendtec's hilarious videos, and many thousands of those viewers have purchased blenders after viewing the videos. A note of caution: of those companies who aren't in the entertainment business who try to create viral videos, 99.9 percent will fail. If you can truly entertain, that's perfect. If not, figure out another way you can provide value to your community.

Flowerama Richfield: Beautiful Pictures That Inspire

Flowerama Richfield is a florist from Saint Paul, Minnesota, that prides itself on providing value to its customers and fans. Every week, Flowerama shares pictures of beautiful floral designs, tips for plant care, and DIY projects. After sharing some interesting DIY projects for wedding planning, one bride private messaged Flowerama and booked her engagement party and wedding. Could the company's articles and pictures have inspired this bride to do it herself? The answer is yes, but the bride loved the website content, and she trusted Flowerama to play a huge part in the most important day of her life.

Likeable: A Daily Blog

Soon after we started our company back in 2007, we wanted to write a blog to share expertise and our point of view and to create and share valuable content about social media and online marketing. Much to the dismay of our small staff, I insisted that the blog be titled "Buzz Marketing Daily." People argued internally, "If you write 'daily' in the title of the blog, you're suggesting we'll have new content daily. What if we can't keep up?"

"We're not a newspaper. We're a marketing firm," one person argued.

Four years later, the title has been changed to "Likeable Content Daily," but we've been able to keep the promise of a new article each weekday. More important, the blog has become one of the most widely read and shared blogs on social media

marketing in the world, and it is a consistent source of new business prospects.

ACTION ITEMS

1. Brainstorm and write down all the ways in which you can provide value to your target audience without focusing on marketing yourself or selling your company to them *at all*. What will help your customers the most: information, entertainment, functionality, or a combination of these?

2. Write down the formats your organization is most capable of using to provide your audience with valuable content on the social Web. Will it be through blog articles you write, videos you create, or a game or application? Or will you comb the Web looking for interesting and useful content based on a particular set of topics and then share your findings?

3. Create several pieces of content you think your customers will find valuable. Before you share the content on Facebook or another social network, share it with two or three friends to test it. Do they find it worthwhile? Equally important, do they see it as pure value or as an advertisement for your organization?

4. Determine the social networks that are most appropriate to house your valuable content. Is it your blog, or Facebook, Twitter, LinkedIn, or somewhere else?

GIVE, AND YOU SHALL RECEIVE

Companies have always sought to provide value for their customers and prospects. In exchange for those efforts, they have wanted *an immediate* return in the form of sales. The challenge on the social Web is to figure out how you can provide valuable content—information, entertainment, and/or applications—without expecting anything back right away. When you give content away for free, there will invariably be people who don't become your customers—but who knows if they would have become your customers anyway? Other prospects will appreciate what you have to offer, share it with their friends, and become customers themselves.

CHAPTER 12

Share Stories (They're Your Social Currency!)

Matthew Weiss, founder and CEO of New York traffic-ticket-fighting law firm 888-RED-LIGHT, told me the following story:

> I had a client—let's call him Jack, as in Jack Rabbit—who was charged with going 140 miles per hour in a 55 zone on the Ocean Parkway near Long Beach, New York. He was driving a Porsche Turbo Carrera late at night when he was pulled over by a Nassau County Highway Patrol Officer.
>
> When we first discussed the case, I told him to bring his toothbrush with him to court. He asked why, and I explained that he could be checking in to the Nassau County Correctional Facility. You see, in New York, a traffic court can impose up to 30 days of jail time for excessive speeding. At our first court appearance, it was readily apparent that this was no ordinary ticket. The Nassau County Traffic Violations and Parking Agency handles over 300 cases a day, many of which are speeding tickets. But it is a rare occurrence to have such a high speed. One jaded court officer whistled in disbelief when he saw what Jack was charged with.

We had no choice but to take this case to trial, as this court does not plea bargain speeding cases 31 miles per hour or more above the limit (let alone ones like Jack's . . . 85 miles per hour over the limit). In preparation for the trial, Jack started to explain to me the details of his case. He adamantly insisted that he wasn't going 140 miles per hour. The following colloquy ensued:

> **Jack:** I was definitely not going 140 miles per hour.
> **Me:** Are you sure?
> **Jack:** Yes. There is no way I was going that speed!
> **Me:** But the officer is going to testify that you were going that speed.
> **Jack:** He is 100 percent wrong!
> **Me:** Well, how do you know he is wrong?
> **Jack:** Because I was actually going 160 miles per hour!

Without hesitation, I responded that I would *not* be allowing him to testify at the trial.

Fortunately, an eloquent plea and a reasonable judge allowed Jack to escape with just a fine and points (keeping his liberty intact). Clearly, though, Jack's explanation of going 160 miles per hour (not 140 miles per hour) qualifies as one of the funniest "defenses" to a traffic ticket I've ever heard.

Weiss's entertaining story wasn't just told to me. It was told to thousands of people through his blog *Confessions of a Traffic Lawyer*. The blog, updated weekly since 2009, is, according to Weiss, "the best storytelling tool I've got." Storytelling, through Weiss's blog, Facebook, and Twitter use, is what is driving his 22 percent increase in business year to year.

WHAT'S YOUR ORGANIZATION'S STORY?

I was sitting in a diner one day in late 2005 with my then-recent fiancée, Carrie, when we began talking about our wedding. I wanted a large one—huge, in fact, as I've always been a public guy, and I hoped to share my big day with as many people as possible. But New York weddings are highly expensive. We both had extensive experience working in marketing and promotions, however, and Carrie came up with a genius idea: we decided to create a promotion around our wedding.

We're both big baseball fans, so we called up the Minor League Mets affiliate team, the Brooklyn Cyclones, and we pitched them the idea of getting married at home plate following a game. We'd secure sponsors to cover the costs of the wedding, and each sponsor would have a part in the promotion before and during the game. Sponsors, and the Cyclones, would likely benefit from the amount of buzz that was sure to surround a wedding with 5,000 guests at a baseball game.

The Cyclones loved the proposal and gave us a shot. The florist 1-800-Flowers.com loved it too, and the company gave us flowers for the event. Then Smirnoff got on board, as did David's Bridal, and a dozen other companies. In July 2006, I married my wife at an amazing wedding in front of nearly 500 friends and family and 5,000 strangers (see Figure 12.1). We raised $100,000

FIGURE 12.1   **Carrie and Dave Tie the Knot**

from sponsors to cover costs and a $20,000 contribution to the Multiple Sclerosis Society.

The event generated *a lot* of buzz. Our sponsors and we were featured in the *New York Times*, on CNBC, CBS's *Early Show*, and ABC's *World News Tonight*, as well as hundreds of other linear and new media outlets. We ended up with not only a dream wedding, but a dream promotion.

A few weeks after the event, we began getting calls from our wedding vendors, thanking us for all the promotion and buzz they received and asking what we were going to do next. Since we couldn't get married again, we decided to start a company around the concepts of word-of-mouth marketing—theKbuzz, now known as Likeable Media, was born.

STORIES BRING YOUR COMPANY TO LIFE

When you hear the story of how a company was born, or you hear a story about the impact an organization has had on a customer's life, or about the unique experience of a group's staff member or partner, you feel an emotional connection with that company. Social media, especially blogs and online videos, allow you to share your stories with your customers, prospects, and the world, further building powerful connections. In the past, storytelling to the masses was expensive and could be accomplished only through television advertising or a public relations executive pitching a major newspaper. Now, storytelling is free, or nearly free, through social media.

Said attorney, entrepreneur, and blogger Matt Weiss, "People love hearing stories. It goes back to primitive tribal times when we used to sit around the campfire. With social media, consumers are in full control the whole time. If you're not captivating, you can lose them at any time. I use storytelling as a vehicle to get people to pay attention and then keep paying attention."

Every company has at least one story to tell, and most companies have lots of them. Ask yourself the following questions to generate some ideas:

- How did our company get started?
- How did we survive the toughest of times?
- Who are some key customers we've had?
- What kinds of funny or interesting things have happened involving customers or staff over the years?
- What employees' lives have been changed as a result of working for us?
- What charitable organizations have we supported?

Stories humanize brands and make them talkable, online and offline. Stories can be told with text, but they are often best told through pictures and videos. They can be told by customers, employees, or managers—they just need to be authentic.

How You Started

No matter how large your company is today, when it started, it was just your founder or founders with a dream and a plan. Every organization has humble beginnings, and by reminding people of this, you connect with your customers, and you keep them from considering your group as a faceless giant, too "corporate" for them to relate to.

You can spend millions of advertising dollars to buy television commercials to tell the story of how you got started, or you can produce gorgeous full-color brochures and mail them out to the world. Or you can tell this story online, using your website, blog, or any social media channels, for little to no cost.

What You Do for Your Customers

If you share stories that are less about you and more about your customers and the emotional experiences they have with your brand, you will create big wins. Consider how your customers have benefited from using your company. How have they grown, and what have you meant to them? How does your product make them feel? Remember, it's not about you. It's about your customers.

At a Word of Mouth Marketing Association conference I attended two years ago, the topic of discussion was creating buzz-worthy, talkable customer experiences. One woman stood up and said, "My company is a storage company. We're totally boring." A man raised his hand, and he replied, "Quite honestly, storage has kept my marriage going strong. You see, I keep every-thing, and my wife usually throws everything out. If it weren't for storage and my ability to keep all of my old baseball cards and Garbage Pail Kids out of sight and mind, things would be a lot tougher for us."

Everyone laughed but took it to heart as well: what's boring to one person might be deeply meaningful to another. Any successful company, no matter what products or services it offers, has lots of stories to share about happy, inspired customers. Whatever your company does or sells, it solves people's problems somehow. You just have to think about what emotional connections your customers make around these prob-lems and how your products or services have truly helped them. By the way, that storage company, Extra Space, now has more than 56,000 fans on Facebook, and it has been successfully using social media to drive leads for three years.

Your Key Staff

The third source of great stories is the staff at your company. Maybe it's a senior executive, or maybe it's someone in the mail-room. It could be someone who worked her way up while going back to school and raising a family. Someone who works for you overcame adversity in his personal life to become a productive member of your team. A staff person who always has a smile on her face when serving customers is a story in itself as well. Maybe it's all of the above.

Your organization, no matter what you sell or what service you offer, has people behind it, and each person has a story to tell. You need to find the compelling stories and share them— through social media. In August 2009, a Facebook fan group popped up entitled "I Love Mary @ McDonalds/Chandler" (see Figure 12.2).

FIGURE 12.2   Mary at McDonald's

The group featured the description "Mary works at McDonald's and is the sweetest *ever!*" and a picture of Mary. Dozens of wall posts and more than 1,400 fans later, the group is still going strong, with comments such as, "I just met Mary today! Yep, she is everything everyone says. She complimented my eyes. What a woman. I wish everyone was like her."

A PICTURE IS WORTH A THOUSAND WORDS, AND A VIDEO IS WORTH EVEN MORE

You've heard the saying, "A picture's worth a thousand words." When telling stories online, pictures and photographs are incredibly powerful tools. A huge reason for Facebook's explosive growth over the past five years is its addictive Photos product—because people naturally love to view and share photos that have been "tagged" to include themselves and their friends. Pinterest and Instagram have also grown into leading social networks thanks to the popularity of pictures.

As an organization, you should harness this feature on Facebook by tagging and sharing photos of customers, staff, and management. Many Facebook pages recognize a "Fan of the Week," for instance, through which one customer's picture is featured on the page, and his or her story is told. In addition to making the Fan of the Week feel special, many selected fans choose to share the news with their friends, thereby increasing the organic virality of the page.

As valuable as pictures are, there is no better storytelling tool than video. Online videos ranging from 30 seconds to two minutes can captivate audiences in ways that only television advertising could in the past. Start by using a flip cam to film short clips of staff, customers, and senior management sharing their stories. If you capture 30 seconds of video from five people in each of those three categories, you'll quickly have at least a few usable videos to share on Facebook, YouTube, and your blog.

One unique feature of Facebook videos that are shared by company pages is that viewers can click inside the video to *like* the page that originally produced it. When you encounter a great video telling a story you want to share, you do so with your Facebook friends, who then have the opportunity to connect to the company that created the video at any point while watching by clicking Like.

CREATING A STORY WHEN THERE ISN'T A NATURAL FIT

Drawing from the three categories of how you started, staff experiences, and customer experiences, you should have lots of great stories to share. However, if you're in a highly regulated industry, such as financial or pharmaceutical, or if for whatever reason you can't find stories that you think will build an emotional connection with consumers, you can always create new stories to tell through your activities and partnerships. Charitable partnerships, giveaways, and promotions are all great ways to create new social stories. Just keep in mind that if they're not core to the customer experience, they're not as valuable.

JPMorgan Chase was the first major corporation to create its own charitable story on Facebook, in 2009. In a program called "Chase Community Giving: You Decide What Matters," it gave Facebook users the chance to support their local charities by voting for them and encouraging their network of Facebook friends to do the same. Users got to choose from the bank's list of more than 500,000 charitable organizations that work on an operational budget of less than $10 million. These nonprofits could make a huge impact in their respective communities performing the good work they do, but they don't have the resources to go around lobbying for grants.

The program was a huge success, garnering millions of supporters on Facebook and sparking hundreds of thousands of conversations about Chase. Since that program, several other major brands have followed suit with charitable voting programs to create stories that drive social buzz. It's a safer way for the brands to go because it creates positive stories worth talking about with little to no risk of anyone saying something bad about the brands. However, there may be less long-term impact as well, because the conversation is not central to a customer's experience with the company. In other words, a bank giving away millions of dollars on Facebook won't make up for practices such as excess fees, poor responsiveness, and bad customer service.

NO MATTER YOUR COMPANY'S SIZE, YOU HAVE STORIES TO TELL

No matter if your company is large or small, new or old, well established or barely known, using stories through the social Web will help garner attention for your organization. Even if your brand has been essentially telling the same story for years, bringing this story online and into the social media conversation breathes new life into it. And if your brand is, well, brand-new, creating a fresh story around your company attracts customers and can invite them to be a part of this narrative. Consider the following two examples.

Auntie Anne's Rewrite: Auntie Anne's Pretzel Perfect Stories

Auntie Anne's, the beloved hand-rolled soft pretzel chain, got its start in 1988 when Anne (yes, there's a *real* Auntie Anne) Beiler bought a stand at a Pennsylvania farmer's market. After perfecting the hand-rolled pretzel, Auntie Anne took her techniques to over 1,500 locations in 48 states and 31 countries. Today, the company's social communities are over 1 million strong. Regardless of how big it grows, it's always about where the company started. The brand continually goes back to its roots and shares with its community how it started, where the company came from, and what values and philosophies go into every store opening and every twist of dough. Whether it's #tbt posts on Instagram highlighting the first signs and machines used to start the business, or it's Facebook and Twitter trivia contests that feature questions about the brand's history, or it's a massive campaign involving the community in the newest story in 2014—Auntie Anne's makes *who it is* part of *what it does* on social media every day. Fans are encouraged to learn and live the brand, not just eat the pretzels.

In May 2014, the brand turned the table on storytelling and encouraged its community to start doing the same. With the launch of the Mini Acts Mighty Impact initiative, Auntie Anne's and its community celebrated everyday heroes whose actions made a difference to those around them. Auntie Anne's has always shared with its fans that one woman starting a pretzel stand made a difference, and so it has created an opportunity for its fans to share their own stories of success and inspiration. During the campaign period, over 60,000 votes for the mightiest act came in for nearly 400 stories.

Dr. Copeland and the Tooth Buggy

Dr. Jerry Copeland is one of the most likeable dentists I've ever met. Dr. Copeland is a pediatric dentist in Tampa, Florida, whose mission is to introduce dentistry to children in a pleasant atmosphere. He and his staff work tirelessly to teach good lifelong dental habits while entertaining their patients. Dr. Copeland doesn't call his patients "patients," however. To Dr. Copeland, they're his friends. Every week, Dr. Copeland tells his friends' stories.

Dr. Copeland gives each of his patients a "Tooth Buggy." The Tooth Buggy is a postcard with his logo on it—a happy red car shining its pearly whites. Dr. Copeland and his staff encourage the children to bring the postcard with them on their family vacations. In August 2014, Dr. Copeland told the story on Facebook of his eight-year-old friend who took the Tooth Buggy on an amazing European vacation. His album *The Tooth Buggy Went to Europe!* read:

> My friend took the Tooth Buggy on an amazing vacation to Europe. I think next year I will have the Tooth Buggy stay in Tampa and work while I go on the same incredible vacation. How many places can you name in this album?

The album got great engagement, and Dr. Copeland inspired more of his friends to share their stories. One of those "friends" even referred a new patient to the office!

ACTION ITEMS

1. Write down your company's founding story. How much do you know offhand about how your organization began? How can you package that story for easy consumption to share on social networks?

2. Research other stories your organization has that would be of interest to your audience. Develop a list of customer experiences, unique staff members, and community involvements that you think the world at large would want to hear about.

3. Determine how you will best share your stories. For instance, will you use a blog or online video? Will you focus on Facebook

and Twitter? Is there a niche social network where your stories would be better received?

4. Decide how you can create new stories for your organization. What partnerships or charitable initiatives can you create that will help to drive them?

SO, WHAT'S YOUR STORY?

Do you have a story well articulated yet? You'll need to determine and polish interesting and enjoyable stories about your company. Then, you'll need to figure out the most effective ways to present your stories on the social Web so that others will digest, enjoy, and share them with their friends. If you use a compelling format to share stories and connect with your customers, you can expect your company's story on social networks to have a very happy ending.

CHAPTER 13

Inspire Your Customers to Share Stories

It was November 16, 2008. A tweet from @MeshugAvi led to a phone call, and suddenly, my wife and I were being pitched on participating in a social media fundraiser that was about to launch. The plan was still pretty loosely defined at the time, but it seemed awfully exciting: people would be asked to share on Twitter what they were thankful for around Thanksgiving, and they would have the opportunity to give a donation to the nonprofit behind the event, Epic Change. The nonprofit seemed great. Its mission is to use storytelling to support projects dealing with people in need who can be helped through financial loans. In this Thanksgiving program, the organization's hope was to use money raised to support Mama Lucy, a chicken farmer in Tanzania who had started a school.

But moreover, the project and its leader, Epic Change cofounder Stacey Monk, were oozing with inspiration. So we volunteered to help with word-of-mouth and social media marketing, and we began to figure out the details with Stacey for what we would call TweetsGiving. Epic Change's plan was to launch and execute the program over the 48-hour period leading up to Thanksgiving Day in the United States, which was just seven days from our first discussion with organizers Stacey Monk and

Avi Kaplan. They scrambled to get a website together, and they planned to get the word out to influential people on Twitter and Facebook, who would hopefully be as excited about the project as we had been and would not only share their stories of gratitude but also spread the word to their online friends and followers.

TweetsGiving came quickly, and it became one of the first successful fundraisers based on social media. Over that 48-hour period in 2008, thousands of people learned of Mama Lucy's story, and they shared their own stories of thanks through tweets, Facebook messages, blogs, and videos. Participants expressed gratitude for their friends and family, their colleagues and staff, their students and teachers, and anyone and everyone important to them. It was amazing to see so many people share stories in just 140 characters in tweets such as, "Thanks for all you have done for me & given me, mom. RIP, greatest mama ever. #tweetsgiving."

Hundreds of people also donated between $1 and $100 to an organization that, prior to that week, none of them had even heard of. In just 48 hours, TweetsGiving raised more than $11,000 in online donations in what would become one of the first successful social media fundraisers. For an organization with no previous database of donors, contacts, or prospects to speak of and for a campaign that was put together from start to finish in seven days, this was an incredible accomplishment.

TweetsGiving 2009, with a little bit more time to plan, raised $35,000 in just 48 hours, and the event in 2010 raised even more money. The enormous success of the project demonstrated the vast power of social media to spread the word quickly about causes, but it also showed the unquestionable power of using social media to inspire people to share their own stories. Just five years later, the ALS Ice Bucket Challenge raised over $100 million in just three months by leveraging social media storytelling, Facebook videos, and YouTube.

THERE'S NOTHING NEW ABOUT THE POWER OF INSPIRATION EXCEPT THE CHANNEL

The only thing that's better than sharing your company's stories on social networks is inspiring your customers and fans to share theirs. TweetsGiving wasn't powerful because of its own story, incredible as it was, but because of the thousands of stories it elicited. Inspiring your customers to share their stories is nothing new or unique to social media. In fact, this idea has always been a key component of word-of-mouth marketing. Social media just allows those stories to spread faster and farther than ever before.

Even 10 years ago, if you wanted to tell your friends about an experience you had with a company, you would call one or two of them on the phone and chat with them. Maybe, if you were particularly inspired, you could share your experience with as many as five or six friends. Today, if you want to tell others about an experience you have had with a company or product, you can update your Facebook status, and with one click, share a story or information with dozens or even hundreds of friends. Essentially, not much has changed from 5 years ago, but in terms of the speed and size of the audience you can disseminate information to, the ante has been upped. *A lot.*

BUILD WORD OF MOUTH INTO YOUR PRODUCTS AND SERVICES

The most effective way of inspiring your customers to tell others about you is to have buzz-worthy, talkable products and services in the first place. These products or features are the types that truly make you say, "Wow!" as a customer or in their very nature create passionate users. Take Facebook itself, for instance. It grew from several hundred users to several hundred million users in just five years, not because of any clever marketing whatsoever but simply because it had built amazing products that people loved and have continued to spread the word about. In fact, when Facebook hit 500 million users in 2010, it celebrated by launching Facebook Stories (FacebookStories.com), which allows people to share ways in which they've used Facebook to reconnect to long-lost friends, reunite with a high school sweetheart, or start a political movement, among many others.

Even if you're not into Apple products yourself, surely you know a bunch of people who are Apple addicts. They talk about

Apple, they write about Apple, they share about Apple, and some of them even sing about Apple. Again, these fans and followers praise the company not because of any marketing initiatives but because its products and features inspire passionate, loyal customers.

It's not always about the products either. Take Zappos.com, for instance. It sells shoes. But anyone who has ever ordered from Zappos.com knows that it doesn't *really* sell shoes—it sells amazing customer service. It sells surprising overnight delivery and free returns. It sells happiness. And it inspires people to share their stories directly or indirectly about Zappos.com every single day.

Do you have a "wow" factor for any of your company's products and services? Is there any aspect of an experience with your company that really knocks your customers' socks off and moves them to tell a friend, or 130 Facebook friends, about you? If not, what little can you do to increase the likelihood of creating "wow" moments? What about you is talkable right now?

FIND THE CUSTOMERS YOU INSPIRE THE MOST, AND GIVE THEM THE TOOLS TO SHARE

Although most people would argue that it's worth doing, not every company is actually able to inspire all of its customers the way organizations like Facebook, Apple, and Zappos.com do. The challenge, then, is to find which of your customers are most inspired by you and what you have to offer them. Then you need to give them the tools and opportunities to share their stories. The social networks themselves allow the stories to take off.

The Fiskateers: A Crafty Use of Social Media for Sharing

Remember, the importance of inspiring stories didn't just start with social media. A favorite pre-Facebook example of this is the Fiskateers. Fiskars, most famous for making scissors, wanted to inspire word-of-mouth marketing opportunities. With the help of its excellent word-of-mouth agency, Brains on Fire, it identified crafters as its most passionate users and "talkers."

In 2005, Fiskars created a crafting community called the Fiskateers. The company gathered the women most passionate about crafting and scrapbooking together, offline, and gave them tools to connect with one another. Of course, the company never told them to promote Fiskars scissors, but as the community grew from year to year, passionate Fiskateers also became passionate Fiskars advocates. Today, the community exists both offline and online, and there are now thousands of people in the Fiskateers community (Fiskateers.com). Many of the members build relationships with one another and share stories through Facebook and Pinterest, while still others bond over crafting at various online and offline events.

Who Are Your Crafters?

Who are your most passionate customers? Is it teenagers, perhaps? Or moms? How about hockey fans? Or CEOs? Maybe music-loving baby boomers? Whatever your customer base, there's a subset of them that includes your raving fans. If you can find these fans, connect them, and inspire them, you have the potential to start a powerful word-of-mouth movement. If you haven't found them yet, fortunately, social media provides you with tools and opportunities that were previously unavailable to do so. All you really need to do is listen to your customers, ask them questions, and get them involved. You can even use Facebook to find your strongest, most vocal supporters.

Keep in mind that you're not trying to find the largest subset of your customers, but the most passionate. For every company, these supporters exist, even if they are as specific as male college seniors, female golfers, young mountain bikers in Texas, or chief technology officers.

Once you've identified your most passionate subset of customers, you'll want to give them as many tools and opportunities as possible to share their stories about you on social networks. A little recognition or encouragement of these customers can go a long way, and once people start seeing other customers posting their stories, it'll remind them of their own experiences that they might want to share. You may also want to consider the influence of this subset of customers and who among *them* is most influential. The reality is that someone with 4,000 Facebook friends sharing a story about you is likely much more valuable to you than someone with 40 friends sharing a similar story about you. Remember to check people's *klout*! (https://klout.com).

RECOGNITION INSPIRES STORIES

People love rewards and recognition, even when they're not monetary in nature. On Facebook, for instance, we've implemented a lot of Fan of the Week or month initiatives for clients, based on who shares the best story, picture, or video. For example, the Franklin Baseball page (Facebook.com/FranklinSports) selected fans of the week based on people uploading pictures of their kids playing Little League baseball or softball.

Uno Pizzeria & Grill selected fans of the week based on pictures or videos uploaded from restaurant experiences (see Figure 13.1). One Purrfect Place, makers of custom cat boxes, asks fans to post photos of their cats, and it features photos and stories about other people's cats. Dunkin' Donuts has steep competition for its Fan of the Week, which is broadcast to its 12 million fans.

In general, fans of the week get their profile pictures added to the sponsoring brand's official pages, which is not only nice recognition for the fans but often leads to those fans sharing the news with their friends. With the average number of Facebook friends per user at 350, and often more active users with even more friends than that, you can imagine how quickly communities can grow around this simple form of recognition.

Prizes Can Inspire Stories Too

Recognition is great, but prizes, including cash, really get people talking. If you can reward your customers with cool, out-of-the-box prizes, you will draw out your most enthusiastic customers to share their experiences. Think "a year's supply of . . . ," or, better yet, "a lifetime supply of . . . ," in exchange for the best poem, video, or picture that showcases how someone is using your product.

FIGURE 13.1	Uno's Fan of the Week

Unlike contests of old, of course, for which submissions were private and you could showcase top entries only by using them in your advertising campaigns, now, through online social channels, all submissions are public and shareable. If someone uploads an unbelievable or entirely unique video submission to a contest on YouTube, chances are it's going to get a lot of views, and if someone shares a hysterical photo submission on Facebook, it's probably going to generate lots of *likes* and comments.

For big brands looking to give away lots of cash, charitable contests can inspire people to share their stories. PepsiCo diverted a huge chunk of its marketing and advertising budget in 2010 toward Pepsi Refresh, a global giving initiative hosted at PepsiRefresh.com, for instance, asking people to nominate causes they believed in and to share their experiences and stories related to these causes. PepsiCo gave away millions of dollars to community groups throughout the year through Pepsi Refresh, built a huge community of supporters, and created an army of people who associate Pepsi with the idea of not just refreshing your thirst but refreshing the world's neediest and most deserving.

Medtronic Share Your Story

Medtronic Diabetes is a world-leading medical device company dedicated to improving the lives of people with diabetes through its core products: insulin pumps and continuous glucose monitoring devices. Medtronic launched its Facebook and Twitter accounts in 2012. As a highly regulated brand in the pharmaceutical space, the company's presence in social media was revolutionary in many ways. However, because many of its indirect (and in some cases, direct) competitors, that is, bloggers, had been able to grow communities, it was critical that Medtronic launch with a campaign that would make a splash and put its customers in the center of everything.

And so Medtronic, along with Likeable Media, introduced a Facebook application designed to inspire loyalty, increase awareness, and cement the company as the branded diabetes destination on Facebook (Figure 13.2). The Share Your Story photo app (launched as the Let's Build Our Timeline Together app) gave the

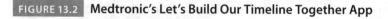

FIGURE 13.2   **Medtronic's Let's Build Our Timeline Together App**

Facebook community a space for sharing their stories with the brand and with the rest of the community. These personal stories were about memorable moments that were made possible with the help of the types of products Medtronic offers its customers.

Never before had a brand in the healthcare space opened its Facebook page to the stories of its customers, and Medtronic took it one step further. When users submitted their stories, they were added to the social editorial calendar, and each story was shared with the growing Medtronic community. During launch, the app received over 250 submissions of stories and photos (80 percent of which the submitters allowed the brand to share with the rest of the Facebook community).

The stories that were then shared continued to be some of the highest-performing posts on the network, creating a residual storytelling effect as users have left comments about their own personal stories as well as words of encouragement to the individuals featured. From day one, the Medtronic Facebook community was about building a real community with the company's customers and people affected by diabetes, and the Share Your Story application helped propel them to enormous success.

Uno Pizzeria & Grill Makes a Happy Birthday for One Fan and Inspires Her to Share Her Story

As discussed in Chapter 4, Uno Pizzeria & Grill is probably best known for its Chicago deep-dish pizza but features a full lunch and dinner menu that can be found at 160 Uno locations across 24 states, the District of Columbia, and several other countries. Uno does, however, have just one location in Southern California, which made the following individual experience a lot easier to pull off successfully.

Kimberly Boynton, Uno's marketing director, ensures that all of the hundreds of monthly comments from more than 100,000 fans are responded to promptly and positively. She looks for interesting stories about customers' experiences and sees on a daily basis how people feel about Uno's services, food, and even online presence and social Web community. One fan posted that she loved Uno so much that she was driving *two hours* to the nearest Uno location in California to celebrate her birthday with family. In addition to responding to the customer with a typical "Thanks for all the Uno love. Have a Happy birthday!" message, Kim decided to take the opportunity to further reward the customer for sharing her strong passion with an attempt at surprise and delight.

One phone call to the restaurant and two hours later, when the customer arrived at the Uno's location with her family, the staff surprised them *upon entering* the restaurant with a song and cake.

"How in the world? . . ." the woman asked.

"You posted on Facebook," the manager replied with a smile. "Happy birthday."

Said Kim, "You can't always give a cake and song to everyone who posts on Facebook. But if you listen carefully, and respond to everyone, and take advantage of opportunities that come up along the way, it can go miles toward building a brand's reputation."

That night, using their mobile phones, the family shared their story through pictures of their experience at Uno with friends on Facebook. But in the weeks that followed, the return on investment for this small action really began to take form, as the family actively posted on Uno's Facebook page, shared a video, and continued to promote the brand. Others were inspired to share their positive experiences and stories as well.

ACTION ITEMS

1. Define your "wow" factor. What aspect of your products or services is truly worth talking about? If there isn't a "wow" factor, what steps can you take to begin to build the "wow" factor into your products, services, or processes?

2. Define your most passionate subset of customers. Who are they, what social networks are they on, how can you reach them, and what tools and opportunities can you give them to encourage them to share their stories?

3. Determine what incentives, if any, might be helpful in order to inspire and accelerate more word of mouth. Will recognition and rewards encourage your customers to share? Will contests, promotions, or giveaways help drive people to share? How about the occasional individual, direct offline interaction?

EMOTIONS GET YOUR CUSTOMERS TO SHARE THEIR STORIES

If you can connect with your customers on a deeper, more emotional level, you'll be much more likely to inspire them to share their stories about you with their friends, family, and their own fans. Consider your target audience and consumers' tastes. Identify your most passionate subset of followers or customers; then recognize them and provide them with some type of incentive. What will make them want to become the most vocal supporters of your organization? How can you make them really happy, or thankful, or appreciative, or excited? How can you make them say, "Wow!"? How can *you* be a part of *their* stories?

CHAPTER 14

Integrate Social Media into the Entire Customer Experience

I was walking to work one day from Penn Station, checking my phone, when I noticed an exciting promotion available through Foursquare, the location-based social network. The promotion inside my Foursquare application read, "Check in at the Marc Jacobs counter at Macy's Herald Square and receive a Marc Jacobs silver tote bag with shower gel and other gifts. Value: $250." Now I don't know much about fashion, but this seemed like an amazing deal, so I texted my team to meet me at Macy's thinking that everyone could enjoy all the cool free stuff, thanks to this social media promotion.

When the 10 of us got to the Marc Jacobs counter at Macy's, however, the clerk there had no idea what we were talking about. We then showed several additional Marc Jacobs staff members our smartphones featuring the Foursquare promotion, and again, they literally had no clue. One staffer said, "I don't know anything about a text message." A couple of others rudely accused us of making up the promotion in order to get free stuff. A full 45 minutes later and two managers into waiting, they apologized and said, "Sorry, we were told that promotion was supposed to be the other day." They gave us fragrance samples to make up for the miscommunication. The Macy's manager took my phone number and e-mail address and said someone from Marc Jacobs would be in touch shortly to apologize.

Nobody called or e-mailed. The experience was disappointing and frustrating for so many reasons. But what was most upsetting was that Macy's and Marc Jacobs went from having an interesting, buzz-worthy social media promotion to creating a memorable, negative customer service experience. Their staff members weren't communicating internally, and they weren't on the same page about a social media promotion that someone within the organization had obviously planned.

SOCIAL MEDIA IS NOT JUST MARKETING

Social media leveraging is not just marketing or public relations. There is no way for an organization to use social media successfully if the organization simply silos the work to marketing or advertising. In order to optimize the results from your social media use, you have to integrate understanding and practice across a diverse group of functions and departments in your organization.

Of course, social media provides outlets for marketing, public relations, and advertising, but it also involves customer service, customer relationship management, sales, operations, human resources, and research and development. Ideally, *anyone at your company who might possibly come into contact with a customer should be trained on the fundamentals of likeable social media*: listening, transparency, responsiveness, and engagement. Furthermore, there are numerous opportunities throughout the customer experience for integration of social networks and social media best practices. The more open and transparent you are with customers throughout the entire customer life cycle, the more comfortable they'll feel about continuing to buy your stuff, hire you, *like* you and your pages, and recommend you to friends.

Put on your consumer caps again, and imagine the following experience. You're at home, logged into Facebook, where you see an ad for a local restaurant your friend has *liked*. You decide to visit for lunch. When you arrive, a sign at the counter tells you to text "like DavesGrill" to "FBOOK" to *like* the restaurant's page and receive a free appetizer. You follow the directions and end up with the free appetizer as promised. You enjoy a meal, and your server, along with your printed receipt, encourages you to share feedback about your experience, good or bad, on the restaurant's Facebook page. You post a mostly favorable review that night but you mention that the dessert was a little disappointing. A manager immediately responds to your post, saying, "I'm sorry," and offers you a gift certificate to come back soon.

Social Media Should Be Integrated Across All Customer-Facing Departments

This type of teamwork, across different roles and departments, is what made the experience so satisfying for you, not social media. Yet everyone you came into contact with had to understand Facebook and be fluent in social media in order for that teamwork to actually function, unlike my team's experience with Macy's. If you have a very small operation, you're used to handling many tasks on your own. But assuming you're part of a larger organization, let's review various departments and consider how each one might integrate and encourage social media in order to optimize the customer experience at every corner:

- **Advertising.** Include social media links and value propositions to customers in all paid linear media. For example, television, radio, print, e-mail, websites, and direct mail should all include social media links, text-to-connect opportunities, or both. The advertising department may also handle social network ads themselves, a growing part of most ad budgets.
- **Marketing.** Determine, create, execute, and measure promotions, contests, giveaways, other marketing programs, and content to be run on Facebook and other social networks. Marketing is where

social media typically lives right now, even though it should have a home in each department.

- **Public relations.** Listen to customer comments on social networks and blogs, and respond in a swift manner. Determine the most influential bloggers and other key customers online, and reach out to them to pitch them on participating in programs.
- **Customer service.** Listen to customer complaints and requests across social networks, and respond. Encourage customers who reach out via traditional channels to share their feedback publicly on social networks.
- **Operations.** Create and implement social media policy. Ensure that all staff members are fluent in understanding company social media links and practices and that signage, receipts, and any other customer touchpoints include opportunities to interact and share.
- **Sales.** Listen carefully to prospects online as well as major potential partners and distributors. Leverage listening to create best-value propositions. Use LinkedIn and individual Facebook profiles to meet and engage prospects.
- **Research and development.** Listen to your customer sentiment and competitors' customer sentiment in order to design new products. Leverage social networks to survey and ask key questions of your customer base.
- **Senior management including the CEO.** Serve as online spokespeople for the brand through Twitter, LinkedIn, video, and blog. Interact publicly with key partners, stakeholders, and media.
- **Information technology.** Ensure that your website is up-to-date with social links, content, plug-ins, and applications. Ensure that social media data is secure. Manage Facebook applications and any other social media and mobile applications.

Customers Don't Care What Department You're In

When should a customer's comment on Facebook be answered by customer service versus sales, versus public relations, versus marketing, versus your agency? That's all up to you. The truth is, the key challenge isn't making sure you know exactly who should answer what kind of comment and when. Instead, the issue is making sure that as many people as possible are fluent in social media, are part of the team, and are treating every customer well!

Customers don't care about your job title or what department you're in. If they have problems, then they want solutions. When you're looking for something specific in a supermarket and you find a staff person and ask for help, a good supermarket will have that staff person trained to walk you to the correct aisle. The employee will help you, with a smile, whether he or she happens to be the butcher, the baker, a cashier, or a janitor. The situation applies to the use of social media too. Try thinking of every post on Facebook, Twitter, or your blog as one that could have been written by the most important celebrity customer you've ever had, and you'll be more likely to treat every customer and every post with great care, no matter your official department or role.

DO YOU NEED A WEBSITE ANYMORE?

As crazy as this may sound, there will definitely be companies and organizations in 2015 and 2016 whose only "official website" will be their Facebook page, Twitter profile, and blog. You already can do just about anything with Facebook that you'd want to do with a traditional website, whether you need order forms, sales carts, or secure data, or you need to utilize any other Web content or functionality. With Facebook, however, you have the added advantage of performing all of these processes in a place where 1 billion or so of your potential customers are hanging out. It's the idea of fishing where the fish are, rather than expecting the fish to come to your boat, or in this case, visit your website.

Skittles, the popular candy brand, briefly redirected all traffic from Skittles.com to its Facebook and Twitter presences in 2009. This transfer was short-lasting, and it was more of a publicity stunt than an attempt at real engagement. But it proved a point: brands no longer have any control of the Web content people see about their companies. So rather than try to show people a prepackaged view of what you think they should see about your company (on a website that nobody will trust anyway), you might consider a total surrender of control and respond to what people are saying, where and when they're saying it. In the meantime, though, you likely do have a website, and it's essential therefore that the website is as integrated with social media as possible. If you have only a tiny link at the bottom of your website to "Join us on Facebook, and follow us on Twitter," you're not leveraging the opportunity to connect to people.

Facebook's social plug-ins, including the Like button and other assorted interactive elements such as Share and Recommend, are imperative to smoothly and deeply integrating Facebook into your Web presence.

Imagine if, for instance, instead of trying to sell people your product or service, whatever it may be, on your website, all you did was try to convince people to *like* your website's content. You'd get fewer sales at first, of course, but over time, more and more visitors to your website would see how many people *liked* you. More important, you'd increase the likelihood that one of the site's next visitors would see that her friend has already given your site, services, products, or content personal approval. *Is there any sales or promotional content anywhere on the Web more valuable than the honest words, "Your friend likes this"?*

HOW CAN YOU MAKE YOUR CONTENT, PRODUCTS, AND SERVICES AS AVAILABLE AS MOBILE FOOD TRUCKS?

New technologies have made it easier than ever for consumers to access what they want. People don't need to go to bookstores to get books, flower stores to get flowers, or shoe stores to get shoes. People also don't need to buy newspapers or magazines to read articles. Thanks to the growth of mobile food trucks, you don't even need to go to restaurants to buy meals anymore in many cities. Now is the best time ever to be a consumer. Just remember, as a marketer, it is necessary that you make it as easy and efficient as possible for people to access your products, services, or content. How can you bring it to them, wherever they are on the Web?

Where in the marketing and communications process can you remind people to engage with you on the social Web? You can integrate your social links and value proposition on your website, in your e-mails, in your linear media, and on your packaging. You can have salespeople, receptionists, customer service people, and the mailroom all finish their phone calls with, "Ask us questions or leave feedback anytime on our Facebook page." Right now, when you call up any big company and wait on hold, you're told to visit its website. But a website is too often a static environment, so why not direct people to an interactive environment where they can quickly get the help they need?

LIKEABLE CUSTOMER SERVICE IS IMPORTANT, AND LIKEABLE EVERYTHING ELSE IS TOO

It doesn't matter how good your marketing is if your customer service doesn't make people smile. It doesn't matter how much you spend on advertising to acquire Facebook *likes* if you don't respond to people's questions or comments. The bigger and more complicated the world gets, the simpler and more connected and transparent it gets as well. So *before* you spend lots of time and money on likeable social media, you've got to make sure you have likeable customer service, likeable salespeople, likeable products, and likeable processes. Whether you do or not, your customers will notice and share their experiences with others. It is worth training every staff person at your organization now and in the future on your social media presence and best practices for communicating with customers and prospects.

Tragically, many companies still don't even allow computer access to Facebook for employees at work. This is disappointing for two major reasons. First, the reality is that most people can access Facebook and Twitter now from their mobile phones, so the idea that limiting computer access to social networking sites will keep productivity up simply isn't practical. Second, and more important, not allowing employees to talk to customers through social networks is like telling all of the staff at a supermarket,

"You're not allowed to talk to customers walking around looking for help. Unless you're in the marketing department, of course."

Dr. Charles Waisbren: A Likeable Doc

Dr. Charles Waisbren has practiced medicine in Milwaukee, Wisconsin, for nearly 30 years. As a general physician, Dr. Waisbren prides himself on "service like it used to be; medical care how it ought to be." In the age where more and more independent practices are being bought out by larger organizations, Dr. Waisbren works tirelessly to maintain a "family feel."

"You always see the same receptionist when you walk in. You always see the same nurses. You always see the same doctor," Dr. Waisbren said. "Trust is so important in this kind of relationship."

Recently, Dr. Waisbren dove head first into social media. When the patient sits down in his chair, he asks her to take out her smartphone and directs her to *like* the practice on Facebook. "It's not about collecting a ton of *likes*," he adds. "It's about adding another direct line of communication between me and patient." He personally fields questions and concerns on the page regularly. When patients don't have a smartphone, Dr. Waisbren takes out his pad and writes a very important prescription: "*Like* FB.com/drwaisbren and ask questions often." (See Figure 14.1.)

San Rafael: Launching a Brand and Building a Community

San Rafael is a brand with a long tradition in Mexico, where it got its start in 1948. It was known first and foremost for selling lunchmeats and hotdogs, but it expanded over the years to include other delicatessen specialties in countries in Central America and the Caribbean. In 2013, the brand introduced a line of quality Mexican cheese to U.S. consumers—its first foray into the United States. Not only was the company launching a product line but it was also essentially launching its brand to a group of consumers who didn't know the name San Rafael. The brand simply didn't carry the equity in the United States that it did in Mexico.

| FIGURE 14.1 | Dr. Waisbren: "Ask Questions Often" |

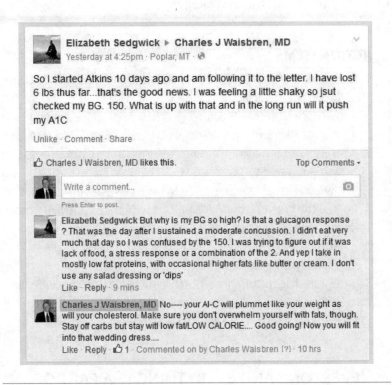

Elizabeth Sedgwick ▶ Charles J Waisbren, MD
Yesterday at 4:25pm · Poplar, MT · 🌐

So I started Atkins 10 days ago and am following it to the letter. I have lost 6 lbs thus far...that's the good news. I was feeling a little shaky so jsut checked my BG. 150. What is up with that and in the long run will it push my A1C

Unlike · Comment · Share

👍 Charles J Waisbren, MD likes this.   Top Comments ▾

Write a comment...   📷
Press Enter to post.

Elizabeth Sedgwick But why is my BG so high? Is that a glucagon response ? That was the day after I sustained a moderate concussion. I didn't eat very much that day so I was confused by the 150. I was trying to figure out if it was lack of food, a stress response or a combination of the 2. And yep I take in mostly low fat proteins, with occasional higher fats like butter or cream. I don't use any salad dressing or 'dips'
Like · Reply · 9 mins

Charles J Waisbren, MD No---- your AI-C will plummet like your weight as will your cholesterol. Make sure you don't overwhelm yourself with fats, though. Stay off carbs but stay witl low fat/LOW CALORIE.... Good going! Now you will fit into that wedding dress....
Like · Reply · 👍 1 · Commented on by Charles Waisbren [?] · 10 hrs

San Rafael launched a Facebook page six months prior to the launch of its product. In the midst of planning all the details of a product launch, the company spent a considerable amount of time perfecting its packaging look and feel to ensure that it would resonate with U.S. consumers. Prominently featured on each variety of cheese's package were the social media credentials prompting users to stay connected with the brand and learn the brand's story. In-store displays and product placements, along with special offers, are what got the U.S. consumers to try the cheese. A great product with a great social media community to match is what kept those customers coming back for more. Today, San Rafael has built up a community of Facebook users who have *liked* its page *and* eat its cheese. Launching a product in the age of social media allows you to quickly establish credibility and trust with your new consumers, so making sure they know where to find you from that first interaction needs to be a key part of the launch strategy.

ACTION ITEMS

1. Determine who else besides you at your organization can have a role in using social media to interact with customers. Form a cross-departmental task force to better integrate social media into all of your business practices and operations.
2. Closely examine all of the available inventory, assets, time, and space you have to promote your Facebook presence. As you grow your Facebook presence, where can you remind people to join the conversation? Where can you share your value proposition for *liking* your company and following you? Have you integrated social media links into your traditional advertising, packaging, and website yet?
3. Integrate Facebook's Like button into as many products and objects on your website as make sense. The easier you make it to be likeable, the more likeable you'll become.

EVERYONE AND EVERYTHING IS A PART OF WORD-OF-MOUTH MARKETING

An argument can be made that every single person at your company who ever talks to a customer has an opportunity to create a word-of-mouth marketing experience, for better or for worse. And every moment that a customer spends looking at any of your materials online or offline is an opportunity to either be likeable or unlikeable. Create as many advocates for social media at your organization as you can, and get help integrating a social media–friendly culture throughout your company. Ensure that you are using social media as fully and as deeply as possible, and you'll also be as likeable as possible.

CHAPTER 15

Use Social Network Ads for Greater Impact

You're relaxing one night at home after work, on the couch, watching some television. Your favorite show cuts to a commercial, and you're about to hit Fast Forward on your DVR to skip the downtime, as you usually do, when you notice something strange. On the upper-right corner of your television screen, you see your friend's name! You hold off on fast-forwarding, examine closer, and read the words, "Your friend Megan Miller likes this ad."

"Wow," you think. "How crazy." You watch the ad and actually find it pretty entertaining. You're glad you paid attention to your friend Megan's approval and didn't skip the commercial.

The next morning, on your way to work, you're listening to the radio, and just before the DJ goes to the commercial break, you hear, "Three of your friends, including Megan Miller, like this next company you'll hear an ad from." Since three of your friends like the company, the ad must be worth paying attention to, so you decide to listen.

You arrive at work, and since you're in charge of scanning the local newspaper for articles of importance to your company, you open up the first page and begin reading. You can't help but notice an advertisement on page 3, because right underneath this ad is printed: "Five of your friends, including Megan Miller, like this company."

None of these advertising examples are possible through traditional, linear media, of course. In fact, they probably seem downright absurd. But can you imagine how incredible it would be if they were possible? The ability to build word-of-mouth endorsements from your friends into personalized advertising units is more powerful than any form of linear advertising ever created, and it's currently possible using Facebook's ad unit.

Because social ads relate people to their own friends and to other real people, they're inherently more powerful than nonsocial ads. In the past, advertisements were about product features and benefits. Today, the content of a social network advertisement can be personalized to have the greatest impact on each user. What copy do you think would have a greater effect: "Our widgets are the best because they're the fastest" or "Your friends Johnny and Susie like our widgets"?

FACEBOOK ADVERTISING

Furthermore, the targeting criteria that are available to marketers through Facebook are so much greater than any previous model that you can literally eliminate all waste. Remember, Facebook has *lots* of data, shared by hundreds of millions of users, so you can target *exactly* the people you want to reach.

The Amazing "Friends of Connections" Ads

Once you have customers who have *liked* your page on Facebook, the best way to grow your fan base and to leverage the organic power of word-of-mouth is to use Facebook ads that target Friends of Connections among your targeting criteria. (See Figure 15.1.) Done right, you essentially use these ads to market your company through your existing customers' and fans' connections and *likes*, gaining their friends' attention instead of

FIGURE 15.1 **Friends of Connections Ad**

Appetude

Like us to discover NYC food news, dish recommendations and food funnies!

👍 Like · Frank Emanuele likes this.

simply marketing to a mass audience or an untargeted group of people.

The average person on Facebook has 350 friends. So even if you just have 100 people who *like* your page to begin with, an ad seen only by friends of connections *has a target audience of roughly 35,000 people*. If you have 1,000 fans, *that's an average target audience of 350,000 people*. The numbers can be astounding, but much more compelling is the fact that every ad served is personalized to tell your prospects which of his or her friends already *like* you inside the ad itself. You cannot receive a better endorsement!

Three Important Types of Ads

In the past few years, Facebook has extended Friends of Connections targeting to its different types of ads. Gone are the days of solely advertising to drive page *likes*. Unlike other advertising media, Facebook allows you to target your precise demographic with the exact call to action to fit the campaign needs. From driving users to download your app to boosting engagement on your content, Facebook allows you to seamlessly advertise on mobile and desktop. Though there are more than a dozen different types of ads, these are three of my favorites:

1. **Driving traffic and leads.** Driving website traffic is the most common use of Facebook advertising. Oftentimes companies use these to drive customers to specific landing pages such as a blog or a "Buy Now" page. In the past, domain ads (which appeared on the right-hand side of your Facebook News

FIGURE 15.2   **Which Ad Is More Powerful?**

Feed) were extremely popular. Nowadays, ads using images and videos in the News Feed are much more successful. Take, for example, the block of ads from my News Feed shown in Figure 15.2. The *Huffington Post* ad with a picture of a wedding (and my friend Tessa's recommendation) is way more powerful than Poland Spring's sidebar ad. When you're marketing, remember to think like a consumer. Ask yourself, "Would this catch my attention? Would I click on that link or *like* this page?"

2. **Post *likes* and engagement.** Post *boosts* have become increasingly important since early 2014. As Facebook's News Feed algorithm continues to evolve and Facebook works to bring in more ad revenue, it's become much more difficult to get your business page's content viewed organically. In fact, fewer than 10 percent of your fans on Facebook will see your posts if they're not boosted. This has huge implications for businesses, both big and small. You've worked hard to build your audience, and it would be a shame for them to miss out on your posts. Facebook allows you to boost content right from the post. With just a few clicks, you can have your Facebook post in front of thousands of your fans—and their

FIGURE 15.3   **A Post Boost**

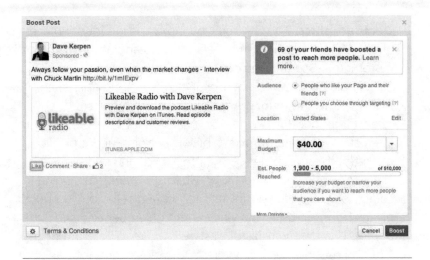

friends. Figure 15.3 is an ad for the Likeable Radio podcast that reached thousands of people for just $40.

3. **App installation ads.** App installation ads have become increasingly more important for brands with mobile apps. Americans alone download millions of apps every day. In fact, Apple recently reported a total of 75 billion app downloads in June 2014 alone. App installation ads allow for users to download applications directly from Facebook on mobile phones. Through *call-to-action buttons*, users are redirected to the app store to complete the download.

Choosing Targeting Criteria

It's great targeting friends of existing *likers*, and chances are many of your customers' friends have a lot in common with your customers. But remember, you can choose exactly what targeting criteria you want to apply to each ad you take out on Facebook. Not all of these will necessarily apply to you, but they're all worth a look. Here's a review of each:

- **Location.** Target people by country, state, city, or town. For local businesses, you can target people in your town, or within a 10-, 25-, or 50-mile radius.
- **Demographics.** This is where you input age, gender, and even ethnic affinity. Ideally, you have an understanding of who your customers are, so that you can target specifically here, as in 23- to 25-year-old Caucasian women, or 56- to 65-year-old Asian men.
- **Interest and behaviors.** Arguably the most important category of ad targeting, this is where you can identify people by their interests. With data on over 1 billion people, Facebook allows marketers to target by interests, both explicit and intrinsic. *Explicit interests* include things like cooking, biking, running, jazz, going to church, or reading fiction. *Intrinsic interests* are behaviors Facebook gleans from the users' activities and profiles. Behaviors include purchase and search history as well as *likes*. There are nearly 1 million possible *likes* and interests to choose from! You can also target by job titles, which is incredibly valuable in the business-to-business space. Reach only CEOs, marketing directors, purchasing managers, or real estate agents, for instance.
- **Birthday.** Self-explanatory. It's nice to wish people "happy birthday" on a day they almost always log in to Facebook.
- **Relationship status and interested in.** Target just singles, married people, people in relationships, or engaged people here. You can also target men interested in women or women interested in men. For obvious reasons, this category is particularly valuable to companies in the wedding industry or dating industry.
- **Language.** Target people who are using Facebook in a specific language. There are more than 200 different languages spoken on Facebook.
- **Education and work.** Target people by their education status or their company. Again, in the business-to-business space, this is particularly valuable. Perhaps you want to reach people at five specific companies in your town or land a new client from one particular company or industry. Maybe you want to get someone's attention to land a new job.

The more specific your target audience, the better. Personalized ads based on these criteria will go so much further in promoting your organization than any traditional mass-media outlet. Use your current fans to create ads that apply to their friends and will therefore attract new customers.

Custom and Lookalike Audiences

Another capability of Facebook ad targeting is creating custom audiences. With the ability to upload e-mail lists or import data from your website's conversion pixels, companies can target more precisely. Say, for example you're an e-commerce brand looking to advertise to women who have purchased from you in the past six months. Using custom audience targeting, reaching those women is easier than ever.

Lookalike Audiences let companies advertise to people who resemble current fans or people who would be interested in your business. All you need is a custom audience list for Facebook to match with other users with similar interests, behaviors, or demographics. For example, if Dr. Ken Redcross (from Chapter 4) wanted to target people who "look like" his current patient base, he just needs to upload his patient's e-mail list.

Seven Cool Things You Can Do with Facebook Ads

Just to get you thinking about all of the potential that's out there, consider these seven possibilities for using Facebook ads:

1. **Target people on their birthdays!** Reach your customers or prospects on their birthday, while they're checking out all of their friends' birthday wishes on their wall. You can offer them a discount or a special prize or simply surprise them by saying "Happy birthday" from your company.
2. **Target your fans with reminders about cool events and promotions, or just to say thank you.** Once you generate *likers*, you can talk to them for free through the information stream on Facebook. But if you have a particular message or offer you want to reinforce to people who you know already *like* you, this is a great, inexpensive way to guarantee that message will be seen.

3. **Target your employees!** Has it been a tough week? Congratulate them for getting through it, or thank them for their hard work! You can do this using the Companies targeting feature, or use job titles combined with companies to target individual departments at your company.

4. **Introduce yourself to a new company.** Just landed a job as a social media specialist at a new firm? Show the company just how cool and social media nerdy you are by introducing yourself to your new coworkers in an ad.

5. **Target your significant other.** You already know everything about this audience. Just input all of the criteria, and you'll get an ad built exclusively for him or her, literally advertising your love. Take a look at the example in Figure 15.4. (I can't believe I was ever in love with a BlackBerry!)

6. **Build potential relationships with key partners.** Target people with "CEO" or "president" and other similar job titles in their profiles at the companies you're interested in building relationships with.

7. **Target specific job titles.** Get connected with the exact employees you want to reach. If you're a marketing software

---

FIGURE 15.4   **Targeted Love Ad**

I love you more   ✕
than

This device. And I'm only miserable when I'm without you. Hope we can unplug for a day soon. I love you.

Unlike
You like this.

company, then targeting the CMO or marketing director will be more beneficial than targeting everyone at said company.

All seven of these practices will help you further build relationships with your customers, prospects, coworkers, employees, and partners online and offline, but these are just a start. What other ways could you target your specific audience through Facebook ads?

Make the Ad Likeable

Once you've selected all of the targeting criteria, you get to actually create the ad, using a headline, a few lines of copy, and a picture. The picture is by far the most important element of a Facebook ad, so you'll want to select a bright, size-optimized image that gets people's attention. You can run an unlimited number of ads under the same budget, so you'll have the opportunity to test out dozens or more of different images, headlines, and copy to see what's most effective in driving *likes*.

You'll need to set a daily budget, which can be as low as $5 and as high as you'd like. You can buy ads through CPM (cost per thousand impressions), CPC (cost per click), or CPA (cost per action). With CPM, your ad may appear many thousands of times, but if nobody clicks on the ad, you'll have nothing to show for your money. With CPC or CPA, you pay only when people click on your ads or take your desired action—so you're only paying for results. CPC or CPA is recommended in order to guarantee how many actions you'll get for your money.

Keep Your Social Ads Social

A lot of companies have failed at using Facebook ads to drive direct sales because people spend time on Facebook to socialize and connect with others, not to buy stuff. The formula for ad success is not just to link ads to your website or shopping cart but to link to your fan page. Connecting users to your page encourages them to engage with you. They might enter a contest or ask you some questions about products, services, or your industry. They have the opportunity to connect with other people in your community. Remember Chapter 5: the object is to engage with your customers or prospects. You'll have ample time to make a great impression on them later—you've just got to get them to *like* you first.

ADVERTISING IN OTHER SOCIAL NETWORKS

Facebook advertisements are the most used and most effective form of social network ads, but they are not the only kind. Both LinkedIn and Twitter, for example, provide direct advertising opportunities as well, with the abilities to target specific audiences and help companies continue to build their online social Web and presence.

Use LinkedIn Ads to Reach Professionals

LinkedIn hosts more than 300 million user profiles, and the users are often more business focused than Facebook's users. Users can either drive traffic to a website or to another page on LinkedIn. While not quite as specific as Facebook's criteria, LinkedIn offers great targeting criteria to reach professionals, including industry, job title, seniority, age, gender, location, skills, and group affiliation. It also offers CPC and CPM models, and it allows for ad budgets as small as $10. LinkedIn ads are often more expensive than Facebook ads on a per-click basis, but then again, you're reaching senior professionals. How valuable is that to your business?

The coolest *social* aspect of LinkedIn ads is that underneath each ad is a link to the profile of the person who took out the ad. It's not as strong an endorsement as a Facebook Friends of Connections ad, but it's a compelling feature. This transparency and subtle invitation to connect is refreshing. Instead of an advertisement coming from a giant faceless organization, it's literally shown as coming from one individual, who's on LinkedIn, just like the person who is viewing the ad. Can you imagine if every ad you saw on television or read in a newspaper had the personal information of the person who took out the ad? That would lead to greater transparency and accountability and likely to better ads being made.

Twitter Ads Allow You to Join the Stream

Twitter has tinkered with a number of different advertising models, but at the moment, Promoted Tweets, Promoted Trends, and Promoted Twitter Accounts all allow advertisers to get their company's most recent tweets in front of people who are using particular keywords on Twitter. Similar to Facebook, Twitter has also increased its objective-based campaigns. This process is most similar to Google's AdWords model, wherein people who search on Google using specific keywords find sponsored listings from advertisers who have preselected (and bought) those keywords. With Twitter, though, it's more about the *conversation* than the search. For instance, try searching on Twitter for doctors in Brooklyn to see what people are saying about their doctors in that area. If a doctor in Brooklyn has purchased specific keywords (such as "Brooklyn," "doctor," "patient," or "care"), her last tweet will show up at the top of your stream.

Twitter ads are particularly useful for driving traffic to your website, driving app installs for your mobile app, and driving lead generation through e-mail list ads.

THE LIFETIME VALUE OF A SOCIAL NETWORK AD

Advertisements have traditionally sought to raise awareness, to increase purchase intent, and to convert passive recipients into customers. At the end of a linear ad, the recipient has become more aware and has decided whether to purchase something or not. Where social network ads differ and can actually be much more valuable, however, is in starting the conversation. All that an ad on Facebook or Twitter really needs to do is generate a *like* or a follower, respectively, for your company. After that point, you have the ability to talk to (and engage with, and eventually sell to!) those fans or followers for the rest of their lives, without any additional advertising expense.

Of course, if you become too marketing or sales heavy in your social network messaging, people can and will "unlike" you or "unfollow" you. To a great extent, that situation has happened with e-mail marketing: e-mail mailing lists aren't usually used to engage or provide value. They're used to sell—and consequently, people who were once fans of a company, often grow to be annoyed by, or even hate, that same company, and eventually they unsubscribe from their e-mail lists.

You have an amazing opportunity to target your ideal customer, and for the price of one click (this can range from $0.50 to $3.00, depending on your targeting criteria), you convert someone to *like* you or follow you and join the conversation. Once he's in your community, you can have his attention literally for the rest of his life, as long as you engage appropriately. What is the lifetime value, then, of that initial ad, *like*, follow, or click?

Likeable's Ads Stumble but Then Build a Business or Two

At Likeable Media and Likeable Local, we've purchased Facebook ads for thousands of clients, and we've used the targeting criteria and Friends of Connections opportunities to grow many communities. But the number one example I'd like to share of how to use Facebook ads comes from our own firm's experience. Facebook ads are the only form of paid advertising we've used, resulting in the growth of a company from literally nothing into $15 million of revenue in seven years. We didn't target correctly at first, but we learned our lesson. And we only spent about $30 per day to do it.

Here's what we did first: we targeted keywords in the Interests category, such as "marketing," "promotions," and "social media." While this generated a lot of fans who were interested in these areas, they may not have been our actual prospects because they likely included students and other people who were interested in these topics but had no decision-making authority at companies. So we shifted gears.

We knew that the decision to hire a marketing agency is made by multiple people at a company, and we could reasonably identify most of them by job title. So we consistently created ads targeting these people: chief marketing officers, vice presidents of marketing, marketing directors, and brand managers. We didn't ask people to call us or even check out our website in ads. Instead, we asked them only to connect to our page on Facebook and join our community. Then, every day, we shared the best content we could find, and we wrote about social media and provided advice about how to best leverage it. The ultimate pull-marketing model eventually worked, and today, dozens of these people have called or e-mailed us asking for our help. Out of the 50,000 fans in our two Facebook communities, more will certainly reach out. But they'll reach out when they're ready to buy, not when we're ready to sell.

Soap.com Uses Facebook Ads to Drive Online Sales

Soap.com is a major online retailer that delivers everyday essentials to people's homes. From shampoo and conditioner to diapers and detergent, Soap.com takes the "dirty work" out of shopping for everyday household items.

In early 2014, Soap.com was looking to acquire new customers, and it experimented with page post link ads. Using the ad shown in Figure 15.5, Soap.com targeted people who had never been to its website before, and it tested different types of creative ad copy. Some of the best-performing ad sets targeted "big city moms" and "beauty product purchasers." Every "big city mom" who saw the ad also saw a call-to-action button encouraging her to "Shop now" or "Learn more." In just four months, Soap.com drove more than $100,000 in sales from Facebook ads. The entire campaign cost less than $10,000—talk about ROI! I think we'd all take a 10-to-1 return on our investment for just about anything!

Pure Barre's Sticky Socks Stick

Pure Barre is a fitness company that uses a unique technique to transform bodies. Using aspects of ballet, pilates, and weights,

FIGURE 15.5   Soap.com's Facebook Ad Targeting People Who Had Never Been to Its Website

the Pure Barre experience is said to be the "fastest, most effective way to change your body." With more than 170,000 fans on Facebook, Pure Barre decided to focus its ads on driving merchandise sales—namely, its "sticky socks."

Pure Barre started by targeting its existing fan base with page link posts to drive fans to their sticky socks landing page. After some trial and error, Pure Barre decided to target the socks to fans who had indicated purchasing behavior—that is, people who had purchased from the website in the past or who had viewed the Shop Now landing page in past weeks (Figure 15.6). The sticky socks sell for $12, and Pure Barre's CPA was $0.50. Once the company nailed down the precise target demographic, selling the socks was effortless and scalable.

FIGURE 15.6   **Pure Barre's Facebook Ad Targeting People Who Had Visited and/or Purchased from Its Website**

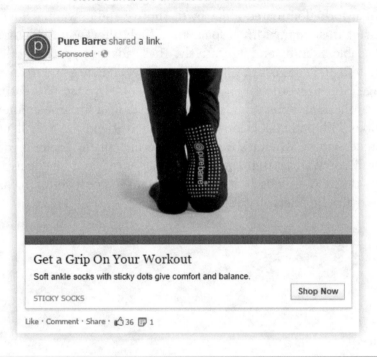

ACTION ITEMS

1. Define your perfect target audience using Facebook's advertising categories to guide you. Determine exactly how big your audience is on Facebook once you've inputted all of the demographic and interests criteria.

2. Test various different creative ideas in advertising. Start with a very small budget and with several different pictures and headlines to determine what works best. (You can begin as low as $5, a budget that anyone can afford.) Link ads to both your Facebook page and your website.

3. Determine whether your organization could benefit from LinkedIn ads or Twitter ads. It's probably not worth it if your organization doesn't yet have a presence on Twitter or LinkedIn. But arguably you should, and it's likely worth testing, especially if you're in the B2B space.

CREATE LIKEABLE SOCIAL ADS

In a world dominated today by disruptive and unwanted advertising in so many forms, social media ads allow you to be more likeable, literally and figuratively. These ads give you the ability to find and connect to your perfect target audience and to leverage built-in word-of-mouth endorsements. Instead of creating transaction opportunities, these ads establish lifetime connections with potential customers—and their friends. In a challenging economy, when it's worth considering cutting back on your traditional advertisements (which may or may not be effective), it's time to look closely at social media ads to boost your fan base and generate new customers.

CHAPTER 16

Admit When You Screw Up, and Then Leverage Your Mistakes

On June 3, 2010, LOFT, a clothing brand owned by Ann Taylor Inc., posted pictures of a tall, blonde catalog model in the brand's new silk cargo pants on its Facebook page with a click-to-buy link in the caption.

Nothing about the post was uncommon in social media, and it certainly was not uncommon for the fashion industry. But for whatever reason, fans responded particularly negatively to this post. While many fans acknowledged that the pants looked good on the model, they complained that the pants were "not universally flattering" and would "look great if you're 5 foot 10 and a stick like the model in the photo." Fans on the page began demanding that LOFT show the pants on "real women."

Many companies, if not most companies, would have done nothing in response to the fans. The entire fashion industry essentially has been built upon images of super-thin models rather than real women, and few protests have changed anything through the years.

But two days later, LOFT posted an "I'm sorry" on its Facebook page along with pictures of "real women" wearing the pants that had been modeled on the page just days earlier. In fact, the female staff of Ann Taylor posted pictures of *themselves* wearing the pants (see Figure 16.1).

The Facebook community rejoiced. Better yet, word spread quickly about what it had done, and LOFT ended up receiving lots of well-earned media attention from the fashion industry and the online world. Years later, a look at the page still shows mostly pictures of skinny models wearing LOFT clothing, but it also shows quick responses from LOFT staff to all comments and questions from fans—the good, the bad, and the ugly. The page also highlights a community that's grown a great deal since June 2010—up to more than 1.5 million fans today.

What did LOFT do? Quite simply, the company admitted a mistake quickly and fixed it. By sharing pictures on Facebook of themselves, in different shapes and sizes, the staff showed they

---

FIGURE 16.1   Loft Staff Models

LOFT Hi! My name is Julie and I am LOFT's Manager of Digital Programs. Yesterday we received a request to show our new silk cargo pants on real women. Through the day we will be showcasing women at LOFT wearing the pant. To get us started I am posting a gallery showing how I wear the pant at work, at night, and on the weekend.

I am 5'3" and a size 6 and a regular shopper of LOFT's petite collection though I shop regular sizes as well.

How I Wear Our New Silk Cargo Pant

June 17 at 11:53am · Like · Comment · Share

43 people like this.

View all 48 comments

were willing to open themselves up to vulnerability and "be real" with their customers and audience. Not only did LOFT make up for its mistake almost immediately but it was able to connect on a personal level to those customers it had offended. It was even able to seize an opportunity the mistake gave it to stand out in a good way.

TWO SIMPLE WORDS GO A LONG WAY

Being able to say "I'm sorry" when you make a mistake goes a long way toward making up for your error. Companies are made up of people, and everyone makes mistakes sometimes, so it's inevitable that companies are bound to do something to upset or otherwise anger their customers occasionally. The issue, and what's particularly frustrating, is when companies don't apologize and take care of the problem with speed.

Any guy who's ever dated someone knows, after listening, being able to say "I'm sorry" is the most important ability in a relationship—it's the same thing for companies. Especially when companies become large, are publicly traded, or have big legal teams, it can be difficult to have someone simply say "I'm sorry." But it's *always* the right thing to do.

HOW TO SAY YOU'RE SORRY

The best way to tell your consumers you're sorry is to have the highest-ranking person at your organization, that is, your chief executive officer, say it through online video in a short film, which addresses the problem and how it's going to be fixed. Having the CEO, or whoever else is your organization's leader, speak tells customers that your company is taking the matter seriously. Responding on video humanizes your company in a way that no press release or letter ever could. And keeping it short and sweet is respectful of your customers' time. Your CEO should be prepared to be as humble and natural as possible.

If your CEO is not good on camera, consider having another high-ranking leader make the video apology instead. This person should still be someone in senior management, and he or she needs to speak on behalf of your whole team. Also, your CEO could write a note, though this is likely to be less effective. Still, if a note is the best option considering your business leaders' on-air personalities, then the letter should be as friendly and genuinely written as possible—try to keep the legalese and corporate-speak out of it.

PLAN FOR THE UNPLANNED

You know your company will make mistakes, but you don't know when they will come, what they will be, and whom they will offend. The best thing to do now, then, is to plan for the unplanned. For many years, companies have had public relations firms or internal PR teams develop crisis communications plans. The major difference now is that word spreads much faster online than ever before. The longer it takes your company to respond to an issue, the worse a problem can skyrocket too. So, before you make the mistakes that you're sure to make, create a cross-departmental team of people who will be able to swiftly handle whatever situation comes up and determine the appropriate social media response.

Teach the Lawyers How to Be Human

Lawyers and corporate communications executives have an uncanny ability to take the words "I'm sorry" and ruin them. And the worst time to argue with your attorneys is in the midst of a crisis. So it's important now that your company plans out what kind of language you will and won't be able to use when a crisis comes. Simple, direct language is almost always better than corporate-speak, *especially* in a social media setting. More relaxed language allows you to be seen as real, vulnerable, and human—and it's way more difficult for customers to be angry at actual vulnerable, real human beings than at an "evil corporation" (as they'd likely see you, even if only at the time of crisis). Just let your lawyers know that in such a situation, you'll want to say, "We're sorry. We screwed up." This alone will make you way more prepared than most companies.

Have Fire Drills

Just as you had fire drills at school so that in the event of a fire, emergency people would know what to do, the only way to prepare for inevitable crises is to have your own drills. Imagine the craziest of challenges. For example, a customer dies while eating at your restaurant, or an employee pulls out a rifle at your store's counter (the crazier or more unlikely, the better). Of course, hopefully nothing like this will actually happen, but something else you haven't imagined will.

So what's the plan? Who meets from different teams—and how quickly? What happens if the crisis occurs on a Friday night? What if the vice president of communications is on vacation at the time? Social media is 24/7/365—you'll need a plan to respond quickly, no matter what. How will you communicate with your customers? What about with your employees, partners, and vendors?

It may seem silly to prepare for something that may never happen, but if you don't prepare for a social media crisis, and you're very slow to respond, or simply respond poorly, when one does occur, serious damage can be caused to your brand. Think about British Petroleum's (BP) response to the 2010 Gulf oil spill, for instance. If BP had responded faster, more seriously, and more genuinely on Facebook and Twitter, it may have much better protected its reputation—and its stock price.

DON'T STOP AT I'M SORRY

Saying you're sorry is just the beginning of how you'll deal with a crisis. More important than ever before is the ability to listen and respond to what people are saying on social networks. Hopefully, you'll have integrated this process into your regular business practices by the time a serious issue occurs, but if for whatever reason you haven't, you'll need a plan to allocate more resources to online community management because your communities on Facebook and Twitter will surely see more traffic during a time of crisis.

Whenever possible, apologize individually to each person's complaint, and continue to follow up. By swiftly responding and showing you care, you can actually take a serious mistake and end up with an even stronger reputation than you had before it happened. Mistakes and crises will come in different shapes and sizes as well—and you'll want to have different levels of responses. But the most important thing to do, no matter what, is to genuinely care, show you care, apologize quickly, and then fix the problem.

JetBlue Messes Up Royally—but Says It's Sorry

Airlines are among the most hated companies in the United States. Air travel is more often challenging than not, and the airlines' brands bear the brunt of customers' frustrations. JetBlue, however, has a strong brand—one that is well regarded and highly rated by its customers. In February 2007, the company experienced a major crisis when a set of storms and a wide variety of internal challenges over the course of one week saw hundreds of flights canceled and thousands of passengers stranded.

What could have been a total disaster for JetBlue's reputation was saved by its fast, appropriate online response. Founder and then-CEO David Neeleman filmed a three-minute YouTube video in which he apologized and made a commitment to customers that nothing like this would ever happen again. The video was shared on Facebook and Twitter, and hundreds of thousands of people saw it. Neeleman followed up the recorded video with traditional media appearances, even including one on the *Late Show with David Letterman*. He was humble and showed that he was committed to fixing things.

Despite one of the worst weeks in any airline's history, this potentially devastating blow to the brand has long been forgotten, and JetBlue quickly was restored as a market leader in customer satisfaction. Over the past few years, as social media has grown, JetBlue has remained one of the top airlines to use tools such as Facebook and Twitter to engage customers.

The Domino's Brand Is Rescued from the Brink of Disaster

In April 2009, two employees of a Domino's Pizza in North Carolina inexplicably filmed a video they shared on YouTube in which they did disgusting things with food they were preparing for customers, including wiping the food against different parts of their bodies. The video had a train-wreck quality to it: since it was so filthy, most people found it hard to eat anything for a while after viewing the footage. Yet hundreds of thousands of people did view the video, and parts of it appeared on national television broadcasts as well.

Domino's responded immediately with a letter on its website apologizing. The company fired the employees and committed to prosecute them to the fullest extent allowed under the law. U.S. Domino's president Patrick Doyle also issued a video apology, although it came a full week after the initial incident. But what else is a brand to do to respond to such a literally filthy crisis? As a quick-serve restaurant, its reputation for food quality wasn't the best to begin with, and this was as horrible a situation as the company and its customers could imagine.

What Domino's ended up doing was starting over, launching an ad campaign, supported by a three-minute-long YouTube and Facebook video, in which it showcased customers talking about how little they liked the taste of Domino's. The video actually quoted people saying they thought the crust tasted like cardboard, along with other highly critical comments. Then the video showcased the Domino's staff working together to create a *brand-new, better-tasting pizza* (see Figure 16.2).

The campaign actually made people feel like Domino's, a corporate giant, was an underdog listening to its customers and trying to become a better company. That's probably because it really was.

| FIGURE 16.2 | Domino's Turns It Around |

The three-minute-long video, too long for television advertising but perfect for YouTube, didn't garner as many views as the disgusting video, of course, but at more than 700,000, it came close. Moreover, it humanized the brand and connected it to customers at a time when it was most needed.

American Red Cross's Rogue Tweet

In February 2011, a member of the American Red Cross social media team accidentally tweeted a confusing, seemingly drunk tweet:

Ryan found two more 4-bottle packs of Dogfish Head's Midas Touch beer . . . when we drink we do it right #gettingslizzerd.

After an hour or so, the director of social media deleted the post and released an apology tweet shedding humor on the situation:

> We've deleted the rogue tweet, but rest assured the Red Cross is sober and we've confiscated the keys.

As an organization that deals with major disasters and devastation regularly, the Red Cross decided to make light of what it called "a silly little mistake." The beer company mentioned in the tweet, Dogfish Beer, also helped to shed light on the situation and encouraged donations to the Red Cross using the hashtag #gettingslizzerd. The Red Cross's calm and humorous reaction put this social media mishap into perspective and actually landed them significant donations!

A Likeable Screwup: The Gap

In October 2010, clothing retailer the Gap unveiled a new logo. The logo was immediately and almost universally hated by vocal customers across several social media channels. Thousands of people called it ugly, protested the logo, and even created fake Twitter accounts poking fun at the Gap.

Despite obviously having spent millions of dollars to create printed materials with the new logo, the Gap quickly realized its mistake, and within a few days, it posted a note on its Facebook page:

> OK. We've heard loud and clear that you don't like the new logo. We've learned a lot from the feedback. We only want what's best for the brand and our customers. So instead of crowdsourcing, we're bringing back the Blue Box tonight.

The informal, humble tone of its message told customers that the Gap was listening to them and cared about what they had to say. The quick decision might not have been possible from a less flexible, more traditional executive team. But in times of crisis, quick decisions are more essential than ever. The whole incident, while costly, improved the Gap's overall reputation and likely saved it from an even costlier mess.

ACTION ITEMS

1. Create a social media crisis plan. What will you do if a customer shares a negative experience on YouTube, or a promotion goes awry, or a planned communication doesn't go as hoped? Who will respond publicly and how? Who will be ultimately accountable for decisions?
2. Work with your legal team and corporate communications team now to establish some guidelines so that if and when a situation arises, you can quickly respond using humble, personal language.
3. Once you have a plan established, conduct a fire drill or two to see how well your organization responds.
4. Make sure you are listening in closely and keeping watch on the online conversation about your company—even on weekends and holidays.

AS LONG AS YOU PLAN FOR THE UNEXPECTED AND CAN SAY YOU'RE SORRY . . .

Humans have an amazing ability to forgive one another for mistakes, and they can even forgive companies too (especially when they're reminded that compassionate, understanding, and reasonable people are behind the company in question). The challenge as an organization comes only when you're not prepared or you are inflexible in your ability to respond when mistakes and crises do emerge. As long as you create a plan in advance, and as long as you're able to publicly, quickly, and authentically say you're sorry, you can maintain a strong brand reputation in the face of any social media challenge.

CHAPTER 17

Consistently Deliver Excitement, Surprise, and Delight

I was at a business conference a couple of years ago, tweeting some of the things I was learning throughout, as I always do. One of the speakers recommended the book *Built to Last*, by Jim Collins, as a must-read. I had heard of it before, and I wanted to remember to buy it while also sharing some of the speaker's wisdom, so I tweeted, "Recommended Biz Book: *Built to Last*. Anyone read it?"

I got a few responses, but my favorite was from Jesse Landry, someone who was following me on Twitter and whom I'd never met, who responded, "I'd be happy to overnight my copy to you if you do not have a copy already."

Not "Great book, Dave, you should check it out," or even "I'd be happy to loan that to you." He offered to overnight it to me. I was immediately wowed. I responded that I certainly didn't need it sent overnight, but that sure, thanks, I would take it, and I gave him my address. Of course, he still overnighted it to me. *Double* wow.

I looked at Jesse's profile and found out he was a consultant for Administaff (now known as Insperity), a company that provides human resources support for small- to medium-size businesses. Jesse didn't pitch me on ever working with him. If he had, I probably would have said, "Thanks, but no thanks," and I would have assumed that he had overnighted the book in order to win my business. Instead, I got excited to see what he did for a living, investigated his company, and determined if he could provide services that I might need someday.

Jesse sent me the book "just because" and received nothing directly in return. As it turns out, of course, months later, I explored the potential of outsourcing Likeable Media's human resources work. Naturally, I turned to Jesse and Administaff to perhaps help solve my problem. But Jesse had no way of knowing I would consider using his services when he sent me the book. *He just sent it.*

If you can figure out ways to do little things for your customers and your online communities, to surprise and delight them, to provide unexpected value, or to add a smile to an individual consumer's face, you will always stand out, be remembered, and win the community's business. If it was important to be remarkable *before* the age of online social media, it's essential to stand out today, when word can spread lightning fast. How can you be remarkable on social networks?

YOU ARE ALREADY AHEAD OF THE COMPETITION

The good news is, simply by doing the basics of likeable social media, such as listening and responding with transparency to everyone's comments about you on Facebook, you're way ahead of so many companies that still maintain a broadcast mentality when using social networks. But eventually the world, and your competition, will catch up and understand social media best practices. On social media now, you're not just competing with your real-life competitors for attention. You're competing with all of your customers' friends and the brands that they are already attached and connected to.

So it's your job to figure out not how you can be better but *how you can be different*. Everything you've read in this book up until now has been about meeting the standards for excellence on social networks. But how do you exceed expectations? How can you do the little things (and the big things) to stand out from your competition? How can you use social networks to be different, to truly create as many "wow" moments as possible? How can you operationalize "surprise and delight"?

The Little Things Matter

Many times it's the little extra things that matter the most. In this chapter's opening story, Jesse definitely didn't need to overnight the book to me—in fact, I hope he got a good deal on it because the shipment may have been more expensive than the book itself. But this action stood out. What little things can you do to separate your company from the pack and have consumers and prospects take notice? The truth is, a lot will depend on the specific nature of your business and your online communities.

One thing you can do is "listen" to conversations that are not necessarily about your company and respond to questions that aren't directly aimed at you. Become part of these conversations, and get involved in the community related to your company or industry, but don't try to push your organization or a sales pitch onto consumers. Listening is particularly easy to do on Twitter, where conversation with strangers is the norm. So if you're a real estate agent, for example, you could listen for people asking questions about getting bank loans for down payments in your town and answer these questions with links to helpful online articles. Or if you're a local bed and breakfast, you might listen for people asking questions about great vacation spots and recommend a few colleagues in exotic locations whom you met at a trade show.

If you can provide unexpected value to people on Twitter and Facebook and expect nothing in return, you can create "wow" moments that collectively will have an impact on your business. Those vacation spots you recommended to others on Twitter will eventually have an opportunity to recommend you to their followers, for instance. Or if the articles you've supplied about loans are extremely helpful, these potential buyers may seek your assistance when purchasing a home.

Best Buy was the first large company to begin delivering unexpected value on Twitter in the form of answering people's questions. It developed the Twelpforce, a group of nearly a thousand employees who have been trained to respond to people's questions on Twitter about electronics products. When one of these hundreds of staff people aren't on the store floor helping an in-person customer, he or she is helping online customers or prospects—and answering any questions about electronics products, *including products not sold at Best Buy.*

The Big Things Matter Too

Especially for larger organizations, big things such as contests and sweepstakes can create "wow" moments as well, if only for participants and winners. If you can create contests that bring people closer to your brand or strengthen that emotional connection, then those contests are more likely to have long-lasting impact.

Franklin Sports, a leading sporting equipment company, is best known as the official batting-glove provider for Major League Baseball (MLB). While its batting gloves and other baseball gear are used by millions of Americans, its fan page was off to a poor start, with only 1,900 fans through its first five months on Facebook.

In September 2010, Franklin leveraged its relationship with MLB and stepped up its efforts with a fan challenge: if it could get to 10,000 fans in the next two weeks, Franklin would give away two playoff tickets to one lucky fan. While this wasn't a prize that everyone would be able to enjoy, it was a prize worth working for, especially for the baseball-crazed fans in the community. Hundreds of fans began suggesting the page to their friends, and within two weeks, Franklin had increased its *likes* more than fivefold, to top 10,000. It gave away the playoff tickets to one excited fan, and it built an energized community in the process.

Cisco, the worldwide leader in networking, is a huge technology company, but it realizes the importance of delighting customers through social media. It's managing to find ways to integrate social media into all of its business practices. In 2013, I talked with Petra Neiger, then social media marketing manager at Cisco, and she told me this:

> We believe engagement needs to happen on multiple levels—from sharing information to conversing, and finding ways to excite, inspire, and nurture our customers and partners. Each approach has its purpose. For example, excitement through special offers and sweepstakes can increase virality, lead to more sales, or increase engagement with your brand. Our Facebook sweepstakes are great examples. Nurturing, if done right, can help take customer and influencer relationships to the next level where they become your ambassadors or ideation team. Our ambassadors are our loyal advocates who, amongst other things, help spread the word, initiate and participate in conversations pertaining to Cisco, correct incorrect information, or even bring important information to our attention. Our engagement efforts so far have also enabled us to tap into the collective wisdom of our target audience and create new opportunities for Cisco.

Cisco understands the need to incorporate both large and small tactics in its social media platform, always focusing on cultivating relationships with customers and partners by standing out and providing something extra. It also does one thing differently from any company I've seen on social networks: for its Cisco Networking Academy fan page on Facebook (https://Facebook.com/CiscoNetworkingAcademy), it actually lets select customers become the administrators of the page, essentially giving them control of the content that goes out to over 800,000 fans along with Cisco's brand reputation. While this move was an extremely risky one, especially for a company of Cisco's size, it has paid off so far. The company has delighted the group of customers it has trusted with its brand's reputation, and it has also found resources from an unlikely source (customers!) to scale the work of community management.

WHEN EVERYONE WINS SOMETHING, YOU WIN EVERYTHING: SHARED PRIZES FOR COMMUNITY GROWTH

Contests and sweepstakes definitely create excitement, but nothing generates more excitement than opportunities for everyone in an audience to win something. Shared opportunity can drive an entire fan page to work together in promoting the growth of its community. The first time we at Likeable Media saw this was with the Cumberland Farms Chill Zone page (https://Facebook.com/ChillZone). Cumberland Farms wanted to capture some of the passion it knew teenagers throughout New England had for its Chill Zone product. Using Facebook social ads, group outreach, and weekly Chill Zone giveaways, the Chill Zone page on Facebook soared to more than 10,000 fans in its first month. To incentivize fans to spread the word and share the fan page with others, it presented a challenge: help us reach 50,000 fans by August 21, 2009, and we'll hold a Free Chill Zone Day (see Figure 17.1).

Less than three months after the launch, the fan base surpassed this goal by more than 20,000 additional fans.

The results were incredible in terms of the numbers of fans joining the community, but the sentiment of people in the community was even more incredible. People posted things like, "I've invited my whole school to become fans," and "I won't rest until we have 50,000 fans. Chill Zone rules!"

The sales results were excellent as well. The first Free Chill Zone Day on June 5, 2009, led to redemptions of 27,000 more units over previous years. The second Free Chill Zone Day as a result of the Free Chill Zone Day Challenge in August increased sales by 23 percent from the previous Friday, and 50 percent of the total sales were attributed directly to Facebook.

FIGURE 17.1 **Free Chill Zone Promotion**

COMBINE AUTOMATION WITH
THE HUMAN TOUCH

As valuable as it is to have tools to manage large groups of *likers*, followers, and conversation, there is no replacement for the human, personalized element of social media. Social network promotions, contests, giveaways, and sweepstakes can entertain and delight thousands or even millions of people at once. But wouldn't a personal, unique response from a real person at a big company really wow you a lot more than even the coolest contest ever?

Unique Words Have Unique Impact

Sometimes, just recognizing people publicly is enough surprise and delight to make someone's day. *Social Media Examiner*, a leading blog about social media for small business, grew its fan base to more than 25,000 *likes* in less than a year without any paid advertising. Its staff does all of the basics, such as responding to any questions or comments and sharing valuable content. But one way it's different from other companies is that it publicly recognizes and thanks someone every 1,000 fans. So when *Social Media Examiner* hit 5,000 fans, it announced its five-thousandth fan to the rest of the community. Then it did it again at 6,000, and it's still celebrating these milestones as it approaches 100,000 fans. It's similar to the millionth-customer promotion at a store—except the fan doesn't get anything except recognition and a personal thank you. Still, it's nice to be recognized among thousands of your peers, and it always serves as a subtle reminder of the growth of the community to the rest of the fans.

Crowdrise, the online donation community founded by actor and philanthropist Edward Norton, uses Twitter to thank people for their posts, donations, and participation. But it also randomly gives away hats, posters, and T-shirts all day long to donors. It says thanks in pointedly different ways from what most people are used to. Give a donation to a worthy cause, and you'll get a tweet from Crowdrise such as, "Have an amazing day," or "Hope you're having the best day ever." No matter what kind of day you're having, you're sure to smile if you're on the receiving end of such a tweet. And you'll probably tell a few friends. Imagine if an accountant always tweeted to new followers, "Hope your day isn't too taxing," or an attorney thanked new LinkedIn connections by sharing, "May the law be with you." What can you say that's even a little different, and remarkable?

Surprise Conversations with Condoms—for Better or for Worse

The New York City Department of Health wanted to create buzz around its NYC Condom campaign in late 2009. The NYC Condom is the first municipally branded condom in the United States. The government program gives away more than

10 million free condoms per year in efforts to promote safer sex throughout New York.

The department wanted to use Twitter to surprise New Yorkers and make them take pause before acting foolishly. So, it created a Twitter account (https://Twitter.com/NYCcondom) that actually tweeted *in the voice of the condom itself.* It began conducting nightly searches on Twitter for people who were talking about going out partying and for New Yorkers who, based on their conversations, were likely to need a condom. It searched using keywords such as "getting laid," "looking to hook up," and "partying all night."

Then, it would respond to people each night with funny tweets from the condom, such as these:

> "Pick me up. I'll keep you covered."

> "Don't leave home without me."

> "If you need me, make sure to wear me tonight."

> "Going out in NYC? Pick me up. I'm easy."

People weren't just surprised. They were shocked. Most people responded, surprised but happy to have had an unexpected "direct conversation" with a condom. Some users actually indicated that they would be picking up an NYC Condom, and they thanked the condom for the reminder. Others shared the health department's wit and wisdom by retweeting @NYCcondom.

A few people also felt surprised in a bad way. Conversation on Twitter is public, but when a government agency operating a Twitter account tweeted back, it reminded them they had been talking online to actual individuals about planning to have sex, and that probably led to a feeling of discomfort. Still, the campaign definitely led to increased buzz, surprised a lot of New Yorkers in the health department's target audience, and affected some people's behaviors. The tweeting condom may have even saved some lives.

ACTION ITEMS

1. Develop a strategy for how you can exceed customers' expectations on social networks to surprise and delight them. To start, write down five ways you, as a consumer, could be surprised, in a good way, by your company's actions.

2. Determine what budget you have for dedicated promotions, contests, giveaways, and sweepstakes on Facebook and Twitter. Depending on your products and services, decide what you can give away to everyone who *likes* you or what you can give away to all of your *likers* if you achieve certain milestones.

3. Create a social network communications plan that includes unique language about talking to your customers and prospects. No matter what your budget, a unique catchphrase can differentiate you, make people smile—and make people spread the word.

OPERATIONALIZE SURPRISE, FOR A GOOD RISE

How can you build systems and processes around making people smile, while generating surprise? How can you encourage a culture of conversation that differentiates you from the growing number of competitors on social networks? If you can truly reward all of your fans and followers, you'll be able to energize a huge group of online advocates. Consistently up the ante for what it means to bring value and delight to your customers and prospects, and not only will they remember you when they need you, but they'll also recommend you when others need you too.

CHAPTER 18

Don't Sell! Just Make It Easy and Compelling for Customers to Buy

It was early December 2009, and my wife and I were cuddled up on the couch, laptops in hand, as any other social-media-happy couple might be. Carrie was logged in to Facebook, checking out all the latest updates from her friends and pages she *liked*, when she saw one about a new scarf from the Limited "as seen on *Oprah*." She thought the update was interesting enough to click, and when she did, the seemingly typical "shopping cart" appeared, with options to purchase the scarf in a wide variety of colors.

One thing that was quite different, though, from other online shopping carts she or I had clicked on before was that the cart was inside the Facebook News Feed, not on the Limited's website. Out of curiosity alone (though the scarf was nice, and it had in fact appeared on *Oprah*), she clicked through the entire shopping process, eventually entering her credit card securely and purchasing the scarf without leaving Facebook. The scarf arrived at our doorstep two days later, but not before my wife had shared with hundreds of Facebook friends how easy it had been to purchase the beautiful scarf.

Carrie *bought* that scarf from the Limited, but it wasn't aggressively *sold* to her. In one of the first business transactions involving physical items within the Facebook platform, the Limited had made the process straightforward and attractive to its thousands of fans. The Limited had created an application through which customers could browse and buy merchandise without ever leaving Facebook, had built up trust in its fan base over several months, and had the credibility of a recent mention on *The Oprah Winfrey Show*. All of those aspects added up, providing the Limited with the opportunity to temporarily turn a social channel into a sales channel, resulting in many thousands of dollars' worth of immediate revenue.

SALES IS NOT A DIRTY WORD, BUT MAKE IT SIMPLE AND EASY (AND EASY DOES IT)

Facebook, Pinterest, and other social networks have grown immensely in a few short years, and, by definition, they are primarily social channels, not sales channels. However, *that doesn't mean you can't use Facebook or Pinterest to directly sell, market, or grow your business*. It does mean that the expectation most people have when they're on Facebook or another social network is that they are there to socialize and connect with others, not to shop. In order to effectively change a social network into a sales channel, you have to make the buying process as effortless and satisfying as possible. You also have to tread carefully: if you push too hard to market or sell, you will erode the all-important trust and likeability you've worked hard to achieve.

The big question on every marketer's mind is how to make money using social media. What is the real return on investment of all the time and money spent in the space? The ROI comes in many forms, of course: brand reputation and credibility, increased loyalty and frequency of purchase, increased recommendations, and decreased need for advertising, to name a few. *But what about direct sales?* The answer is, if you follow all of the strategies presented in Chapters 1 through 17 of this book, it's OK, even advisable, to sell to people across social networks. Make the sales process as easy, fun, and shareable as possible, and *never get too pushy*.

Think about the situation this way: if you engage your prospects online, have a great product or service targeted toward the right people, and make it painless and compelling to buy whatever you're offering, then you don't really have to do any selling at all. Selling and marketing are usually disruptive, unwanted experiences, while buying is normally considered a fun, rewarding, and sometimes even exciting experience. So how can you create social buying opportunities instead of social sales and marketing opportunities?

There are a number of ways to directly sell your products or services through your social media networks and pages. Table 18.1 gives a few examples of Facebook applications that will help you set up shop!

Mind the Apps

Most important, you need to focus on the technology around the buying process. The smoother it is to buy from you, the greater

TABLE 18.1   Five Facebook Apps to Sell Your Stuff

APP	WEBSITE	PROS
8thBridge	8thBridge.com	Portable, personal, and participatory: create your e-commerce platform
Payvment	Payvment.com/facebook	Launch an enterprise-grade storefront on your Facebook page
Shop Tab	ShopTab.net	Set up shop on Facebook easily, quickly, and inexpensively
Shoutlet	Shoutlet.com	Build, engage, and measure your social media marketing communication in one platform
Show & Sell	NorthSocial.com/store/show-sell	Turn your Facebook page into a store

the percentage of your fans, followers, and users will become customers. Create or personalize a simple but highly functional Facebook, iPhone, or mobile application. Better yet, create all three. Make sure you have an easy-to-use shopping cart on your Facebook page or website. Or, for those of you who don't have the inclination or the ability to go high tech (for example, doctors, lawyers, and accountants are unlikely to ever have a shopping cart service), simply make sure you have the best, most engaging, and friendly employees answering phones or greeting people at doors.

The more seamless the buying process, the more completed sales you'll generate, and the more buzz you'll create for future sales opportunities.

TWEET Doesn't Include Selling—or Does It?

At Likeable, we suggest our clients follow a brief set of guidelines when using Twitter, based around an acronym we came up with for TWEET:

- Trust building. Build relationships.
- Wisdom. Learn from industry leaders and your customers.
- Ears open. Listen to the conversation.
- Establish your brand. Create a strong presence.
- Teach. Tell the world about what you do.

Of course, there's nothing in this mnemonic device about selling. There's nothing even there about marketing. But if you do a great job listening, learning, and building trust with the right people, if you establish your brand with the right fan base, and if you share what it is you and your organization do, you won't have to sell. People will already know your product and service, and they will come to you when they are ready to buy. The less friction in the buying process, the better, and the clearer and simpler the checkout or order process, the more likely your customer will be satisfied.

Ultimately, you still have to make sure your fans and followers know what you do or sell and give the customer a buying opportunity. You could be the most engaging, transparent, responsive, and attentive company in the world, but if you never actually educate people about what you sell and, without hitting them over the head, tell them how to buy, you won't be optimizing your social network presence.

THE FACEBOOK SALES FUNNEL DOES INCLUDE SALES

The traditional sales funnel includes awareness, intent, trigger, and then purchase. The Facebook or social media sales funnel still includes purchase—it's just a longer path to get there (see Figure 18.1). First, you must generate awareness, and a *like*. Then, you'll take the prospects through a series of interactions, engaging them and providing them with interesting, educational, or valuable content. When the customers are ready to buy, as long as you have given them a clear, simple path to purchase, the sale can be triggered.

FIGURE 18.1   Facebook Sales Funnel

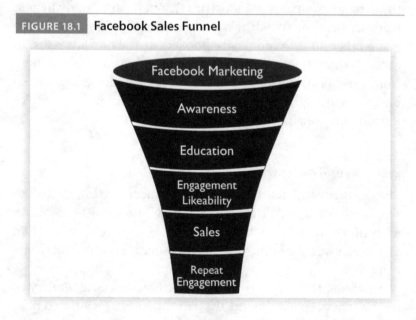

But the best part of the Facebook sales funnel, as compared to the traditional sales funnel, is that it doesn't end in one sale. The customer, still a *liker*, is eternally connected to you, unless he or she *unlikes* you. So after the sale, you can still engage with the customer, giving him or her value outside of directly purchasing your product. Staying connected with your customers on social networks after an initial sale also gives you a huge new advantage—the power of leveraging your customers' social graph and introducing yourself passively to *their* friends and followers. While the sales process through Facebook is clearly a longer one, it also yields greater frequency of purchase and increased awareness of you to your customers' networks.

USE SOCIAL NETWORKS AND INVENTORY MANAGEMENT TO SELL OUT

When you have a limited supply of inventory and a need to sell it quickly at a discount, there is no faster or more efficient way to do so than through social media. Airlines, hotels, and theaters are examples of industries that can particularly benefit from this use of social networks, especially right before the plane takes off, the rooms are booked, or the curtain rises. In general, though, any type of company or business can benefit from careful inventory management, price control, and distribution, utilizing the large social network community they've tapped into or helped grow.

Dell Sells on Twitter with Likeable Results

The company that has had the greatest success using Twitter to sell inventory is Dell. Through its @DellOutlet Twitter account, with more than 1.4 million followers, it has sold more than $7 million worth of refurbished computer and other electronic equipment.

How has Dell done this? When it has excess inventory of products, it deeply discounts the items, then shares a timed offer on Twitter with a link to purchase. This setup results in immediate sales but also creates word of mouth about the great deals. In turn, more Twitter users become Dell followers, and therefore, more sales opportunities are created the next time the company shares an offer.

Have you ever wondered why last-minute flights get expensive instead of cheaper? Last-minute travelers either pay an extraordinary amount to fly, or they are forced to make other travel arrangements, typically leading to lots of empty seats or half-empty flights. JetBlue was the first airline to solve this "empty seats" problem using social media. It created @JetBlueCheeps, a Twitter account dedicated solely to sharing great limited-inventory, last-minute deals on airfares. While earning $39 to $89 a ticket is not a tremendous amount of revenue for JetBlue, it's better than flying with empty seats. Customers who can be flexible about waiting for deals on Twitter can also leverage this to the fullest degree.

Do you have inventory you could deeply discount to give away quickly? Remember, in addition to driving immediate sales, you'd gain the advantage of creating a buzz on a medium in which word spreads lightning fast. You are also likely to generate returning, and new, customers.

SODASTREAM PUTS ITS FANS FIRST—WITH GREAT RESULTS

When it came time for the at-home carbonated beverage machine company SodaStream to launch its holiday contest in 2013, the staff went to the drawing board with Likeable Media, the company's social media agency. What SodaStream walked away with was an idea that tapped into the strongest sales generator for its organization: word of mouth and referrals. Taking the traditional marketing tactic and breathing new life into it, SodaStream encouraged fans to Fizz It Forward.

What the brand did was simple. It asked the community of over a half a million fans to tell *their friends* about SodaStream—and to nominate them to win their own soda-making machine. They took word of mouth and supercharged it with social media. Besides the

13,000 entries and 5 million impressions during the most crowded time of the year for brands on Facebook, the subtle nudges made not only by the brand but by the brand's most enthusiastic fans drove over $1 million in e-commerce revenue. SodaStream never told its community to go out and buy its products. It just reminded them of a great product that was a click away.

Game On: How Disc Replay Won the Referral Game

Disc Replay is a franchise of video game and electronic stores in Indiana. In the summer of 2014, owner Alan Jackson dove head first into social media as a means to boost his marketing efforts. Disc Replay prides itself on buying and selling high-quality video games and DVDs and constantly delighting its customers. As a Likeable Local customer, Disc Replay participated in a social media referral program. Through sharing authentic content on social media and providing an exceptional experience online and off, Disc Replay landed 16 referrals through its Facebook page alone. A few "Refer a Friend" Facebook posts and approximately $30 in post boosts amounted to hundreds of dollars in video game sales and 16 new loyal customers.

BUYING OPPORTUNITIES + ENGAGING FACEBOOK UPDATES = GREATER SALES SUCCESS

If the object of the social media game is to create engaging, valuable, and likeable content and experiences for your community and if the object of the business game is to create compelling buying opportunities for your prospects, consider pairing those two objectives via one Facebook update. For instance, let's say you're responsible for marketing and selling shoes. An example of an engaging Facebook update to your community might be this: "What do you think the most common women's shoe size is in the United States?" An example of a compelling sales update could be this: "Click here to enjoy 50 percent off on our newest line of women's shoes [link]."

Remember, though, that Facebook's News Feed algorithm is such that updates need to generate comments and *likes* in order to remain at the top of people's feeds. So in order for people to even *see* the 50 percent discount offer, you'll have to be at the top of people's News Feeds. Hitting people over the head on Facebook with offers will not lead to sales, but it may very well lead to people *unliking* you or unsubscribing from your feed. Thus, try combining the two objectives to create a best-of-both-worlds scenario: "What do you think is the most common women's shoe size? After you guess, click the link to find out the answer, and enjoy 50 percent off select shoes [link]."

By engaging your community, you're creating value and optimizing for people's Facebook feeds. Combining this engagement with a compelling offer, you give your fans a great buying opportunity, and thus you provide your company with an equally great sales opportunity.

1-800-Flowers.com Will Win Because It "Gets" Likeable, Social Sales

The company 1-800-Flowers.com won the national floral space when it became the first florist to have a memorable 1-800 phone number. It then continued to win the space by establishing a strong e-commerce platform through its website before any other flower company. Now, 1-800-Flowers.com will continue to dominate the national floral space because it understands the conjunction of e-commerce and social media.

Through third-party technology company 8thBridge, 1-800-Flowers.com was the first major retailer in the world to establish a Facebook store, in 2009. Commerce, from start to finish, can take place within the Facebook platform at Facebook.com/1800Flowers, creating an easy, compelling buying experience. More important, the company has grown a sizable fan base of more than 1 million customers on Facebook. It offers weekly promotions and contests, asks questions, and listens to the feedback it receives. The company is responsive and transparent about customer inquiries, it inspires customers' stories, and it surprises and delights random fans. It engages!

It's the combination of positive social media practices and easy, compelling buying opportunities that will help 1-800-Flowers.com continue to thrive in business. How can you model your practices after it, and Dell, and JetBlue? How can you create the most likeable buying process online?

ACTION ITEMS

1. Conduct an assessment of your current online buying processes. How simple and compelling is your online sales cart? How interested and capable would you be as a consumer in buying from your company?

2. Research Facebook applications for sales, and choose one of the apps listed in Table 18.1 or discussed elsewhere in the chapter to integrate into your page. Depending on your business, develop simple mobile applications, as well, to drive buying opportunities wherever people find you and need you.

3. Write five sample Facebook updates that combine an engaging question or valuable content with an irresistible offer, and link to your website to buy or learn more. Test, track, and measure the results in order to optimize them for future ROI.

KEEP ON YOUR CONSUMER CAP, THINK BUYING, NOT SELLING, AND THE SALES WILL COME

The days of push-marketing tactics are quickly coming to an end, ushering in better times for consumers everywhere. Always think the way your consumer does, create buying opportunities that you yourself would want to leverage, and make purchasing simple and easy. Be patient, and continue to provide value for your communities. Develop simple, user-friendly opportunities for customers to buy from you, wherever and whenever they choose to. The sales *will* come.

Just Be Likeable

A major paradigm shift in marketing, media, and communications is well under way. Facebook and social networks have ushered in a new era marked by increased transparency and the most empowered consumer of all time. There is no doubt that this shift creates massive opportunities for the organizations that are most able to adapt their thinking and strategies to successfully implement plans via social media.

All of the new social networking tools and sites can be overwhelming, and so-called experts, sharing opposing information or telling you to emphasize different priorities, make it even more challenging. In your company or organization, you're driven and measured by results. Since the results of leveraging social media are often not immediately apparent, it is tempting to rely on traditional marketing tactics that have been proven to generate immediate results instead of utilizing social media. Resist that temptation.

KEY CONCEPTS TO REMEMBER

An understanding of the 18 concepts outlined in this book will guide you in your conceptualization, creation, and implementation of a social media plan. Familiarizing yourself with Facebook, LinkedIn, and the other social networks that your customers use can help guide your decisions about where and how to allocate your resources. And knowing the tools available through social media will make your job easier. But the process can be overwhelming. The contents of this book alone are likely difficult to digest and implement, so I suggest that when you first explore all the possibilities social media has to offer, you concentrate on these four key concepts: listen, be transparent, be responsive, and be likeable.

Listen Up

The biggest paradigm shift of all that social media represents is that it gives you the ability to listen to what your customers and prospects are saying publicly. You can start listening today for free, and your ability to do so will inform and prepare you to best accomplish all of your social media marketing and advertising objectives. Acknowledging to your customers that you're listening can endear you to them forever. Before you talk, be sure to listen, and once you start talking, never stop listening.

Transparency Is the New Default

People like it when others are honest and transparent. You like it when other people are honest and transparent. Yet somehow, so many companies and industries are secretive, even dishonest, about aspects of their business. Embrace transparency and openness. Be honest when you mess up and when things don't go as planned. The Internet becomes more transparent with every day that goes by. For you as a consumer, this situation is incredibly beneficial, and it can also be a great thing for you as a marketer, if you can embrace it.

Respond to Everyone

The world is talking about you and to you. People everywhere are discussing their problems that you can solve better than your competitors. The world is telling you about their wants and needs that your organization can help them with.

Every time a customer or prospect talks publicly on a social network, it's an opportunity for you to respond and engage. Whenever you don't respond, you either make a negative impression or you give a competitor an opportunity to reply. Whenever you do respond, you have an opportunity to make a positive impression on customers, prospects, and on all of their friends.

Just Be Likeable

In the end, succeeding on social networks amounts to your ability to be likeable. There are two fundamental aspects to this term: likeable business practices and likeable content. Adopting *likeable business practices* means treating customers the way you'd like to be treated. You need to follow the Golden Rule in each decision you make affecting your customers. Posting *likeable content* means that you share only those updates on Facebook or Twitter that would make you click the Like button if you were on the receiving end. Create and share stories, text, photos, videos, links, and applications that you as a consumer would want to *like*, comment on, and share. To be likeable, you must always respect and add value to your community.

THIS ISN'T THE END; IT'S THE START

Now it's time to get out there and apply the contents of this book. Use social media to grow your company and meet your organization's objectives. And I meant what I wrote at the beginning of this book: if you have questions, suggestions, compliments, or complaints, tweet to me anytime at https://Twitter.com /DaveKerpen, or Facebook-message me at https://Facebook .com/LikeableLocal. I hope to have the opportunity to prove to you that I'm as transparent, responsive, and likeable as I know you will be.

Be amazing, and be likeable. I'll see you on Twitter!

A Refresher Guide to the Social Networks That Matter Most

My wife, Carrie, and I bought a new home a few years ago and have since made several renovations. As I watched Carrie fall down the rabbit hole of home renovations, decorating, and furniture shopping, I got to observe how she, as a consumer, used social media to investigate and make purchase decisions, what networks affected her choices, and how.

Every social media user has his or her own pattern, or "social DNA," for how to use each network. My wife (and now more than 1 billion others!) uses Facebook for her actual friends, past and present. If you've met Carrie in "real life," chances are she'll friend you on Facebook. She uses Twitter, however, to connect with celebrities (her guilty pleasure is reading the tweets of Justin Bieber, Ashton Kutcher, and Heidi Montag!) and with people she doesn't know but with whom she shares commonalities: moms, social media agency leaders, and people who live in our town. She also connects with brands she loves through Twitter. LinkedIn acts as a Rolodex of every professional contact she's ever had, and Instagram serves as her photo album of her favorite moments with our family, friends, and employees. Pinterest is where she gets ideas for home projects and crafts and cooking with the kids. YouTube is a place where she can learn how to do things she's never done before. As an active Internet and social media user, she also uses other social sites and tools as needed.

Now that you've got Carrie's social DNA, let's look at it in action. Her first step in our new home renovation was to find contractors who would do the physical work on our house. Three big things happened here.

First, she Googled. Through her search, she found ServiceMagic (now called HomeAdvisor), a social review site for home services providers, where she was able to check reviews on contractors.

Second, she posted to her Facebook friends, asking if anyone knew anything about repairing a roof (or if they knew anyone who knew anything about repairing a roof and could make any recommendations).

Third, she threw the same question out to her followers on Twitter. When she got her replies, she cross-referenced the comments she had received from her Facebook friends (which she viewed as the most valuable) with the comments from her Twitter followers. She then looked up the recommended contractors on ServiceMagic to check their reviews. Carrie would end up posting her own review about the wonderful work the contractor performed, and, thanks to the Facebook integration on ServiceMagic, she was able to share the review with her Facebook friends. The post received 10 *likes*.

Now, on to decorating. My wife and I have a ton of books, and we were fortunate to purchase a home with a traditional parlor that has floor to ceiling bookshelves. In Googling ideas for creating the perfect library, Carrie stumbled upon a website called Houzz, a small niche social network where decorators and designers create slide shows of their suggestions, categorized by subject. She found about six slide shows devoted entirely to libraries, and she tweeted each image to her friends, asking for feedback. She even got to know some of the other folks in the Houzz network.

Later, as Carrie was on Facebook, socializing away, she saw an interesting post come into her News Feed from a furniture store she had previously liked, Raymour & Flanigan: "Want to create a dream library in your home? Click here for perfect accents for your quiet space." The status linked to pieces that worked for a library or study, including the electric fireplace that now sits in our home in Port Washington.

Was it luck that Raymour & Flanigan decided to place that post right at the time that Carrie was making purchasing decisions about buying home accessories? No. Carrie had decided to become a fan of Raymour & Flanigan's Facebook page weeks before simply because she knew that the company sold furniture and that she was moving.

Raymour & Flanigan used smart marketing to engage with Carrie—the same way any designer who was searching for tweets about furnishing a library could engage with her on Twitter or any Houzz designer could have asked to evaluate her empty space and offer suggestions. These networks are ripe for connecting with consumers; you just need to figure out how your customers and target audience are using these sites, and then connect with them in the way that's most natural.

Once we moved in, Carrie used YouTube to learn how to arrange the perfect bookshelves—and I have to admit, we had a lot of fun that night, drinking wine, going through our books, and creating a useful and picturesque arrangement. Thanks, YouTube, for a romantic evening at home. In the years since then, Carrie and I have made several renovations to the home, and we have Pinterest and Facebook to thank for all of Carrie's ideas (and the bills).

Four years later, for the rewrite of this book, I have the opportunity to demonstrate just how fast-moving social networks are. We just completed another round of extensive renovations on our home, including a new patio and outdoor fireplace. The inspiration for my wife's latest decision? Pinterest, of course—a network that didn't even exist when I wrote the first edition.

THE NETWORKS AND THEIR USES

As our home furnishing story demonstrates, the integration of many social networks is now commonplace in our lives. Surely, you and your friends use social networks each day to influence your own behavior and decisions as a consumer. But to utilize them effectively for your own marketing and advertising purposes, you must first fully understand the tools at your disposal.

Each person uses social media and social networks in different ways—we all have our own specific social DNA. Though some believe Facebook is the most important social network for companies to consider, at the end of the day, every user is looking for the same thing—to connect and to engage, to be heard and to listen. It's just that they choose different networks for different engagements. There are hundreds of niche social networks, so it's worth looking at what communities might exist around the needs your company or organization serves.

Since we can't look into all of those niche networks, I provide the following information as a refresher about the major ones that have emerged, their basic uses, and some advice on how marketers can get started in incorporating social media networks into their plans. Whatever networks you choose, you should consider integrating them with Facebook and using it as a hub for your social strategy. Your Facebook presence will be infinitely richer, and your results that much stronger. If you're in B2B, consider using LinkedIn as the hub for your social networking activities.

This primer for social media newcomers and refresher for social media veterans will help you better understand the 18 concepts outlined throughout the book. Take a close look at the information and statistics that follow because even social network veterans may find some likeable content to help them further understand the abilities, tools, and powers of harnessing online social media.

FACEBOOK: ONE BILLION PEOPLE CAN'T BE WRONG

BEST USES: Connect with and engage your target audience

Facebook is the number one social network in the world, with more than 1.3 billion people using the service and a growth rate of nearly 1 million users per day. Facebook features three entities: individual profiles, groups, and pages.

- **Profiles.** This entity is how each individual signs up for the service, identifies himself or herself, and interacts with others. When two people who have written individual profiles "friend" one another, they have equal access to each other's streams of information. When two individuals connect on Facebook, they are considered "friends."
- **Groups.** Groups can be started and joined by any individual around any topic or interest. While some groups are official in nature (for example, "Official Group to Elect Barack Obama President"), many groups are more unofficial, and sometimes just silly (for example, "Join this group and I'll quit smoking," or "Mean people suck," or "I love my Pop-Pop"). One great use for Facebook groups is for internal communication among employees, departments, clubs, or other groups of people. Both of our companies, Likeable Local and Likeable Media, use Facebook groups to communicate during and after work. Groups can be public, private, or even secret so that no activity whatsoever is shared outside of the group.
- **Pages.** Also commonly referred to as "company pages" or "business pages," pages are intended to be the official representation and voice of companies, nonprofits, brands, governments, and celebrities and other public figures. Within the Facebook platform, it is through pages that you will have the most opportunities to build a responsive, transparent, engaging brand for your customers and prospects. Facebook pages operate similarly to individual profiles, with a few notable exceptions. First, pages are one-way connections—when an individual connects to a company page, he or she has access to the business's stream, but the business doesn't have access to the individual's profile. Second, pages have increased Web functionality—Facebook applications can be added to a business's page to replicate just about anything a business would want on its own website. Third, and arguably most important, the terminology is different for pages. When an individual connects to a page on Facebook, he or she *likes* the business, public figure, or other entity represented by the page, as compared to becoming "friends" with the individual.

As fellow wordsmiths would agree, language is important, and it hasn't always been this way for Facebook or other social networks' use of different terminologies. Myspace, for instance, didn't differentiate between individuals and non-individuals, calling all connections "friends." This terminology ultimately makes little sense. You are friends with people you know, but no matter how much you love your favorite cereal brand, it's not your friend. Even Facebook originally differentiated between individuals and organizations by asking people to "become a fan" of pages. While this setup worked for certain categories (you may be a "fan" of the New York Mets, Conan O'Brien, and Ashton Kutcher), again, you'd be a lot less likely to become a fan of Cheerios than to *like* Cheerios. When Facebook changed the terminology from "become a fan" to "*like*," millions more clicked Like. Today there are tens of millions of pages representing companies and organizations, and the average person *likes* between 5 and 50 pages—with some people *liking* hundreds of pages.

Liking Content: Pages and Friends

In February 2009, Facebook added the function to *like* any content your friends or fan pages shared. This lightweight action allows people to express approval of or endorse content without having to type a full comment to say, "I like this." In an increasingly time-starved world, adding the Like button to all content on Facebook encourages a greater deal of interactivity and, with every click on Like, it gives your friends, and Facebook, a better picture of who you are and what content you find valuable.

A Lot More to Like

In 2010, Facebook added three more key features—community pages, social plug-ins, and places—in its quest to reorganize the social Web:

- **Community pages.** These pages are not created by any entity, and yet they represent millions of entities. Think of community pages as the unauthorized version of fan pages. In April 2010,

Facebook automatically generated 6.5 million of these pages from their users' stated interests, *likes*, schools and jobs, and comments.

These community pages often have a *Wikipedia* entry included, and they display any public posts about the company, organization, or topic at hand. Take a look at the accompanying screenshots that follow, and you'll see Likeable Media's (one of our companies) official timeline page (Figure A.1) as well as its community page (Figure A.2). These community pages added millions of socially connected links to the social Web, allowing people to find others with whom they have common interests, education, and jobs.

- **Social plug-ins.** This feature took Facebook from being an enormous social network to being the body reorganizing the entire Internet around your social graph. In April 2010, Facebook released what it called "social plug-ins," allowing websites to add, with very simple lines of code, buttons to layer people's Facebook information into their own website experience. The Like button is by far the most prominent example of these buttons—in the years since the Like button was released, more than 10 million distinct websites have added it to their websites. (You can do it too—at Developers.Facebook.com.) The Like button allows people to endorse a website, product, article,

FIGURE A.1   **Likeable Media's Official Facebook Timeline Page**

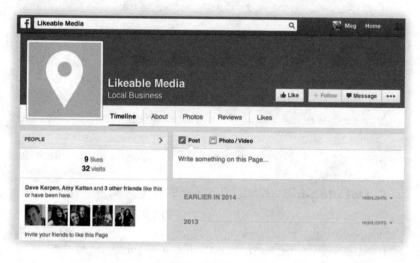

FIGURE A.2   Likeable Media's Facebook Community Page

picture, or video to all of their Facebook friends with one click. Future visitors to the website see how many people have *liked* this page or object before, but more important, they see if any of their friends have *liked* it.

- **Facebook places.** Introduced in late 2010, Facebook "places" allows every physical location to have its own "place" page on Facebook and to offer "deals" to customers who "check in" virtually. This function is particularly important if you have brick-and-mortar locations for your business and Facebook's graph search. Remember, you have the ability to claim a place page as your own if you own or are responsible for marketing for that physical location. In other words, if your organization has any physical presence whatsoever, you may claim the place pages as applicable to your organization, and you may then use these pages for communications and marketing.

Facebook's Timeline

In March 2012, Facebook launched Timeline for brands, as an update to the brands' fan pages. Timeline is different from fan pages in a number of key ways. First, there is much greater emphasis on a brand's "cover photo," a large banner your company can design that sits across the top of your page. True to the word *timeline*, you can also update the stories of your company over time, through Milestones located at the far right of the Timeline. In order to keep content highlighted at the top of your page, you can now "pin" posts for up to seven days. Finally, landing "tabs" have been eliminated, but you can still have tabs that help your Facebook page act as a mini-website, and tabs are better showcased than in the past, with larger icons right beneath your cover photo, linked to your tabs. Timeline allows for better storytelling than past iterations of Facebook's fan pages, rewarding you more for sharing pictures and videos. Facebook allows brand Timelines to target content to their fans by age, job title, company, and more—criteria that previously has been reserved for advertising. Now brands can tell one story to women 18 to 24, and another, more relevant story to men 35 to 44, for instance. Facebook continues to make aggressive changes to keep up with other growing social networks.

With the addition of these features, this personalized Web is much more appealing than the impersonal, link-driven Web that Google had previously organized. And it's very powerful. The best way to fully understand *like*'s potential is to experience it, so put the book down if you're near your computer or smartphone, and visit RottenTomatoes.com. This film review site has added a deep integration of the Facebook social plug-ins, what Facebook calls "instant personalization." As long as you're logged into Facebook when you visit the site, you'll see all the movies your friends have *liked*, reviewed, or talked about online. Would you rather see movie reviews from critics or from your own friends, family, and connections, many of whom share your interests and tastes?

The implications of the Like button are vast, as close to a billion people are now publicly *liking* their favorite brands, companies, celebrities, and ideas. We can all agree that word of mouth among friends is the strongest form of marketing, and now, Facebook has made it easier than ever to see what your friends recommend and have to say about anything you'd search for on the Web. Remember, also, that this is just in the early stages of growth. As people continue to join Facebook, and a greater number of website owners integrate the Facebook plug-ins into their user experiences, the Web will become more personalized, and it will be easier to find people, places, and things your friends have already *liked*.

The two most important features to consider on Facebook are your fan page and the implementation of Facebook's social plug-ins on your company's website. On your fan page, you can have *tabs* where visitors land and are introduced to your page. Check out the tabs of a few examples in Table A.1.

Once people *like* your page, it's all about engaging your community—through status updates, pictures, videos, links, and applications like virtual gifts, contests, and promotions (see Table A.2).

You can truly incorporate any functionality you'd want on an interactive website within your Facebook fan page.

Social plug-ins are incorporated on your website. Think of them as bringing the Facebook platform to your website,

TABLE A.1   Ten Great Fan Pages on Facebook

BRAND	FACEBOOK SITE
Dairy Queen	https://www.facebook.com/dairyqueen
Dove	https://www.facebook.com/DoveUS
Dunkin' Donuts	https://www.facebook.com/DunkinDonutsUS
Seamless	https://www.facebook.com/seamless
Vitamin Water	https://www.facebook.com/vitaminwater
LSU	https://www.facebook.com/geauxlsu
Ocean City, MD	https://www.facebook.com/OceanCity
Medtronic	https://www.facebook.com/medtronicdiabetes
Target	https://www.facebook.com/target
Century 21	https://www.facebook.com/century21

TABLE A.2	The Five Most Engaging Facebook Status Updates
Photos	
Videos	
GIFs	
Links with images	
Interactive applications (polls and quizzes)	

whereas pages bring your brand to Facebook. The most popular plug-in is the Like button, but other plug-ins include the Share button, the Recommend button, and Livestream. For a complete list of the latest social plugins available from Facebook to add to your website, visit Developers.Facebook.com/docs/plugins.

The best tools and tactics for Facebook change a lot, as Facebook is constantly innovating, and companies are always working hard at better optimizing the tools available. Keeping up is hard work, but take a look at Table A.3 to check out five blogs worth reading in order to stay as current as possible on Facebook and to learn how to best leverage Facebook's changes to your advantage.

Facebook is certainly the biggest game in town, and it likely will be for a long time to come. But it's not the only game in town.

TABLE A.3	Five Blogs to Read to Keep Up with Facebook Changes
BLOG	**WEBSITE**
Facebook Blog	Blog.facebook.com
All Facebook	Allfacebook.com
Likeable Media	Likeable.com/blog
Likeable Local	Blog.LikeableLocal.com/blog
Mashable	Mashable.com/social-media/facebook

TWITTER: REAL-TIME CONSUMER ENGAGEMENT FOR BETTER OR FOR WORSE

BEST USES: Consumer insight, customer service, real-time communication

You've heard before of the giant cocktail party that is social media. If Facebook is a consumer's high school reunion, her book club, and her playgroup—well, Twitter is her rave, a flashy, trippy sort of place where you can talk to anyone about anything at any time, connected through a series of 140-character exchanges. Twitter was born in 2006, and media and celebrities have helped drive the network to more than 645 million users worldwide within eight years. Twitter still suffers from what I call "cereal syndrome"—if you're like many people, you may think Twitter is a bunch of celebrities and narcissists running around, inundating people with the minutiae of their lives, such as what they had for breakfast. While Twitter surely has its share of such people, many others are there to learn, share, and grow, just as they might at a cocktail party.

There are three types of ways to share on Twitter: general updates, @replies, and direct messages:

- **General updates.** Also known as "tweets," these messages go out into the stream of everyone who's signed up to follow your account.
- **@Replies.** Such messages are meant to get the attention of one or more accounts on Twitter without bothering other users. For instance, if you begin a tweet with @DaveKerpen (my "Twitter handle"), the only people who will see your tweet are me and anyone who's following both you and me. This arrangement keeps noise to a minimum and allows you to effectively tweet an unlimited amount of times without annoying others not directly involved in the conversation, as long as most of your messages are directed @ individuals. Therefore, tweeting @ individuals keeps your Twitter stream relevant. Many people don't realize the difference between starting a tweet with @DaveKerpen (just the people who follow

both of us and I will see your tweet) and .@DaveKerpen (starting
with the dot means all of your followers will see the tweet).

- **Direct messages.** These updates are private messages between
  two accounts, similar to text messages or private messages on
  Facebook. This comes in handy if you need to share or solicit
  private information, such as an account number or phone
  number.

One of the main distinctions of Twitter versus Facebook is
that Twitter's conversations are typically much more public.
While people on Facebook mostly share with friends they know,
fewer than 5 percent of all Twitter users keep their updates
private since most of them opt for all-inclusive, completely open
conversations. Because of this, marketers are able to search
conversation on Twitter and see all the conversations currently
taking place. Twitter search is like the Google of conversation
and provides insight to countless companies.

Before you even think about a social media strategy,
you should head to Twitter to find out what your current
social media presence actually is. Don't think you have
one? Whether they're mentioning your brand by name or
they're mentioning experiences related to using your brand,
consumers are talking about interactions with your company
or other companies like it, and you need to know what they're
saying before you begin your specific strategy. What words
do people use when describing the problems your company
solves? These are the words worth searching. Use "advanced
search" to look at only specific geographic areas if only certain
places apply to you.

Twitter is also an incredible customer service tool. You can, as
a brand, send a direct message to someone who's following you
on Twitter. The other reason that Twitter works for customer
service is simply because the customer has decided it does.
Customers increasingly expect you to provide customer service
on Twitter, and that expectation will only grow over time. Check
out the five companies listed in Table A.4 that are using Twitter
well for customer service.

TABLE A.4	Five Prominent Companies Utilizing Twitter
COMPANY	TWITTER HANDLE
JetBlue	@Jetblue
Seamless	@Seamless
Zappos	@Zappos
Nike	@NikeSupport
Starbucks	@Starbucks

You might consider using Twitter during live offline events or when hosting live chats. Twitter works well for conversations in which people want to address specific individuals and a general group at once. For example, if you are to tweet someone directly, addressing a message to one person's Twitter handle, only this specific user will receive the tweet. If you use someone's Twitter handle in the text of a tweet you are sending out to a group, for example, congratulating a user, then both the entire group and the individual will receive the message.

You can also use Twitter to host contests and promotions. Twitter can get overwhelming quickly to the novice user, so I suggest using a wide variety of applications to make your Twitter experience easier and richer. See the list in Table A.5.

The best way you can learn about Twitter and all its potential, though, is to join today or if you've already joined, to commit to spending more time using the platform. Try the following:

TABLE A.5	Five Twitter Applications
APPLICATIONS	WEBSITE
Hootsuite	Hootsuite.com
TweetDeck	TweetDeck.com
TweetChat	TweetChat.com
Social Mention	SocialMention.com
Twellow	Twellow.com

- Spend 30 minutes per day at Twitter.com.
- Follow 20 to 30 accounts from people and organizations you like and want to interact with.
- Download a Twitter app for your smartphone.

Within two weeks, you'll understand Twitter for business far better than you do today.

LINKEDIN: FROM ONE PROFESSIONAL TO ANOTHER, TO 300 MILLION MORE

BEST USES: Recruitment, retention, industry collaboration, B2B business development

You may not be the most organized professional on the planet. And I'll be the first to admit that people have looked at my business card holder and cringed. It's stuffed to the brim with cards, exploding out of every angle. This mess used to be my bible—one of the things I'd grab first if my office were on fire. Although you may always keep your business card book, it's quickly becoming irrelevant thanks to LinkedIn. The largest social network that's "strictly" professional, LinkedIn boasts more than 300 million users, in a space that's not for sharing pictures of your kids or talking about sports or music.

A business card doesn't tell someone when her former colleague left financial planning to become a singer and song-writer. Nor does a business card tell you when a former assistant at your first job made partner at a top law firm. LinkedIn does. That's what's appealing about it to users. What's appealing about it to businesses? Well, essentially the same thing.

LinkedIn, when used properly, is a recruiter's dream. Every individual is no further than about six degrees away from any person who would be a good candidate to recruit to join her team, or to talk with about a business deal or partnership. In addition, LinkedIn can be used to position your company as the single best place to work in the industry. Consider working with your HR department to create a dynamic company profile, with videos that you share on YouTube about the corporate culture of your organization.

LinkedIn is especially useful for marketers in the business-to-business space. Executives and prospective customers, vendors, and partners feel safer networking on a website created just for business than they feel about networking on Facebook. Consider creating a space for your company to be the thought leader in your field. Do you run an accounting firm? Create a LinkedIn group where CPAs can connect and collaborate about new tax laws. Own a chain of restaurants? Create a LinkedIn community for restaurant management professionals. In 2011, LinkedIn launched LinkedIn Today, now called Pulse, a curated news product that allows users to see what articles are resonating most with their LinkedIn connections. As the product has grown, it's made LinkedIn a place where people spend more time, making it more appealing to marketers.

In 2013, LinkedIn launched the LinkedIn Influencer program where business and world leaders published articles on a weekly or monthly basis. I was lucky enough to slip into the program, and I've been blessed to write alongside Richard Branson, Bill Gates, and Barack Obama. In fact, I've generated over 20 million page views with my posts, more than any other Influencer. Even though I'm much less famous, accomplished, or smart than the other Influencers, I've been more successful—proving that content itself is more important than the person writing the content on LinkedIn. In the spring of 2014, LinkedIn opened up its publishing platform to all of its users. Now, you too can publish your content and articles on LinkedIn. It's similar to a blog—only there are 300 million fellow professionals who can potentially read any article you publish on LinkedIn, and they're all connected by varying degrees to your own network. I've published three articles with over 1 million views each!

Now, of course, you can use Facebook in many of these ways, but remember, you want to engage others in ways that are consistent with a target's DNA. Many potential job candidates won't take kindly to your posting on their Facebook wall about an upcoming position at your company—especially if they are Facebook friends with their boss. Many senior executives, even if they're on Facebook, might consider Facebook only for personal use and stick to LinkedIn for all of their business networking, business activity, and decision making. It's simply a matter of the users applying the tools in the ways that work best for them.

SLIDESHARE: THE INSTAGRAM OF LINKEDIN

Founded in 2006, Slideshare is a presentation-focused social media network for businesses. Slideshare was initially meant to host strictly business presentations, but it has exploded as a fun, interactive, social marketing platform in recent years and has become a lead driver. In fact, Slideshare is the number 2 lead driver for Likeable's businesses—just behind LinkedIn. Presentations posted to Slideshare entertain, inspire, and educate. In 2012, LinkedIn acquired Slideshare for $118.75 million.

From small businesses to major brands, and every business in between, marketers have a unique opportunity to share beautiful PowerPoint presentations, webinars, and videos on Slideshare. In 2015, Slideshare is expanding its mobile and video capabilities, making it perhaps the YouTube for business videos. No longer will small business videos have to compete with videos of babies dancing to Beyonce or kittens on skateboards; Slideshare will be an uninterrupted, business-focused video and presentation hub. If you're focused on selling and marketing to other business professionals, you should definitely take a look at Slideshare.

YOUTUBE AND VINE: IF A PICTURE'S WORTH A THOUSAND WORDS, HOW MANY IS A VIDEO WORTH?

BEST USES: Demonstrate corporate culture or product uses

YouTube, owned by Google, is one of the largest search engines in the world in its own right. It is the largest video-sharing website in the world by far, with hundreds of millions of videos housed on its servers and millions more being added each month. Use YouTube to showcase your corporate culture and your coolest products, services, and expertise so that when people search for keywords related to your business, your videos will appear.

A FEW HINTS ABOUT ONLINE VIDEO

1. Content is more important than production quality. A good flip cam will do.
2. Short and sweet is almost always better. A good rule of thumb is 30 to 90 seconds per video.
3. Have fun. Video is a great way to showcase your brand's personality.
4. Don't just post it on YouTube. Post your video on Facebook, Vimeo, and other sites. Consider using a service such as TubeMogul to syndicate videos across many sites.
5. Answer people's comments. Just as you should be responsive on other social networks, so should you respond to people's comments and questions on YouTube.

There is no better way to tell a story than through video, as evidenced by the rise of television advertising as the largest segment of the marketing and advertising industry by far (television accounts for more than 43 percent of all global advertising spending[1]). Yet through YouTube, and other online video channels, your videos can be seen for a lot less money than what you would spend for traditional television advertising. Are you a trusted advisor to your audience, creating valuable how-to videos? Are you completely customer focused, capturing video of users and allowing them to speak about your products or services? Whoever you are, consider taking the things your brand fans love most about you and bringing them to life on YouTube. See Table A.6 for a list of five companies that have been able to harness the power of YouTube in creating their own video content and channels.

Think about why you search online. It's usually because you want to know something—how to do something or where to find

TABLE A.6	Five Amazing YouTube Channels
COMPANY	YOUTUBE SITE
GoPro	https://www.youtube.com/GoProCamera
Rainbow Loom	https://www.youtube.com/TwistzBandz
Nintendo	https://www.youtube.com/Nintendo
Rolex	https://www.youtube.com/WorldOfRolex/
Heineken	https://www.youtube.com/heineken

something. Consider creating videos that answer those questions relating to your products or customer experiences.

Also, forget the notion that YouTube is about creating "viral videos" and getting millions of views. Is it possible to create videos on YouTube that will go viral? Sure. But think of the last 10 viral videos you've seen on YouTube. Chances are few of them, if any, were created by or for a business. Most of these videos take off organically. Videos that are "produced" don't tend to go viral. What makes content viral is that very thing that often can't be produced: the spontaneity of human experience. Even parody videos are based on an initial experience that was captured on video and released to the world, then deemed "viral."

You will receive far more relevant views answering questions focused on your customers or prospective customers than if you try and force virality. Remember, it's not about reaching the most people with your video. It's about reaching the right people.

In January 2013, Dom Hofmann, Rus Yusupov, and Colin Kroll founded Vine, a short-form video network owned by Twitter. Vine is to video marketing as Twitter is to blogging: short and sweet. Vines are six-second videos that users record on their phones and post to the app as well as to Facebook and Twitter. Although they last just a few seconds, these videos have been used by brands and marketers to tell amazing stories.

Using relevant hashtags, brands have seen great success creating videos in real time. Companies like Dunkin' Donuts and Oreo are known for their real-time vines during Super Bowls and awards shows (Table A.7). The great thing about Vine is that

TABLE A.7	Three Amazing Brand Vine Examples
BRANDS	**VINE SITE**
Dunkin' Donuts	https://vine.co/dunkindonuts
Coca-Cola	https://vine.co/ccfreestyle
Oreo	https://vine.co/oreo

now every marketer with a smartphone is a producer. Unlike ever before, companies have the opportunity to bring their brands to life.

GOOGLE+: THE SEARCH GIANT IS SOCIAL

BEST USES: Driving better search results for your company; collaborating with customers and coworkers through live video

For many years, Google struggled with how to best handle social media, with its first social network Orkut enjoying only moderate success in Brazil, and Google Wave and Google Buzz both failing. Google+ launched in July 2011, and in its first year, Google+ amassed a whopping 100 million users across the globe. After undergoing several design changes, the Google+ interface looks a lot like, well, Facebook—with two key differences: circles and hangouts.

Circles: You Decide What Conversations to Have with Whom

While Twitter and Facebook both offer lists to sort your connections, Google+'s circles are the best iteration yet of a solution to the social networking problem that we all have different sorts of relationships with different people. You decide what circles to list each of your connections with, and then, for each piece of content you share, you decide which circles to share that content with. For instance, individuals might have a circle for high school friends, another for college friends, another for colleagues, and another for senior management. More important, businesses might have one circle for customers, another for VIP customers, and another for prospects. Then you can share different content for each category—you probably wouldn't share the same thing about your business with a VIP customer that you would with a brand-new prospect, for instance. Remember, individuals cannot see what circle they're in—only that you've circled them.

Hangouts: Live Video + Up to 10 Participants = One Great Online Party

The best, most useful feature of Google+ for businesspeople is the hangout, Google's new group chat feature. Instead of directly asking a friend to join a group chat, users instead click "Start a hangout" and they're instantly in a video chatroom alone. At the same time, a message goes out to their social circles, letting them know that their friend is "hanging out." Friends can then join the hangout as long as they have been placed in a circle that was invited by the person who created the hangout.

You can "hang out" with up to nine other participants at a time, making the feature great for internal collaboration or customer service or support. Live video allows you to get closer to the customer than anything except real-life, face-to-face contact, and in the social network setting, it is a lot more scalable. For instance, if you're a ceramic artist, you can do a live demo with nine customers watching and participating. Just as important, the entire hangout video on Google+ is automatically recorded and archived for YouTube, if you want to share it. The hangout feature was even used successfully in January 2012 by President Barack Obama, who live-chatted with five Americans while hundreds of thousands submitted their own questions and watched online.

While circles and hangouts differentiate Google+ from the other social networks, the most important thing to remember about Google+ is that it's a product of Google, which means that there are huge search implications. When people search on Google.com while they are logged in, they now get "personalized" results based on their Google+ connections and what's been shared the most on the search company's fledgling

TABLE A.8	Five Brands Using Google+ Well
BRANDS	**WEBSITE**
Sephora	plus.google.com/+Sephora
Burberry	plus.google.com/+Burberry
Toyota	plus.google.com/+toyotausa
Virgin	plus.google.com/+Virgin
New York Times	plus.google.com/+nytimes

social network. This means that if you want to show up in search results when your customers and prospects are searching, you'd be wise to get on Google+ and begin creating circles, curating and share content, and conducting hangouts. You can learn from other businesses that are using Google+ successfully. Table A.8 features five of the best brands using Google+ for business.

PINTEREST: CONTENT CURATION AT ITS BEST

BEST USES: Curating visual content, driving e-commerce

Pinterest is a pinboard-esque social network that allows users to curate images and videos around categories based on interests, themes, hobbies, and so on. Cofounded by CEO Ben Silbermann, Pinterest's mission is to "connect everyone in the world through the things they find interesting." The platform launched in March 2010, but it experienced a heavy spike in popularity in January 2012, reaching 11.7 million unique users and becoming the fastest site in Internet history to reach the 10 million mark. In March 2012, it became the fourth largest social network in the United States. Among the key demographic of Pinterest users are females ages 25 to 34, and popular interests are crafts, cooking, gifts, fashion, and interior design.

On Pinterest, users are able to easily curate by "pinning" images and videos that interest them from other websites (hence the name: pin + interest = Pinterest). Images can be pinned via a "Pin it" button or the iPhone app. A user can share an image pinned by another user in an action called *repinning* or by simply liking another user's image. Pins can be organized by topics called *boards*. Like Twitter, users can follow fellow users and see their interests in a feed.

This social network isn't just for millions of women to pin designer shoes or plan their fairytale weddings. Pinterest offers a new way for brands to connect with current customers and attract new ones. Furthermore, brands are using Pinterest to link images to product pages on their websites and driving direct sales through the growing social network. Consumers are very visual, and brands have an opportunity with Pinterest's emphasis on the visual to inspire current and potential customers to make a purchase. The platform has even developed a price display feature to generate a price tag banner across the image of a product. Online marketplace Etsy has taken advantage of this feature to make it easier for its more than 50,000 followers to buy what they see and like. Check out Table A.9 for 10 other brands thriving on Pinterest.

TABLE A.9 **Ten Brands Thriving on Pinterest**

BRAND	PINTEREST
Kate Spade	Pinterest.com/katespadeny
HGTV	Pinterest.com/hgtv
Whole Foods	Pinterest.com/wholefoods
Chobani	Pinterest.com/chobani
J. Crew	Pinterest.com/jcrew
The Today Show	Pinterest.com/todayshow
Travel Channel	Pinterest.com/travelchannel
Men's Health	Pinterest.com/menshealthmag
Audi	Pinterest.com/audiusa
GAP	Pinterest.com/gap

As a brand, the first step is to begin following, repinning, and liking others' relevant content. Build your audience, and figure out what interests them. From there, explore these Pinterest strategies.

Create Boards Beyond Your Products or Services

Successful brands expand their Pinterest board horizons beyond just pinning images of their own products. Create boards with unexpected themes, and curate content that is still relevant to your brand but more relevant to your customers. Take Chobani's "We Would Like to Eat with You" board, for instance. Chobani is able to connect with customers on another level and show off an extra dimension of personality with its board dedicated to unique images of spoons.

Go Behind the Scenes

Give your followers a more intimate connection with your brand by offering a behind-the-scenes look. For example, *The Today Show* shares exclusive shots of the show on its "Anchor Antics" board.

Humanize

Pinned pictures have the ability to reveal the human side to your brand. With images and videos sharing the stories of its 1,200 farm families, Cabot Cheese's Pinterest board "Farmers and Farms" reveals the people behind the brand.

Crowdsource

You will be able to better understand your customers' wants and needs if you crowdsource your curated content. Ask your customers to pin relevant pictures and tag your brand. From there, you can repin content on a special board—for example, Bergdorf Goodman's "I Have a Weakness For" board, which shows what its Facebook fans crave.

INSTAGRAM: TURNING EVERYONE WITH A SMARTPHONE INTO AN EXCELLENT PHOTOGRAPHER

BEST USES: Bringing your brand to life through photos; social networking from your smartphone

If the success of Pinterest demonstrates the power of pictures on the social Web, Instagram demonstrates the power of pictures on the mobile Web. Instagram is a free photo-sharing app that was launched in October 2010. The service allows users to take a photo, apply a digital filter to it, and then share it on a variety of social networking services, including Instagram's own. The service, available only for smartphones and not for the dot-com Web, grew quickly to 200 million users. In April 2012, in its largest acquisition deal to date, Facebook made an offer to purchase Instagram, with its 13 employees, for approximately $1 billion in cash and stock. Instagram accepted the offer, and Facebook plans to keep Instagram independently managed.

Facebook bought Instagram for a whopping $1 billion before it had earned $1 in revenue, perhaps because Facebook CEO Mark Zuckerberg realized that the future of the social Web is the mobile Web and that Instagram had conquered the mobile Web better than anyone. For Instagram users, it's all about sharing "on the go"—taking pictures around you, applying a filter to make the pictures look as likeable as possible, and then sharing those pictures.

For business users, Instagram is best when you have something beautiful to share. So industry categories that are excellent candidates for Instagram include fashion, food, and travel. For busy small business owners, it's exciting as well because you do not need a computer to use it. In fact, you can't use Instagram on your computer! It's all about your iPhone or Android device, snapping photos, selecting a filter, and sharing.

Similar to Twitter, Instagram uses the @ symbol to tag other users, and the # hashtag symbol to tag categories and keep track of them for later. Some brands have used Instagram for contests, others for crowdsourcing stories through photography.

TABLE A.10	Seven Noteworthy Brands Using Instagram Well
BRAND	**WHAT YOU CAN LEARN FROM THEM**
Warby Parker	Integrate promotions with live events.
Red Bull	Create hashtags such as their #FlyingFriday.
Puma	Work with popular Instagrammers to take and share photos for you.
Boston Celtics	Give fans access to exclusive real-time photos.
Tiffany's	Don't make it about your product, but instead about the emotions your product evokes (e.g., for Tiffany's, Love).
NH Hotels	Use contests to elicit great fan photos.
Sharpie	Inspire passion from otherwise boring products.

Table A.10 shows seven noteworthy brands using Instagram, and lessons you can apply to your business.

FOURSQUARE: REACH YOUR CUSTOMERS WHERE THEY ARE

BEST USES: Reaching your customers when they're at or near your locations; understanding consumer behavior at the point of purchase

There is no doubt that location-based social networking is a major trend in social media and in marketing. Foursquare, founded in 2009, was the pioneer of location-based social networking. The idea behind location-based networks is that you "check in" using your smartphone device wherever you go, letting friends know where you are and earning various rewards for sharing your location. This leads to serendipitous experiences and the ability to generate localized deals.

In the past few years, other social networks have adapted to the growing location-based, "checking-in" marketing trend. In fact, 20 times as many people as all of the other services combined use Facebook Places to check in. Nevertheless, despite Foursquare's 20 million users and billions of check-ins worldwide, it was forced to pivot, and in 2014, Foursquare launched its new app called Swarm. The app removed the business-to-consumer (B2C) aspect of Foursquare's services and pivoted to a consumer-to-consumer (C2C) approach. "Keep up and meet up" is the new mission, and the app aims to connect people and places at once. In the first several months after its initial launch, however, Swarm was confusing to consumers, and the rate of adoption was low.

TUMBLR: SHARING IN HYPERDRIVE

BEST USES: Expanding content, reaching a specific demographic, strengthening relationships

Tumblr is a microblogging platform that allows users to create text, audio, image, and video content in a short-form blog. Launched by David Karp in February 2007, the platform became popular with the teenage and twenty-something demographic. As of July 2012, Tumblr was host to 64.7 million blogs and more than 27.5 billion total posts. Today, it is owned by Web giant Yahoo!, and it continues to grow.

Tumblr is an incredibly user-friendly blogging platform that makes it easy to start building a community. Users are given a Dashboard which, similar to Facebook's News Feed, allows them to see recent posts from Tumblr blogs they follow. Posts can then be reblogged or liked.

Businesses, especially in retail or media, can use this microblogging platform as a sort of social media hub, facilitating content curation and enabling them to expand their Facebook and Twitter content by feeding it into the vast Tumblr ecosystem. Brands can also build content directly onto Tumblr, offering unique content to help build a strong following. The *Economist*, for instance, teases content from upcoming issues in its Tumblr posts.

TABLE A.11	Five Brands Using Tumblr Effectively
BRAND	**TUMBLR SITE**
DKNY	Dknyprgirl.tumblr.com
Sesame Street	Sesamestreet.tumblr.com
E!	Eonline.tumblr.com
Rolling Stone	Rollingstone.tumblr.com
New York Times	livelymorgue.tumblr.com

Even if your brand isn't image based, you have the opportunity to post or reblog relevant photos. Matt Silverman of Mashable described to me that Tumblr is "sharing in hyperdrive," with a multitude of recycled content being churned daily. Make sure to highlight your products using high-quality photos that don't sell aggressively to consumers. Urban Outfitters does a great job of letting its Tumblr images speak for themselves.

Another strategy is to give users an inside look into your brand to strengthen your relationship and foster loyalty. For example, the New York City restaurant Boqueria uses video posts to show its followers how to make particular dishes from its menu. And on "NBA Through the Lens," the NBA shows games from different angles and allows followers to view scenes from the locker room. See Table A.11 for five brands using Tumblr effectively. With Tumblr, brands can reach a young demographic, expand the reach of their content, and reinforce their relationships with consumers.

THE BLOGOSPHERE: EVERY BLOGGER IS "THE MEDIA" NOW

BEST USES: Connecting more deeply to your target audience; positioning yourself as a thought leader in your industry

A *blog* is a website or part of a website that features articles or entries displayed in reverse chronological order. There are more than 150 million blogs in the world.[2] In order to be successful with a blog, you need to provide valuable content for your target audience, write consistently (at least twice a week), and provide a truly interactive atmosphere. Table A.12 provides a list of the best blogging platforms for you to get started.

Many company blogs are unsuccessful because they are updated infrequently, and too often they're updated with broadcast materials that read like press releases, rather than being valuable resources or content. With a blog, you have the opportunity to include longer text updates than you're able to through Facebook or Twitter. A blog also allows you to incorporate photos, videos, polls, and other multimedia. You can also tell stories at your own pace and on your own terms.

Building a successful blogging strategy is twofold. It includes both the creation and growth of your own blog as well as interaction with other bloggers writing for your target audience and/or about similar topics. By solidifying a large audience for your blog, you can, in effect, become your own publisher or media network and cut out or reduce the so-called media middleman. Many blogs today have larger audiences than a great deal of newspapers, for instance, so you can use blog content to grow your own media outlet.

Five Reasons Your Company Should Be Blogging

Of the many reasons your company should be utilizing blogs, the following five are the strongest and will provide you with ideas on how to start, and continue, the blogging process:

TABLE A.12   **Four Best Blogging Platforms**

PLATFORM	WEBSITE	PROS
WordPress	Wordpress.com	Variety of themes and plug-ins on your own or as a WordPress-hosted blog
Tumblr	Tumblr.com	Ultimate microblogging platform combining blogs and Twitter
Medium	Medium.com	Built-in audience introduces your content to others like you
Blogger	Blogger.com	Easy to use instantaneous setup

1. **Extend the conversation.** A corporate blog is the perfect outlet for long-form communication with your audience and/or clients. Twitter and Facebook are ideal platforms for quick, short-form messaging—and they are incredibly important—but a blog allows you to really dive into the topics and trends that matter in your industry.

   Also, blogging aids you in being transparent and providing the "insider look" your audience craves. Someone researching your company will be able to glean more information from the company blog than is available in the standard website "About" section and in Twitter and Facebook updates. While these forms of communication heavily involve proactive response to questions and concerns, a blog stands as a channel for sharing in-depth ideas, practices, and stories that make your company unique . . . and amazing. You can even use your blog as a platform for crowdsourced information.

   Developing a new product? Ask your blog audience for input and ideas, getting the targeted consumers involved in the development process!

2. **Attract future customers.** Blogs influence purchasing decisions—whether you are giving your readers a behind-the-scenes look at how a product was conceptualized and made or showing your products in action, consumers will have an added reinforcement as to why your products rock. In this sense, a product can be literal, such as a camera, or figurative, if your company provides services rather than tangible goods. You can think of your company's blog as a cost-effective extension of your sales calls or advertisements. In reality, twenty-first-century consumers have come to expect the brands they purchase from to be available to them in the online social world, and having a corporate blog where they can research and interact with you is one of the first steps to take in meeting that expectation.

3. **Attract future employees.** A company or brand is only as good as the talent it recruits to represent it. By providing potential employees a look into your corporate structure—life at the company, how ideas are formed, and the exciting things that are happening—you are essentially dangling the carrot.

Let your target employee base know why working for you would be an amazing opportunity, and they will come to you.

4. **Position yourself as a leader.** As a brand, you want to be seen as innovative—a thought leader in your industry. To see how competitive companies in your industry are getting involved in the blogosphere, check out the resources listed in Table A.13.

   Blogging allows you to share your company's best ideas and intelligent commentary for what's happening in your space. Having a well-written blog will help you stand out from, or above, your competitors. By allowing multiple people to contribute either posts or simply ideas for the posts, everyone in your company has a voice—and I'm sure they have a lot of great things to say.

5. **Search engine optimization (SEO).** Ideally, blogs are updated regularly, which inherently lends itself to great SEO. HubSpot has reported that companies that have active blogs receive up to 55 percent more traffic—including higher rates of both organic search and referral traffic.[3] By utilizing appropriate keywords, sharing "link love" with others, and submitting your blog to directories, you will help drive more eyes to your page. Once you post the content on your blog, it will live there indefinitely. Someone searching for a specific topic can stumble upon a post from months, or even years, ago. Blog content continues to work for you long after it's been published. And of course, more eyes on your company's blog and website ultimately will lead to higher customer conversions down the road.

TABLE A.13   **Five Great Resources to Find Blogs in Your Industry**

RESOURCE	WEBSITE
BlogDash	BlogDash.com
Blogdigger	Blogdigger.com
Google Blogs	BlogSearch.Google.com
IceRocket	IceRocket.com
Technorati	Technorati.com

FLICKR, MYSPACE, YELP, AND THE HUNDREDS OF OTHER NICHE SOCIAL NETWORKS

BEST USES: Connecting to a highly targeted audience

You know your audience. That's your job—as a marketer. If you don't, it's time to go back to step 1 and start listening and understanding your customer. If you do, then it's definitely in your best interest to do a little research on niche networks for your heavy-user group. While most of your customers are probably using Facebook, Twitter, and YouTube, some of your most passionate customers might be using smaller, niche social networks. There is literally a community for every interest, so if you know what your customers are into, you can build a presence in the niche community that makes the most sense.

Into taking photos? Flickr is for you. All about music? Check out Myspace—which was once the king of social media. Love vampires? Try VampireFreaks.com. Love dogs? Dogster.com. Are your customers the wealthiest people in the country? Check out Affluence.org. There's even a rumor about a site for secret agents in the United States called A-Space.

Yelp, TripAdvisor, and Angie's List are three of many "review style" social networks. User reviews are still one of the most trusted forms of marketing, with more than 70 percent of Web users trusting this form of consumer engagement.[4] Whether you should devote your resources to any of these niche sites depends on what you're marketing and who your audience is.

Yelp, a review site for restaurants and other local service providers, and TripAdvisor, a review site for travel, are just two of dozens of review sites for different niches and topics. As a marketer, you have a responsibility to ensure that any reviews you solicit are honest and come from real customers. The best way to receive such reviews is simply to ask for them. When I get a receipt that asks me to fill out a survey about my experience for a chance to win a $10 gift card, I am perplexed. Why not ask me to share my review on Yelp, or TripAdvisor, or some other appropriate review site? If the review is good, it helps the brand infinitely more. If the review is bad, it's echoing what many are feeling, and it gives the opportunity for the brand to respond publicly.

Niche networks aren't always as brand friendly as Facebook or Twitter, but they are worthwhile nonetheless. Begin by researching how the community works, and ask community leaders about how to best get involved. It's a smaller net you're casting, but an incredibly valuable one if you engage in a way that works for the group. Remember, your goal is to find your audience, wherever they are, listen to them, engage them, and join them.

CHAPTER 2

1. Source: http://Investor.FB.com, accessed January 12, 2015.
2. Source: http://internetlivestats.com/twitter-statistics, accessed January 12, 2015.

CHAPTER 8

1. Aaron Sorkin, interview with Stephen Colbert, The Colbert Report, Comedy Central, September 30, 2010, available at http://thecolbertreport.cc.com/videos/h7gmgz/aaron-sorkin, accessed January 12, 2015.

APPENDIX

1. Source: http://www.adweek.com/news/advertising-branding/north -american-ad-spending-could-top-pre-recession-levels-year-160026, accessed January 12, 2015.
2. Source: http://www.wpvirtuoso.com/how-many-blogs-are-on-the -internet/, accessed January 12, 2015.
3. Source: http://blog.hubspot.com/blog/tabid/6307/bid/5014/Study -Shows-Business-Blogging-Leads-to-55-More-Website-Visitors.aspx, accessed January 12, 2015.
4. Source: http://www.nielsen.com/us/en/insights/news/2012 /consumer-trust-in-online-social-and-mobile-advertising-grows .html, accessed January 12, 2015.

Index

Dave Kerpen is the founder and CEO of Likeable Local, a social media software company serving thousands of small businesses, as well as the chairman and cofounder of Likeable Media, an award-winning social media and word-of-mouth marketing agency.

Following Dave's sponsored wedding that raised over $100,000 including $20,000 for charity, he and his wife Carrie started and transformed the KBuzz (founded in 2007) into Likeable Media, the only three-time WOMMY Award winner for excellence from the Word of Mouth Marketing Association (WOMMA) and one of the 500 fastest growing private companies in the United States, according to *Inc.* magazine for both 2011 and 2012.

Named by *Entrepreneur* magagine as one of 10 up-and-coming leaders, Dave has been featured on BBC, CNBC's *On the Money*, ABC's *World News Tonight*, CBS's *The Early Show*, in the *New York Times*, and in countless blogs. Dave has also keynoted at dozens of conferences across the globe including Singapore, Athens, Dubai, San Francisco, and Mexico City.

Likeable Social Media: How to Delight Your Customers, Create an Irresistible Brand, and Be Generally Amazing on Facebook and Other Social Networks," was Dave's first *New York Times* bestselling book. Dave followed *Likeable Social Media* with two more books, *Likeable Business* and *Likeable Leadership*. He is now working on his fourth, "The Art of People."

Dave lives in Port Washington, NY, with his wife and children.

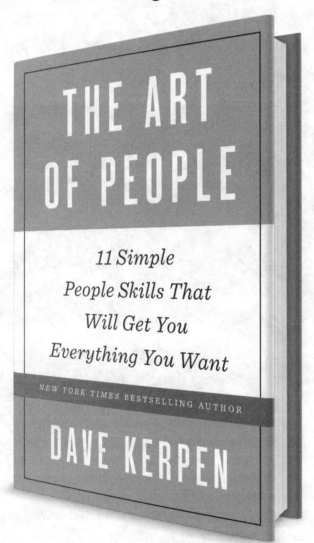

◉likeablelocal

The Social Media Solution
TO EMPOWER YOUR BUSINESS TO SUCCEED

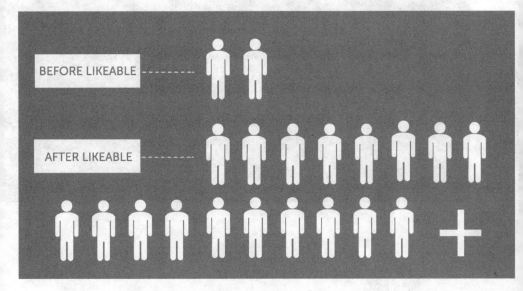

BEFORE LIKEABLE

AFTER LIKEABLE

Start to Build, Engage, and Grow
YOUR ONLINE PRESENCE TODAY

Learn more at LikeableDemo.com

Contact@LikeableLocal.com
LikeableLocal.com
212.359.4347

likeable media

We create, curate, and promote content that gets your brand results.

WHAT WE DO

Create
Our team of writers, designers, and multimedia artists use insights to craft frequent and captivating content.

Curate
Around-the-clock community management responds proactively and reactively on behalf of your brand.

Promote
We develop and execute social ad campaigns that deliver on your unique objectives with unmatched success.

To learn more about Likeable Media, including free resources and blog, please visit **likeable.com**.

To learn more about Dave as a speaker, please visit **davekerpen.com**.